JERUSALEM

YOTAM OTTOLENGHI

JERUSALEM

SAMI TAMIMI

EBURY
PRESS

Additional text by Nomi Abeliovich and Noam Bar

Food photography by Jonathan Lovekin

Location photography by Adam Hinton

Contents

Introduction

One of our favourite recipes in this collection, a simple couscous with tomato and onion, is based on a dish Sami's mum, Na'ama, used to cook for him when he was a child in Muslim east Jerusalem. At around the same time, in the Jewish west of the city, Yotam's dad, Michael, used to make a very similar dish. Being Italian, Michael's dish was made with small pasta balls called ptitim. Both versions were beautifully comforting and delicious.

A dish just like Michael's is part of the Jewish Tripolitan (Libyan) cuisine. It is called shorba, and is a result of the Italian influence on Libyan food during the years of Italian rule of the country, in the early twentieth century. So Michael's ptitim was possibly inspired by Tripolitan cooking in Jerusalem, which in turn was influenced by Michael's original Italian culture. The anecdotal icing on this cross-cultural cake is that Michael's great uncle, Aldo Ascoli, was an admiral in the colonial Italian navy that raided Tripoli and occupied Libya in 1911.

Confusing? This is Jerusalem in a nutshell: very personal, private stories immersed in great culinary traditions that often overlap and interact in unpredictable ways, creating food mixes and culinary

combinations that belong to specific groups but also belong to everybody else. Many of the city's best-loved foods have just as complicated a pedigree as this one.

This book and this journey into the food of Jerusalem form part of a private odyssey. We both grew up in the city, Sami in the Muslim east and Yotam in the Jewish west, but never knew each other. We lived there as children in the 1970s and 1980s and then left in the 1990s, first to Tel Aviv and then to London. Only there did we meet and discover our parallel histories; we became close friends and then business partners, alongside others in Ottolenghi.

Although we often spoke about Jerusalem, our hometown, we never focused much on the city's food. Recently, however — is it age? — we have begun to reminisce over old food haunts and forgotten treats. Hummus — which we hardly ever talked about before — has become an obsession.

It is more than 20 years since we both left the city. This is a serious chunk of time, longer than the years we spent living there. Yet we still think of Jerusalem as our home. Not home in the sense of the place you conduct your daily life, or constantly return to. In fact, Jerusalem is our home almost against our wills. It is our home because it defines us, whether we like it or not.

The flavours and smells of this city are our mother tongue. We imagine them and dream in them, even though we've adopted some new, perhaps more sophisticated languages. They define comfort for us, excitement, joy, serene bliss. Everything we taste and everything we cook is filtered through the prism of our childhood experiences: foods our mothers fed us, wild herbs picked on school trips, days spent in markets, the smell of the dry soil on a summer's day, goat and sheep roaming the hills, fresh pitas with minced lamb, chopped parsley, chopped liver, black figs, smoky chops, syrupy cakes, crumbly cookies. The list is endless — too long to recall and too complex to describe. Most of our food images lie well beyond our consciousness: we just cook and eat, relying on our impulses for what feels right, looks beautiful and tastes delicious to us.

And this is what we set out to explore in this book. We want to offer our readers a glimpse into a hidden treasure, and at the same time explore our own culinary DNA, unravel the sensations and the alphabet of the city that made us the food creatures we are.

In all honesty, this is also a self-indulgent, nostalgic trip into our pasts. We go back, first and foremost, to experience again those magnificent flavours of our childhood, to satisfy the need most grown-ups have to relive those first food experiences to which nothing holds a candle in later life. We want to eat, cook and be inspired by the richness of a city with 4000 years of history, that has changed hands endlessly and that now stands as the centre of three massive faiths and is occupied by residents of such utter diversity it puts the old tower of Babylon to shame.

IT IS MORE THAN 20 YEARS SINCE WE BOTH LEFT THE CITY. THIS IS A SERIOUS CHUNK OF TIME, LONGER THAN THE YEARS WE SPENT LIVING THERE

Jerusalem food

Is there even such a thing as Jerusalem food, though? Consider this: there are Greek Orthodox monks in this city; Russian Orthodox priests; Hasidic Jews originating from Poland; non-Orthodox Jews from Tunisia, from Libya, from France or from Britain; there are Sephardic Jews that have been here for generations; there are Palestinian Muslims from the West Bank and many others from the city and well beyond; there are secular Ashkenazi Jews from Romania, Germany and Lithuania and more recently arrived Sephardim from Morocco, Iraq, Iran or Turkey; there are Christian Arabs and Armenian Orthodox; there are Yemeni Jews and Ethiopian Jews but there are also Ethiopian Copts; there are Jews from Argentina and others from southern India; there are Russian nuns looking after monasteries and a whole neighbourhood of Jews from Bukhara (Uzbekistan).

All of these, and many, many more, create an immense tapestry of cuisines. It is impossible to count the number of cultures and sub-cultures residing in this city. Jerusalem is an intricate, convoluted mosaic of peoples. It is therefore very tempting to say there isn't such a thing as a local cuisine. And indeed, if you go to the ultra-Orthodox neighbourhood of Me'ah She'arim and compare the prepared food sold in grocery shops there to the selection laid out by a Palestinian mother for her children in the neighbourhood of A-tur in the east of the city — you couldn't be blamed for assuming these two live on two different culinary planets.

However, if you take a step back and look at the greater picture, there are some typical elements that are easily identifiable in most local cuisines and crop up throughout the city. Everybody, absolutely everybody, uses chopped cucumber and tomatoes to create an Arab salad or an Israeli salad, depending on point of view. Stuffed vegetables with rice or rice and meat also appear on almost every dinner table, as does an array of pickled vegetables. Extensive use of olive oil, lemon juice and olives is also commonplace. Baked pastries stuffed with cheese in all sorts of guises are found in most cultures.

EVERYBODY, ABSOLUTELY EVERYBODY, USES CHOPPED CUCUMBER AND TOMATOES TO CREATE AN ARAB SALAD OR AN ISRAELI SALAD, DEPENDING ON POINT OF VIEW

Then there are looser affinities, those shared by a few cuisines but not all of them — bulgar or semolina cases stuffed with meat (kubbeh), burnt aubergine salads, white bean soups, the combination of meat with dried fruits. Eventually, these separate links between the different groups link all of the groups together to one clear and identifiable local cuisine.

Aside from that, there are the local ingredients. Jerusalemites tend to eat seasonally and cook with what grows in the area. The list is endless. It is made up of dozens of vegetables — tomatoes, okra, string beans, cauliflower, artichokes, beets, carrots, peppers, cucumbers, celeriac, kohlrabi, courgettes, aubergines; and fruit — figs, lemons, peaches, pears, strawberries, pomegranates, plums and apricots; herbs, nuts, dairy products, grains and pulses, lamb and chicken.

The passion in the air

The diversity and richness of Jerusalem, both in terms of the cooks and their disparate backgrounds and the ingredients they use, make it fascinating to any outsider. But what makes it doubly exciting is the emotional and spiritual energy that this city is drenched in. When it comes to people's emotions it is hard to overstate how unique it is as a city.

Four thousand years of intense political and religious wrangling (SEE PAGE 18) are impossible to hide. Wherever you go — in Jewish parts in the city centre or within the walls of the ancient old city — people are zealously fighting to protect and maintain what they see as their piece of land, their endangered culture or their right for a certain way of life. More often than not, this is pretty ugly. Intolerance and trampling over other people's basic rights are routine in this city. Currently, the Palestinian minority bears the brunt with no sign of it regaining control over its destiny, while the secular Jews are seeing their way of life being gradually marginalized by a growing Orthodox population.

The other, more positive, side of this coin is that the inherent passion and energy that Jerusalemites have in abundance results in some fantastic food and culinary creativity. The best hummus joints, where methods have been perfected over generations, are in the city (and locals are happy to go into some seriously heated debates about the best one), as are some of the country's most creative modern restaurants. There is something about the heated, highly animated spirit of the city's residents that creates unparalleled delicious food. It also has a very obvious effect on the flavours, which are strong and bold, with lots of sour and sweet. The Jerusalem Palestinian hummus is patently sharp, as are the Friday night Sephardi soups.

On top of that, there is a spirit of warmth and generosity that is sometimes almost overbearing. Guests are always served mountains of food. Nothing is done sparingly. 'Eat more' is a local motto. It is unthinkable not to eat what you are served. Going into a friend's restaurant, or a friend of a friend, you are never expected to pay. It is a combination of the famous Middle Eastern hospitality that goes back to the days of Abraham and the typical Jewish Ashkenazi way of always showering guests and relatives with delights, lest they 'go home hungry'. Heaven forbid.

Alas, although Jerusalemites have so much in common, food, at the moment, seems to be the only unifying force in this highly fractured place. The dialogue between Jews and Arabs, and often between Jews themselves, is almost non-existent. It is sad to note how little daily interaction there is between communities, with

IT TAKES A GIANT LEAP OF FAITH, BUT WE ARE HAPPY TO TAKE IT, TO IMAGINE THAT HUMMUS WILL EVENTUALLY BRING JERUSALEMITES TOGETHER, IF NOTHING ELSE WILL

people sticking together in closed, homogenous groups. Food, however, seems to break down those boundaries on occasion. You can see people shop together in food markets, or eat in each other's restaurants. On rare occasions, they work together in partnership in food establishments. It takes a giant leap of faith, but we are happy to take it — what have we got to lose? — to imagine that hummus will eventually bring Jerusalemites together, if nothing else will.

The recipes

Our selection of recipes here includes traditional, age-old dishes, cooked just as they should be, with no change or modern touch. Others are fairly traditional, but we allowed ourselves poetic licence and updated them to suit the times or our sensibilities. And then there are recipes that are just loosely inspired by the flavours of Jerusalem — delicious concoctions that could have easily fitted on many Jerusalem dinner tables but have yet to become local classics.

We don't mean to cover all of the city's foods, or even substantial parts of it, nor all of its communities. This is impossible. Smarter people have delved deep into Jewish and Arab cuisines and have documented both extensively. Other communities in the city have also had their foods written about. So a lot is omitted. Some typical local dishes like kugel (slow-cooked noodle cake), bagel (Arab or Jewish), pashtida (savoury flan), pastelikos (little Sephardi meat pies), tchulent or hamin (everything cooked in one pot overnight for Shabbat), strudel, challah (sweet Shabbat bread) — all are left neglected. Ashkenazi foods particularly are under-represented. This has to do with our personal backgrounds and the types of flavours we tend to cook and eat.

As we draw deep inspiration from Jerusalem and its food but are in no way trying to represent its realities, the justification for this collection of recipes is our preferences and cooking habits and those of our readers. The cooks who like our style and flavour combinations lead a (usually) western, modern lifestyle. They have a certain set of ingredients available to them and a 21st-century mindset (use less oil in the food, spend less time in the kitchen...). We can only hope that through our haphazard, often eccentric selective process and through our modifications we have succeeded in distilling the spirit of the place that made us and shaped us.

Finally, a comment about ownership

In the part of the world we are dealing with everybody wants to own everything. Existence feels so uncertain and so fragile that people fight fiercely and with great passion to hold on to things: land, culture, religious symbols, food — everything is in danger of being snatched away or of disappearing. The result is fiery arguments about ownership, about provenance, about who and what came first.

As we have seen through our investigations, and will become blatantly apparent to anyone reading and cooking from this book, these arguments are futile.

Firstly, they are futile because it doesn't really matter. Looking back in time or far afield into distant lands is simply distracting. The beauty of food and of eating is that they are rooted in the now. Food is a basic, hedonistic pleasure, a sensual instinct we all share and revel in. It is a shame to spoil it.

Secondly, you can always search further back in time. Hummus for example, a highly explosive subject, is undeniably a staple of the local Palestinian population, but it was also a permanent feature on dinner tables of Allepian Jews who have lived in Syria for millennia and then arrived in Jerusalem in the 1950s and 1960s. Who is more deserving of calling hummus their own? Neither. Nobody 'owns' a dish because it is very likely that someone else cooked it before them and another person before that.

Thirdly, and this is the most crucial point, in this soup of a city it is completely impossible to find out who invented this delicacy and who brought that one with them. The food cultures are mashed and fused together in a way that is impossible to unravel. They interact all the time and influence each other constantly so nothing is pure any more. In fact, nothing ever was. Jerusalem was never an isolated bastion. Over millennia it has seen countless immigrants, occupiers, visitors and merchants — all bringing foods and recipes from four corners of the earth.

As a result, as much as we try to attribute foods to nations, to ascertain the origin of a dish, we often end up discovering a dozen other dishes that are extremely similar, that work with the same ingredients and the same principles to make a final result that is just ever so slightly different, a variation on a theme.

FOOD IS A BASIC, HEDONISTIC PLEASURE, A SENSUAL INSTINCT WE ALL SHARE AND REVEL IN. IT IS A SHAME TO SPOIL IT

History

The complexity and vibrancy of the food in Jerusalem stems from its location as a meeting point between Europe, Asia and Africa and the incredible richness of its history. Jerusalem was traditionally depicted, as in this medieval map (below), as the centre of the universe, surrounded by three continents. Indeed, there are few places in the world to match its importance. Yet Jerusalem has never been a great metropolis. It has never had temples as big as those of Luxor, art as refined as Greece, or public buildings as magnificent as those of Rome. It didn't possess large imperial courts like those of China or India, or busy commerce hubs as in central Asia. It has always been a rather small and crowded city, built of the stone of its surrounding hills.

The energy of Jerusalem is introspective. It is born out of an interplay between the peoples that have been coming and going for millennia, and the spirit that seems to hover among the olive trees, over the hills and in the valleys. It is not through anything material but through faith, learning, devotion and, sadly, fanaticism, that Jerusalem gained its importance.

When King David founded it as his capital, in a[...] was, as it is now, a collection of rugged hills with l[...] or water. David was a warrior, and chose his capital for [...] reasons — it was at the centre of his kingdom. His son, Solo[...] most glorious Jewish king, built the first temple in Jerusalem, a[...] sanctified its place as Temple Mount. Following Solomon's death [...] the young Jewish kingdom was broken up by squabbling relatives, and often attacked from the north. This culminated in 587 BC, when Babylon attacked Jerusalem, burnt the city and the temple, and dispersed its inhabitants.

It is then that we first see one of the greatest emotions attached to Jerusalem — yearning. We are told of two Jewish leaders, Ezra and Nehemiah, who successfully made it their life mission to restore the temple in Jerusalem and the Jewish nation in its homeland. This yearning will play out again and again, in Jews, Muslims and Christians, from all parts of the world. Indeed it is so strong that psychiatrists have identified the Jerusalem Syndrome — pilgrims who break down when their life goal, the long-anticipated journey to the holy city, is accomplished.

In 332 BC the Persian empire fell to Alexander the Great, and a few centuries of Hellenistic influence followed. A protracted war of cultures took place between the modern, frivolous and inter-marrying Hellenistic Jews, and the more traditional Jews. For a while, a rebellion of Jewish traditionalists — Maccabees — gained the upper hand and managed to control the religious life. This revolt gave us Hanukkah, the festival of lights, based on the story that, upon restoring the temple to its Jewish traditions, a little jug of oil could miraculously feed the sacred light of the temple for eight days.

While for many the Maccabean revolt is a story of liberation and inspiration, some scholars see it as another episode in a centuries-long struggle between traditionalists and cosmopolitan Jews. This is another pattern that is played out in Jerusalem again and again, nowadays manifested as the struggle between the orthodox and the secular Jews in the city.

The Romans — following hot on the heels of the Hellenistic influence — first appeared in Jerusalem in 63 BC, and then gradually asserted their authority against Jewish resistance, which culminated in a failed revolt in 70 AD, when the second, and last temple was destroyed. This event is painfully etched in Jewish history as the onset of a slow process of decline that would not end until the advent of Zionism.

Jesus Christ lived some decades before this momentous event, at a time of great political, military, cultural and spiritual upheaval. His presence is of course still evident in many monuments in the city, first and foremost in the Church of the Holy Sepulchre, the site of the resurrection. This is a collection of dimly lit caves, buildings and churches, encompassing 17 centuries, each attributed to a different creed of Christianity but all connected. As usual in

… IN 587 BC … BABYLON ATTACKED JERUSALEM, BURNT THE CITY AND THE TEMPLE, AND DISPERSED ITS INHABITANTS. IT IS THEN THAT WE FIRST SEE ONE OF THE GREATEST EMOTIONS ATTACHED TO JERUSALEM — YEARNING

...lem, there is no splendour there, but there is, in the crowds ...pilgrims; the secluded little corners where people kneel and ...to the light of a candle; the glimpses of exquisite art; and the ...aning loaded onto every stone — a truly moving experience, ...rhaps even a transcendental one.

Alongside the slow development of the nascent religion, the Roman–Jewish conflict continued to simmer, and came to a head in another revolt, in 132 AD, after which Jews were banned from the city — bar one day a year — for many centuries. The city was renamed Aelia Capitolina, and with the Christianization of the Byzantine Empire it was adorned with Christian churches, and became a veritable Christian city, devoid of any Jewish presence.

This, and similar periods, are considered by Palestinian historians as proof that not only the Jews, but also the Palestinians (many of whom are Christian), have a long-lasting historical claim on the city. In fact, some Palestinians claim that they are descendants of the Jebusites, the original inhabitants of Jerusalem, who were deposed by King David.

Islam was born in the 7th century, and with it came another claim on the city. Jerusalem, or 'Al-Quds' in Arabic, meaning 'The Holy', is the third holiest site for Sunni Muslims. It is from here, believe Muslims, that the prophet Mohammad ascended to heaven. After the death of the prophet the Muslims went on a conquering spree of a huge scale, Jerusalem included. Temple Mount, the site of the long-demolished Jewish temple, was consecrated by Islam with the building of two large mosques, one of them the golden dome of the rock, which still dominates the skyline of the old city. Temple Mount remains exclusively Muslim, with Jews only using the Western Wall, also called the 'Wailing Wall' — remnant of the ancient wall that surrounded the Jewish temple's courtyard and a place where some still weep over the temple lost 2000 years ago.

Over a millennium of Muslim control followed, with different Muslim powers vying for power. Christians staked a new claim for the city in the Middle Ages, when the Catholic Church managed to bring together forces from all around Europe to recapture the Holy Land. It was an ambitious project, with knights coming from as far away as Norway. The crusaders controlled the city from 1099 to 1187, but then lost it again. During the crusaders' rule a network of markets was built along ancient Roman paths in the old city that survives to this day. In each of the three alleys specific produce was sold: at the herb market you could find fresh produce, malquisinat was the fast food market, offering meals to the many pilgrims that flocked to the city, and 'the covered market' was used by cloth vendors.

Jerusalem then became a rather neglected place, changing hands as the (mostly) Muslim rulers came and went. The Muslim authorities were, by and large, quite tolerant, certainly more tolerant than the Christians. Jews were allowed to stay in the city and Christians

> DURING THE CRUSADERS' RULE A NETWORK OF MARKETS WAS BUILT ALONG ANCIENT ROMAN PATHS... AT THE HERB MARKET YOU COULD FIND FRESH PRODUCE, MALQUISINAT WAS THE FAST FOOD MARKET... AND 'THE COVERED MARKET' WAS USED BY CLOTH VENDORS

allowed to worship there. In the 19th century, under Ottoman control, Jerusalem still enjoyed some glory due to the wide, if sparse, international presence. However, it was described by most visitors as a miserable, congested and squalid provincial town.

The British conquered Jerusalem in 1917, during the First World War, and the city became anything but sleepy. The Brits brought a definite push for modernization, and this was intertwined with the growth of the Palestinian national identity and the Zionist reclaim of Israel. Jerusalem has since been at the heart of the struggle between these two fierce nationalistic movements, and when the UN decided in 1947 to divide Palestine between them, Jerusalem was given to international administration. But a war, rather than peaceful division, is what followed. Interestingly, this war has different names: for the Jews it is the War of Independence, an assertive act of bravery after the trauma of the holocaust; for Arabs, however, it is called a nakba — 'the catastrophe'. The young Israeli state managed to hold on to the western part of the city while losing

its eastern, ancient part, which has been densely populated by Arabs. Eastern Jerusalem was controlled by Jordan until the 1967 war, when Israel took over the whole of Jerusalem, along with the surrounding areas.

The population grew quickly throughout the 20th century. Arabs settled in the city as part of a general urbanization trend, and Jews arrived from around the world to the re-founded national home. Entire communities immigrated and usually settled in particular areas, maintaining their traditions. This insular tendency, combined with the fact that most families — both Jewish and Arab — have many mouths to feed and not a lot to live on, creates a real microcosm of tradition.

Jerusalem is claimed by Israel as the 'eternal capital of the Jewish people' and by the Palestinians as the capital of their state. The question of this city is at the heart of the Israeli–Palestinian conflict and its resolution is essential for achieving that elusive dream of peace in the Middle East. Perhaps naively, we hope that the city can be acknowledged by all as part of the world heritage — undoubtedly a true reflection of reality — and provide the key for sharing, acceptance and coexistence.

VEGETABLES

Roasted sweet potatoes & fresh figs

Figs are abundant in Jerusalem and many trees, bearing the most delectable fruit, actually belong to no one, so anybody can help themselves. Summer months are always tinted with the smell of wild herbs and ripe figs. The mother of Sami's childhood neighbour and friend, Jabbar, used her roof to dry the glut of figs (and tomatoes) in the hot summer sun, spending hours cleaning and sorting them meticulously. Poor Um Jabbar — Sami and her son never wasted time and used to sneak up to her roof regularly, stealing her figs at their peak and causing havoc. This wasn't enough for Jabbar though. The boy had such a sweet tooth that he always carried around with him an old match box full of sugar cubes, just in case. Unfortunately, this habit had clear ramifications, evident in his 'charming' smile.

---

4 small sweet potatoes (1 kg in total)
5 tbsp olive oil
40ml balsamic vinegar (you can use a commercial rather than a premium aged grade)
20g caster sugar
12 spring onions, halved lengthways and cut into 4cm segments
1 red chilli, thinly sliced
6 fresh and ripe figs (240g in total), quartered
150g soft goat's cheese, crumbled (optional)
Maldon sea salt and black pepper

This unusual combination of fresh fruit and roasted vegetables is one of the most popular at Ottolenghi. It wholly depends, though, on the figs being sweet, moist and perfectly ripe. Go for plump fruit with an irregular shape and a slightly split bottom. Pressing against the skin should result in some resistance but not much. Try to smell the sweetness. The balsamic reduction is very effective here, both for the look and for rounding up the flavours. To save you from making it you can look out for products such as balsamic cream or glaze.

Preheat the oven to 240°C/220°C Fan/Gas Mark 9.

Wash the sweet potatoes, halve them lengthways and then cut each again similarly into 3 long wedges. Mix with 3 tablespoons of the olive oil, 2 teaspoons of salt and some black pepper. Spread the wedges out on a baking sheet, skin-side down, and cook for about 25 minutes until soft but not mushy. Remove from the oven and leave to cool down.

To make a balsamic reduction, place the balsamic vinegar and sugar in a small saucepan. Bring to a boil then reduce the heat and simmer for 2–4 minutes, or until it thickens. Be sure to remove the pan from the heat when the vinegar is still runnier than honey; it will continue to thicken as it cools. Stir in a drop of water before serving if it does become too thick to drizzle.

Arrange the sweet potatoes on a serving platter. Heat the remaining oil in a medium saucepan and add the spring onions and chilli. Fry on a medium heat for 4–5 minutes, stirring often, making sure not to burn the chilli, and then spoon the oil, onions and chilli over the sweet potatoes. Dot the figs among the wedges and then drizzle over the balsamic reduction. Serve at room temperature with the cheese crumbled over, if using.

Na'ama's Fattoush

200g Greek yoghurt and 200ml full-fat milk or 400ml of buttermilk (replacing both yoghurt and milk)

2 large stale Turkish flatbread or naan (250g in total)

3 large tomatoes (380g in total), cut into 1.5cm dice

100g radishes, thinly sliced

3 Lebanese or mini cucumbers (250g in total), peeled and chopped into 1.5cm dice

2 spring onions, thinly sliced

15g mint

25g flat-leaf parsley, roughly chopped

1 tbsp dried mint

2 garlic cloves, crushed

3 tbsp lemon juice

60ml olive oil, plus extra to drizzle

2 tbsp cider or white wine vinegar

¾ tsp coarsely ground black pepper

1½ tsp salt

1 tbsp sumac or more according to taste, to garnish

Arab salad, chopped salad, Israeli salad — whatever you choose to call it, there is no escaping it. Wherever you go in the city, at any time of the day, a Jerusalemite is most likely to have a plate of freshly chopped vegetables — tomato, cucumber and onion, dressed with olive oil and lemon juice — served next to whatever else they are having. It's a local affliction, quite seriously. Friends visiting us in London always complain of feeling they ate 'unhealthily' because there wasn't a fresh salad served with every meal.

There are plenty of unique variations on the chopped salad but one of the most popular is Fattoush, an Arab salad that uses grilled or fried leftover pita. Other possible additions include peppers, radishes, lettuce, chilli, mint, parsley, coriander, allspice, cinnamon and sumac. Each cook, each family, each community has their own variation. A small bone of contention is the size of the dice. Some advocate the tiniest of pieces, only a few millimetres wide, others like them coarser, up to 2cm wide. The one thing that there is no arguing over is that the key lies in the quality of the vegetables. They must be fresh, ripe and flavoursome, with many hours in the sun behind them.

This fabulous salad is probably Sami's mother's creation; Sami can't recall anyone else in the neighbourhood making it. She called it fattoush, which is only true to the extent that it includes chopped vegetables and bread. She added a kind of home-made buttermilk and didn't fry her bread, which makes it terribly comforting.

Try to get small cucumbers for this as for any other fresh salad. They are worlds apart from the large ones we normally get in most UK supermarkets. You could skip the fermentation stage and use buttermilk instead of the combination of milk and yoghurt. For a typical chopped salad, try the Spiced chickpeas and fresh vegetable salad, PAGE 56, omitting the sugar and the chickpeas.

If using yoghurt and milk, start at least three hours and up to a day in advance by placing both in a bowl. Whisk well and leave in a cool place or in the fridge until bubbles form on the surface. What you get is a kind of home-made buttermilk, but less sour.

Tear the bread into bite-size pieces and place in a large mixing bowl. Add your fermented yoghurt mixture or commercial buttermilk, followed by the rest of the ingredients, mix well and leave for 10 minutes for all the flavours to combine.

Spoon the fattoush into serving bowls, drizzle with some olive oil and garnish generously with sumac.

Baby spinach salad with dates & almonds

1 tbsp white wine vinegar
½ medium red onion, thinly sliced
100g pitted Medjool dates, quartered lengthways
30g unsalted butter
2 tbsp olive oil
2 small pitas, about 100g, roughly torn into 4cm pieces
75g whole unsalted almonds, roughly chopped
2 tsp sumac
½ tsp chilli flakes
150g baby spinach leaves, washed
2 tbsp lemon juice
salt

Pitas are allotted the shortest of shelf lives in Jerusalem. Ideally, you'd eat them within a couple of hours of baking. Crunchy pita croutons make good use of leftover pita. We use them for soups and scatter them over salads and other mezzes. They will keep for at least a week in an airtight container. Serve this salad as a starter; its sharp freshness really whets the appetite.

Put the vinegar, onion and dates in a small bowl. Add a pinch of salt and mix well with your hands. Leave to marinate for 20 minutes, then drain any residual vinegar and discard.

Meanwhile, heat the butter and half the olive oil in a medium frying pan. Add the pita and almonds and cook them on a medium heat for 4–6 minutes, stirring all the time, until the pita is crunchy and golden brown. Remove from the heat and mix in the sumac, chilli and ¼ teaspoon of salt. Set aside to cool.

When you are ready to serve, toss the spinach leaves with the pita mix in a large mixing bowl. Add the dates and red onion, remaining olive oil, lemon juice and another pinch of salt. Taste for seasoning and serve immediately.

The humble aubergine

Few ingredients have reached the level of veneration achieved by the humble aubergine or have found their way to almost every table in Jerusalem, for breakfast, lunch and dinner. Everybody loves to be associated with the aubergine — it's like a little local celebrity. The number of people who claim to have invented the baba ghanoush (SEE PAGE 76), or at least elevated it to the level of fine food, is extraordinary.

At the markets in the city, the aubergines come in a wide range of shapes and sizes, from the regular kind, elongated and uniform in size; to zebra — streaked on the outside and pure white on the inside; baby aubergines; globe aubergines and the baladi, a local heirloom variety that is wide, flat and resembles the shape of a fan.

Aubergines, depending on variety, lend themselves to pickling, stuffing, cooking in sauce, frying, baking, roasting, charring, burning, puréeing and even cooking in sugar and spice to make a festive jam (Moroccan) or fruit mostarda (Allepian) — a type of candied fruit conserved in a spicy syrup. They also marry beautifully with the flavours so typical of the city: tahini, pine nuts, date syrup, tomatoes, chickpeas, potatoes, lemon, garlic, lamb meat, fresh cheese and yoghurt, olive oil, sumac and cinnamon.

Arabs first brought aubergines to Italy and Spain but it was the Jews who are said to have introduced them to these cuisines when moving and trading among the Arab Moorish culture and the Christian cultures in the 15th and 16th centuries. Sephardi Jews have always been identified with aubergines, as were Arabs, even when Europeans were quite suspicious about them and were reluctant to use them, believing that 'mad apples', as they were known, helped induce insanity.

Roasted aubergine with fried onion & chopped lemon

2 large aubergines, halved lengthways with the stem on (about 750g in total)
150ml olive oil
4 onions (about 550g in total), peeled and thinly sliced
1½ green chillies
1½ tsp ground cumin
1 tsp sumac
50g feta, broken into large chunks
1 medium lemon
1 garlic clove, crushed
salt and black pepper

Sharp, salty and mildly sweet all intermingle here to make a wonderfully rich starter that can be followed by a light and simple main course, like Turkey and courgette burgers with spring onion and cumin (SEE PAGE 200). Good aubergines should be light in weight, with not many seeds inside, and have a tight, shiny skin. Having some moisture in the oven when roasting them prevents the aubergines from going dry and crisp as they cook and colour. If the oven is pretty full that isn't a problem because of the natural moisture of food. But if you are roasting a single tray of aubergines we recommend placing a shallow tray with some water at the bottom of the oven.

Preheat the oven to 220°C/200°C Fan/Gas Mark 7.

Score the cut side of each aubergine with a criss-cross pattern, brush the cut side with 100ml of the oil and sprinkle liberally with salt and pepper. Place on a baking tray, cut-side up, and roast in the oven for about 45 minutes, until the flesh is golden brown and completely cooked.

While the aubergines are roasting, add the remaining oil to a large frying pan and place on a high heat. Add the onions and ½ a teaspoon of salt and cook for 8 minutes, stirring often, so that parts of the onion get really dark and crisp. Deseed and chop the chillies, keeping the whole one separate from the half. Add the ground cumin, sumac and one chilli and cook for a further 2 minutes before adding the feta. Cook for a final minute, not stirring much, then remove from the heat.

Use a small serrated knife to remove the skin and pith of the lemon. Roughly chop the flesh, discarding the seeds, and place the flesh and any juices in a bowl with the remaining chilli and the garlic.

Assemble the dish as soon as the aubergines are ready. Transfer the roasted halves to a serving dish and spoon the lemon sauce over the flesh. Warm up the onions a little and spoon over. Serve warm or set aside to come to room temperature.

Za'atar

If there is one smell to match the emblematic image of the Old City of Jerusalem, one odour that encapsulates the soul of this ancient city nestling in the Judean Mountains, it is the smell of za'atar. It is hard to describe the flavour of za'atar. It hovers in the general area where herbs like oregano, marjoram, sage or thyme reside, but is quite unique. Za'atar is sharp, warm and slightly pungent, almost at one with the smell of goats' dung, smoke from a far-off fire, soil baked in the sun, and — dare we say it — sweat. Like most of the local plants, it is full of fragrant etheric oils which are released when the hardy, dry bushes are trampled underfoot.

—

ZA'ATAR IS PART AND PARCEL OF THE PALESTINIAN HERITAGE AND THE SMELL OF HOME TO ANYONE WHO GREW UP EITHER IN JERUSALEM OR ELSEWHERE IN THE MOUNTAINOUS REGIONS OF THE HOLY LAND

—

The small bushes grow wild in those mountains and have been used for millennia to give flavour to the local bread. Za'atar is part and parcel of the Palestinian heritage and the smell of home to anyone who grew up either in Jerusalem or elsewhere in the mountainous regions of the Holy Land. For millennia this pervasive plant, known in English as hyssop, has been picked throughout Palestine and used fresh during the spring and early summer or dried and then rehydrated for use later on in the year.

Typically, the leaves would be used to make a salad with fresh tomatoes, spring onion, olive oil and lemon juice. In Sami's family fresh radishes were served on the side. Another use was mixing the leaves into plain bread dough, along with ground turmeric, to bake into fragrant, light loaves.

When Sami and his brothers used to visit his uncle, who lived outside the city, they climbed the rocks surrounding the house to pick large bundles of fresh za'atar that grew in between the nooks and crevices.

To most, though, za'atar is known in the form of a spice mix consisting of powdered dried za'atar leaves, ground sumac, toasted sesame seeds and some salt. This olive-green powder is familiar to any visitor to East Jerusalem who buys the light, sesame-crusted local Arab bagels. These are almost obligatory (they just fly off the wooden carts on which they are sold), and are always accompanied with a little pouch made of old newspaper and containing a generous serving of za'atar mix. Dip and chew, dip and chew, the combination is fragrant and tasty.

In Palestinian cuisine za'atar mix is sprinkled over labneh (STRAINED YOGHURT, SEE PAGE 302), hummus (SEE RECIPE PAGE 114),

chicken, various salads and is particularly popular when applied to a flat piece of dough, covered with tons of olive oil and then baked to make Manakish, a hugely popular Levantine flatbread.

Za'atar is a key ingredient in the Palestinian diet and has become central to modern Israeli cuisine. The spice mix is sold in all supermarkets and grocery shops and cooks sprinkle it liberally to add a certain zest to dishes. Regrettably, za'atar has joined the long list of thorny subjects poisoning the fraught relationship between Arabs and Jews, when Israel declared the herb an endangered species and banned picking it in the wild. Though a compelling argument was made about preserving the dwindling population of wild za'atar, the decree was taken without any form of dialogue with Arabs, who see it as a deliberate violation of their way of life.

Roasted butternut squash & red onion with tahini & za'atar

1 large butternut squash
(1.1kg in total), cut into
2cm x 6cm wedges
2 red onions, cut into
3cm wedges
50ml olive oil
3½ tbsp light tahini paste
1½ tbsp lemon juice
1 small garlic clove,
crushed
30g pine nuts
1 tbsp za'atar
1 tbsp roughly chopped
flat-leaf parsley
Maldon sea salt and black
pepper

This is a highly versatile dish that is quite simple to prepare but boasts some very substantial flavours. It is ideal as a starter, a vegetarian main course or as a side to serve with a simple main course such as Lamb shawarma (SEE PAGE 210) or Chicken sofrito, minus the potatoes (SEE PAGE 190). The tahini sauce is quite dominant — though we love this, you may want to use a little less of it when finishing the dish. Just taste it and decide.

Preheat the oven to 240°C/220°C Fan/Gas Mark 9.

Put the squash and onion in a large mixing bowl, add 3 tablespoons of oil, 1 teaspoon of salt and some black pepper and toss well. Spread on a baking sheet with the skin facing down and roast in the oven for 30–40 minutes until the vegetables have taken on some colour and are cooked through. Keep an eye on the onions as they might cook faster than the squash and need to be removed earlier. Remove from the oven and leave to cool.

To make the sauce place the tahini in a small bowl along with the lemon juice, 2 tablespoons of water, the garlic and ¼ teaspoon of salt. Whisk until the sauce is the consistency of honey, adding more water or tahini if necessary.

Pour the remaining oil into a small frying pan and place on a low-medium heat. Add the pine nuts, along with ½ teaspoon of salt and cook for 2 minutes, stirring often, until the nuts are golden brown. Remove from the heat and transfer to a small bowl, along with the oil, to stop the cooking.

To serve, spread the vegetables out on a large serving platter and drizzle over the tahini. Sprinkle the pine nuts and their oil on top, followed by the za'atar and parsley.

Broad bean kuku

500g broad beans,
  fresh or frozen
2 tbsp caster sugar
45g dried barberries
3 tbsp double cream
¼ tsp saffron threads
5 tbsp olive oil
2 medium onions, finely
  chopped
4 garlic cloves, crushed
7 medium free-range eggs
1 tbsp plain flour
½ tsp baking powder
30g dill, chopped
15g mint, chopped
salt and freshly ground
  black pepper

This frittata-like dish is characteristic of the Iranian Jewish cuisine. Barberries, another typical ingredient, are tiny sharp berries. Try looking for them online or in specialist Middle Eastern and Iranian shops, otherwise substitute with chopped up dried sour cherries. Serve this as a starter with Yoghurt with cucumber (SEE PAGE 299).

Preheat the oven to 180°C/160°C Fan/Gas Mark 4. Put the broad beans in a pan with plenty of boiling water. Simmer for 1 minute, strain, refresh under cold water and set aside.

Pour 75ml of boiling water into a medium bowl, add the caster sugar and stir to dissolve. Once this syrup is tepid, add the barberries and leave them for about 10 minutes, then strain.

Bring the double cream, saffron and 2 tablespoons of water to the boil in a small saucepan. Remove immediately from the heat and set aside for 30 minutes to infuse.

Heat 3 tablespoons of the olive oil in a 25cm non-stick, ovenproof frying pan for which you have a lid. Add the onions and cook on a medium heat for about 4 minutes, stirring occasionally, then add the garlic and cook and stir for a further 2 minutes. Stir in the broad beans and set aside.

Beat the eggs well in a large mixing bowl until frothy. Add the flour, baking powder, saffron cream, herbs, 1½ teaspoons of salt and ½ a teaspoon of pepper and whisk well. Finally stir in the strained barberries and the broad beans and onion mix.

Wipe clean your frying pan, add the remaining olive oil and place in the oven for 10 minutes to heat well. Pour the egg mix into the hot pan, cover with a lid and bake for 15 minutes. Remove the lid and bake for another 20–25 minutes, or until the eggs are just set. Remove from the oven and rest for 5 minutes, before inverting onto a serving platter. Serve warm or at room temperature.

Raw artichoke & herb salad

2–3 large globe artichokes
(700g in total)
3 tbsp lemon juice
4 tbsp olive oil
40g rocket
15g torn mint leaves
15g torn coriander leaves
30g pecorino toscano or
romano, thinly shaved
Maldon sea salt and black
pepper

Artichokes are the most extraordinary vegetable; nothing tastes quite as magical. Many cooks tend to be finicky when it comes to artichokes, easily shunning the effort involved in preparing them. In Jerusalem, some housewives buy many kilograms of artichokes when they are in season, in early summer, and allocate a couple of hours to trimming and cleaning them, before storing them in the freezer for a rainy day. If you can spare the time, we'd encourage you to adopt the habit. If you can't, prepare just a couple and make this refreshing salad, the ideal pairing to anything fatty or hearty. Try it with Lamb shawarma (SEE PAGE 210), *Latkes* (SEE PAGE 92), *or Jerusalem mixed grill* (SEE PAGE 174).

Prepare a bowl of water mixed with half of the lemon juice. Remove the stalk from the artichoke and pull off the tough outer leaves. Once you reach the softer, pale leaves, use a large sharp knife to cut across the flower so that you are left with the bottom quarter. Use a small sharp knife or a vegetable peeler to remove the outer layers of the artichoke until the base, or bottom, is exposed. Scrape out the hairy 'choke' and put the base in the acidulated water. Discard the rest then repeat with the other artichoke(s).

Drain the artichokes and pat dry with paper towels. Using a mandolin or large sharp knife, cut the artichokes into very thin slices, about 1mm thick, and transfer to a large mixing bowl. Squeeze over the remaining lemon juice, add the olive oil and toss well to coat. You can leave the artichoke for up to a few hours if you like, at room temperature. When ready to serve, add the rocket, mint and coriander to the artichoke and season with a ⅓ of a teaspoon of salt and plenty of freshly ground black pepper. Toss gently and arrange on serving plates. Garnish with the pecorino shavings.

Mixed bean salad

String beans are in season in summer and early autumn and are a symbol of the Jewish New Year (Rosh Hashana), particularly with Sephardi Jews. You would expect the fruit and vegetable market, Machne Yehuda, to be bustling the last two days before Rosh Hashana, a holiday on which a seminal family meal takes place. Often, though, the market is eerily calm. A taxi driver explained to us that the smart and canny housewives shop well before the holiday, when the prices are low, preparing and cooking whatever can be made in advance, and that only 'mugs' go shopping last minute, just before the holiday.

280g yellow beans, trimmed (if unavailable, double the quantity of French beans)
280g French beans, trimmed
2 red peppers, cut into 0.5cm strips
3 tbsp olive oil, plus 1 tsp for the peppers
3 garlic cloves, thinly sliced
50g capers, rinsed and patted dry
1 tsp cumin seeds
2 tsp coriander seeds
4 spring onions, thinly sliced
10g tarragon, roughly chopped
20g picked chervil leaves (or a mixture of picked dill and shredded parsley)
grated zest of 1 lemon
salt and black pepper

*Yellow beans are wonderfully tender. We would suggest making an effort to find them, because they make a contribution to the general texture and the look of the dish, but you are perfectly fine substituting as suggested. Serve this salad alongside Polpettone (*SEE PAGE 202*) or Roasted chicken with Jerusalem artichoke and lemon (*SEE PAGE 180*).*

Preheat the oven to 220°C/200°C Fan/Gas Mark 7.

Bring a large pan with plenty of water to the boil and add the yellow beans. After 1 minute add the French beans and cook for another 4 minutes, or until the beans are cooked through but still crunchy. Refresh under ice-cold water, drain, pat dry and place in a large mixing bowl.

Meanwhile, toss the peppers in 1 teaspoon of olive oil, spread on a baking tray and place in the oven for 5 minutes or until tender. Remove from the oven and add to the bowl with the cooked beans.

Heat the 3 tablespoons of olive oil in a small saucepan. Add the garlic and cook for 20 seconds, add the capers (careful, they spit!) and fry for another 15 seconds. Add the cumin and coriander seeds and continue frying for another 15 seconds. The garlic should have turned golden by now. Remove from the heat and pour the contents of the pan immediately over the beans. Toss and add the spring onion, herbs, lemon zest, ⅓ of a teaspoon of salt and black pepper. Serve, or keep refrigerated for up to a day. Just remember to bring back to room temperature before serving.

Lemony leek meatballs

What is a meat recipe doing in the vegetable section? Well, what makes these fritters so special is how well the flavour of the leeks holds its own against the meat, while the latter is more in the background. This is a reversal of roles when compared with other meatballs. The result is feather-light texture, and a sharp lemony flavour.

The recipe was given to us by Tamara Meitlis, who is a fine Turkish Jewish cook and a great friend. It is highly typical of the Jews of Izmir. As with most other Turks, you don't mess about with Tamara's recipes. 'Sure, you can do it differently if you like,' she tells us with a generous smile, 'but only if you want it to come out wrong!' Tamara is right. Sephardi recipes, particularly Turkish, which is a mature and confident cuisine, have been perfected over generations and are best adhered to religiously. When you come to think of it, this is true of most Jerusalem cuisines, and you should really only deviate from a traditional recipe once you have made sure there isn't any senior mama looking over your shoulder.

---

6 large trimmed leeks
 (about 800g in total)
250g minced beef
90g breadcrumbs
2 medium free-range eggs
2 tbsp sunflower oil
200–300ml chicken stock
80ml lemon juice
 (about 2 lemons)
80g Greek yoghurt
1 tbsp finely chopped flat-
 leaf parsley
salt and black pepper

These make a wonderfully light starter after which you can serve almost anything. As a variation, you can finish them off while frying them in the pan. Just cook them longer, without braising in the stock, and serve hot with a wedge of lemon.

Cut the leeks into 2 cm slices and steam them for approximately 20 minutes, until completely soft. Drain and leave to cool, then squeeze out any residual water with a tea towel. Process the leeks in a food processor by pulsing a few times until well chopped but not mushy. Place the leeks in a large mixing bowl, along with the meat, breadcrumbs, eggs, 1¼ teaspoons of salt and 1 teaspoon of black pepper. Form the mix into flat patties, roughly 7cm x 2cm — this should make 8. Refrigerate for 30 minutes.

Heat up the oil over a medium–high heat in a large heavy-based frying pan for which you have a lid and sear the patties on both sides until golden brown; this can be done in batches if necessary.

Wipe out the base of the pan with a paper towel and then lay the meatballs back inside, slightly overlapping if needed. Pour over enough stock so the patties are almost covered, but not quite. Add the lemon juice and ½ teaspoon of salt. Bring to the boil, then cover and simmer gently for 30 minutes. Remove the lid and cook for a few more minutes, if needed, until almost all the liquid has evaporated. Remove the pan from the heat and set aside to cool down.

Serve the meatballs just warm, or at room temperature, with a dollop of Greek yoghurt and a sprinkle of chopped parsley.

Kohlrabi salad

Kohlrabi is a weird vegetable. We don't like saying it but it is. It is a cabbage with a swollen stem that looks like a bumpy green or purple apple and with a texture and flavour not dissimilar to a radish or cabbage heart. It is weird because of its look — it is like an alien vegetable, with a round, squat base from which straight leafy stems spew out haphazardly — and because people in the West, Germany excepted, have no clue what to do with it. Perhaps because of its oddity and eccentricity, or maybe because it is so easy to grow and tastes so fresh, people in Israel love it. Jerusalemites mainly use kohlrabi for refreshing and crunchy salads, sometimes in combination with other firm vegetables and fruit, such as fennel, radish, cabbage and apple. But they also cook with it, adding it to stews and creamy gratins and sometimes even stuff it.

---

3 medium kohlrabies
  (750g in total)
80g Greek yoghurt
70g soured cream
50g thick double cream
1 small garlic clove,
  crushed
1½ tsp lemon juice
1 tbsp olive oil
2 tbsp finely shredded
  fresh mint
1 tsp dried mint
20g baby watercress
¼ tsp sumac
salt and white pepper

This salad was first made in our London West End restaurant, NOPI. It is simple, fresh and makes for a great way either to open or end a meal. You can also serve it alongside a selection of other seasonal salads or cooked vegetables to make a light meal. Choose kohlrabies that are small and hard with tight-looking skin.

Peel the kohlrabies, cut into 1.5cm dice and put in a large mixing bowl. Set aside and make the dressing.

Put the yoghurt, soured cream, double cream, garlic, lemon juice and olive oil in a medium bowl. Add ¼ teaspoon of salt and a healthy grind of pepper and whisk well. Add the dressing to the kohlrabi, followed by the fresh and dried mint and half the watercress. Gently stir and place on a serving dish. Dot the remaining watercress on top and sprinkle with the sumac.

Root vegetable slaw with labneh

3 medium beetroot
(450g in total)
2 medium carrots
(250g in total)
½ a celeriac (300g in total)
1 medium kohlrabi
(250g in total)
4 tbsp lemon juice
4 tbsp olive oil
3 tbsp sherry vinegar
2 tsp caster sugar
25g coriander leaves,
roughly chopped
25g mint leaves, shredded
20g flat-leaf parsley leaves,
roughly chopped
½ tbsp grated lemon zest
200g Labneh (see page
302) or shop-bought
salt and coarsely ground
black pepper

We make this salad in the winter or early spring, before any of the summer crops are around. It is incredibly fresh, ideal for starting a hearty meal. It is also great served alongside grilled oily fish. The labneh can be substituted with Greek yoghurt, well seasoned with some olive oil, crushed garlic and salt and pepper. It can also be left out all together, if you prefer to keep it light and simple. This recipe was inspired by a dish from Manta Ray, a great restaurant on the beach in Tel Aviv.

Peel all the vegetables and slice them thinly, about 2mm thick. Stack a few slices at a time on top of each other and cut them into matchstick-like strips. Alternatively, use a mandolin or a food processor with the appropriate attachment. Place all the strips in a large bowl and cover with cold water. Set aside while you make the dressing.

Place the lemon juice, olive oil, vinegar, sugar and 1 teaspoon of salt in a small saucepan. Bring to a gentle simmer and stir until the sugar and the salt have dissolved. Remove from the heat.

Drain the vegetable strips and transfer to a paper towel to dry well. Dry the bowl and replace the vegetables. Pour the hot dressing over the vegetables, mix well and leave to cool. Place in the fridge for at least 45 minutes.

When ready to serve, add the herbs, lemon zest and 1 teaspoon of black pepper to the salad. Toss well, taste and add more salt if needed. Pile onto serving plates and serve with some labneh on the side.

Fried tomatoes with garlic

3 large garlic cloves,
    crushed
½ a small hot chilli, finely
    chopped
2 tbsp chopped flat-leaf
    parsley
3 large, ripe but
    firm tomatoes
    (about 450g in total)
2 tbsp olive oil
Maldon sea salt and
    coarsely ground black
    pepper
rustic bread, to serve

These tomatoes, eaten by Palestinians any time of the day when tomatoes are in season, are not an earth-shattering revelation but they are quietly and surprisingly fantastic when served with simply grilled fish (SEE GRILLED FISH SKEWERS WITH HAWAYEJ AND PARSLEY, PAGE 226), *simple rice* (SEE BASMATI RICE AND ORZO, PAGE 103) *or other grain dishes with a clear savoury note* (SEE MEJADRA, PAGE 120). *To keep it simple, serve them with a thick slice of good bread. Adjust the cooking time and temperature to the softness of the tomatoes: a soft tomato should be cooked on a higher heat for a shorter time. In any case, use only good, flavoursome tomatoes.*

Mix the garlic, chilli and chopped parsley in a small bowl and set aside. Top and tail the tomatoes and slice vertically into thick slices, about 1.5cm thick.

Heat the oil in a large frying pan placed over a medium heat. Add the tomato slices, season with salt and pepper and cook for about a minute, then turn over, season again with salt and pepper and sprinkle with the garlic mixture.

Continue to cook for another minute or so, shaking the pan occasionally, then turn the slices again and cook for a few more seconds, until soft but not mushy.

Turn the tomatoes over onto a serving plate, pour over the juices from the pan and serve immediately.

Puréed beetroot with yoghurt & za'atar

Beetroot is one of very few vegetables that have a strong presence in the cuisine of almost any group in Jerusalem: it colours pickling juices on the Arab table (SEE PAGE 307) and is used in most mezze selections, it is the base for Ashkenazi borscht and hamitsa, a refreshing cold version of the soup, and it forms the basis for another soup, of Jewish-Iraqi and Kurdish origin, where the famous semolina kubbeh is served (SEE PAGE 162).

Beetroot also crosses cultural lines with the flexibility of an acrobat. On Yotam's tour of the city when filming a documentary about Jerusalem food, he met Michal Baranes and Yakub Barhum. They are a mixed couple, she is Jewish with Moroccan ancestry and he is a Muslim from the Arab village of Ein Raffa, on the outskirts of the city. At their restaurant, Michal, the chef, does some cross-cultural fireworks with her food, featuring elements from her Moroccan heritage, alongside very current Israeli themes and many traditional Palestinian dishes she learns from her cooks, who are mostly local. One of Michal's most useful tools is chrein, the horseradish and beetroot relish used in practically every Ashkenazi household. She puts it in her prawn 'falafel' — minced prawns and chrein, rolled in panko crumbs and deep-fried — making scrumptious fishcakes that look like falafel but taste nothing like it.

900g medium beetroots (500g in total after cooking and peeling)
2 garlic cloves, crushed
1 small red chilli, deseeded and finely chopped
250g Greek yoghurt
1½ tbsp date syrup
3 tbsp olive oil, plus extra to finish the dish
1 tbsp za'atar
salt

TO GARNISH

2 spring onions, thinly sliced
15g toasted hazelnuts, roughly crushed
60g soft goat's cheese, crumbled

You will be surprised how well beetroot works with chilli and za'atar. Its sweetness takes on a seriously savoury edge which makes it one of the most popular salads among Ottolenghi's customers. You can serve it as a dip or a starter, with bread, or as part of a mezze range. If the beetroot is watery and the dip ends up runny and doesn't hold its shape, consider adding a little mashed potato to help thicken it. Date syrup can be replaced with maple syrup.

Preheat the oven to 200°C/180°C Fan/Gas Mark 6.

Wash the beetroot and place in a roasting tin. Put them in the oven and cook, uncovered, until a knife slices easily into the centre, approximately 1 hour. Once they are cool enough to handle, peel and cut each one into about 6 pieces. Allow to cool down.

Place the beetroot, garlic, chilli and yoghurt in a food processor bowl and blend to a smooth paste. Transfer to a large mixing bowl and stir in the date syrup, olive oil, za'atar and 1 teaspoon of salt. Taste and add more salt if you like.

Transfer the mash onto a flat serving plate and use the back of a spoon to spread the mixture around the plate. Scatter the spring onion, hazelnut and cheese on top and finally drizzle with a bit of oil. Serve at room temperature.

Swiss chard fritters

400g Swiss chard leaves,
  white stalks removed
30g flat-leaf parsley
20g coriander
20g dill
1½ tsp grated nutmeg
½ tsp sugar
3 tbsp plain flour
2 garlic cloves, crushed
2 medium free-range eggs
80g feta, broken into small
  pieces
60ml olive oil
1 lemon, cut into 4 wedges
salt and black pepper

The intense green colour of these fritters, originally Turkish, is paralleled by a wonderfully concentrated 'green' flavour of chard and herbs. They are a truly marvellous way to start a meal. Spinach makes a good substitute for chard: increase the quantity by 50 per cent and just wilt it in a pan instead of boiling it.

Bring a large pan of salted water to the boil, add the chard and simmer for 5 minutes. Drain the leaves and squeeze them well until completely dry. Place in a food processor along with the herbs, nutmeg, sugar, flour, garlic, eggs, ⅓ teaspoon of salt and some black pepper. Blitz until smooth and then fold the feta through the mix by hand.

Pour a tablespoon of oil into a medium frying pan. Put over medium–high heat and spoon in a heaped tablespoon of mixture for each fritter. Press down gently to get a 7cm wide and 1cm thick fritter. You should be able to fit about three at a time. Cook for 3–4 minutes in total, turning once, until the fritters have taken on some colour. Transfer to kitchen paper then keep each batch warm while you cook the remaining mixture. Serve at once with a wedge of lemon.

Spiced chickpeas & fresh vegetable salad

100g dried chickpeas
1 tsp bicarbonate of soda
2 small cucumbers
  (280g in total)
2 large tomatoes
  (300g in total)
240g radishes
1 red pepper, deseeded and
  white flesh removed
1 small red onion, peeled
20g coriander leaves and
  stems, roughly chopped
15g flat-leaf parsley,
  roughly chopped
90ml olive oil
grated zest of 1 lemon, plus
  2 tbsp juice
1½ tbsp sherry vinegar
1 garlic clove, crushed
1 tsp caster sugar
1 tsp ground cardamom
1½ tsp ground allspice
1 tsp ground cumin
Greek yoghurt (optional)
salt and black pepper

The inspiration for this salad didn't come directly from Jerusalem but rather from Morito, a wonderful London tapas bar owned and run by Samantha and Samuel Clark, whose food is inspired by southern Spain, North Africa and the Middle East, very much echoing the same voices that can be heard in Jerusalem's kitchens. The combination of the cold and fresh salad with the warm chickpeas is surprisingly enticing. You can serve this dish as it is, with just a thick, fresh pita. Still, a plate of Hummus (SEE PAGE 114) alongside, or perhaps Cauliflower with tahini (SEE PAGE 60) would complement it fantastically well. The salad also works on its own without the chickpeas (just omit the sugar).

Soak the dried chickpeas overnight in a large bowl with plenty of cold water and the bicarbonate of soda. The next day, drain, place in a large saucepan and cover with water twice the volume of the chickpeas. Bring to the boil and simmer for about an hour, skimming off any foam, until completely tender, then drain.

Cut the cucumber, tomato, radish and pepper into 1.5cm dice; cut the onion into 0.5cm dice. Mix everything together in a bowl with the coriander and parsley.

In a jar or sealable container mix 75ml of the olive oil, the lemon juice and zest, sherry vinegar, garlic and sugar and mix well to form a dressing, then season to taste with salt and pepper. Pour the dressing over the salad and toss lightly.

Mix together the cardamom, allspice, cumin and ¼ teaspoon of salt and spread on a plate. Toss the cooked chickpeas in the spice mixture in a few batches to coat well. Heat the remaining olive oil in a frying pan and over a medium heat lightly fry the chickpeas for 2–3 minutes, gently shaking the pan so they cook evenly and don't stick. Keep warm.

Divide the salad between four plates, arranging it in a large circle, and spoon the warm spiced chickpeas on top, keeping the edge of the salad clear. You can drizzle some Greek yoghurt on top to make the salad creamy.

Chermoula aubergine with bulgar & yoghurt

Historically, bulgar was generally the rural people's food in the Middle East, while rice was for more affluent city folk. Still, bulgar — boiled wheat that has been dried and cracked or ground — was staple to many Palestinians. Today, this differentiation is less relevant, with bulgar gaining popularity with everybody, particularly for salads and mezzes.

2 garlic cloves, crushed
2 tsp ground cumin
2 tsp ground coriander
1 tsp chilli flakes
1 tsp sweet paprika
2 tbsp finely chopped
  preserved lemon skin
  (see recipe page 303,
  or shop-bought)
140ml olive oil, plus extra
  to finish
2 medium aubergines
150g fine bulgar
50g sultanas
10g fresh coriander,
  chopped, plus extra
  to finish
10g fresh mint, chopped
50g pitted green olives,
  halved
30g flaked almonds,
  toasted
3 spring onions, chopped
1½ tbsp lemon juice
120g Greek yoghurt
salt

Chermoula is a powerful North African paste that is brushed over fish and vegetables giving them the perfumed aroma of preserved lemon, mixed with heat and spice. Here, the aubergines flavoured with chermoula, drizzled with cold yoghurt, make a luscious way to start any meal. Combine it with the sweet and salty bulgar salad and you have a modest vegetarian feast.

Preheat the oven to 200°C/180°C Fan/Gas Mark 6.

To make the chermoula, mix together in a small bowl the garlic, cumin, coriander, chilli, paprika, preserved lemon, two thirds of the olive oil and ½ a teaspoon of salt.

Cut the aubergines in half lengthways. Score the flesh of each half with deep, diagonal criss-cross scores, making sure not to pierce the skin. Spoon the chermoula over each half, spreading it evenly, and place on a baking sheet cut-side up. Put in the oven and roast for 40 minutes, or until the aubergines are completely soft.

Meanwhile, place the bulgar in a large bowl and cover with 140ml boiling water.

Soak the sultanas in 50ml of warm water. After 10 minutes drain the sultanas and add them to the bulgar, along with the remaining oil. Add the herbs, olives, almonds, spring onion, lemon juice and a pinch of salt and stir to combine. Taste and add more salt if necessary.

Serve the aubergines warm or at room temperature. Place one half per portion on a serving plate. Spoon bulgar on top, allowing some to fall from both sides. Spoon over some yoghurt, sprinkle with chopped coriander and finish with a drizzle of oil.

Fried cauliflower with tahini

This dish is usually served in the context of a large mezze assortment, laid out on the table at the beginning of a substantial meal. This type of dining is now familiar in the West and has become quite popular — the communal tables in Ottolenghi provide good evidence — but it is hard to overstate how deeply rooted it is in the culture and the temperament of Jerusalem and the wider region.

For Jerusalemites, Arabs and Jews alike, the idea of dining on one's own is abhorrent. Eating is a celebration, a feast, it is about breaking bread and about conviviality, it is about abundance and sharing. As no one is particularly fussy about decorum and good table manners, the meal is always destined to turn into a lively gorge, with everybody sharing everything, happy to dig into each other's plates, to grab and move plates around until truly satisfied. It is not a particularly orderly or calm way to eat, but it is certainly a very happy one.

500ml sunflower oil
2 medium cauliflower heads (1kg in total), divided into small florets
8 spring onions, each divided into three long segments
180g light tahini paste
2 garlic cloves, crushed
15g flat-leaf parsley, chopped
15g chopped mint, plus extra to finish
150g Greek yoghurt
60ml lemon juice, plus grated zest of 1 lemon
1 tsp pomegranate molasses, plus extra to finish
about 180ml water
Maldon sea salt and black pepper

For many in the West who have been brought up on cauliflower cheese and other similar dairy-heavy dishes, it is hard to fathom different, sharper and fresher treatments of cauliflower. This salad keeps the creamy element that helps make cauliflower comforting but without tasting in any way greasy or unctuous. It will keep in the fridge for a day. Just remember to bring it back to room temperature and re-season before serving.

Heat up the sunflower oil in a large saucepan placed on a medium–high heat. Using a pair of metal tongs or a metal spoon, carefully place a few cauliflower florets at a time into the oil and cook them for 2–3 minutes, turning them over so they colour evenly. Once golden brown, use a slotted spoon to lift the florets into a colander to drain. Sprinkle with a little salt. Continue in batches until you finish all the cauliflower. Next, fry the spring onion in batches but only for about 1 minute. Add to the cauliflower. Allow both to cool down a little.

Pour the tahini paste into a large mixing bowl and add the garlic, chopped herbs, yoghurt, lemon juice and zest, pomegranate molasses and some salt and pepper. Stir well with a wooden spoon as you add the water. The tahini sauce will thicken and then loosen up as you add water. Don't add too much, just enough to get a thick, yet smooth, pourable consistency, a bit like honey.

Add the cauliflower and spring onion to the tahini and stir well. Taste and adjust the seasoning. You may also want to add more lemon juice.

To serve, spoon into a serving bowl and finish with a few drops of pomegranate molasses and some mint.

Roasted cauliflower & hazelnut salad

1 head of cauliflower,
  broken into small florets
  (660g in total)
5 tbsp olive oil
1 large stick of celery, cut
  on an angle into 0.5cm
  slices (70g in total)
30g hazelnuts, with skins
10g small flat-leaf parsley
  leaves, picked
50g pomegranate seeds
  (from about ½ a medium
  pomegranate)
⅓ tsp ground cinnamon
⅓ tsp ground allspice
1 tbsp sherry vinegar
1½ tsp maple syrup
salt and black pepper

Cauliflower, raw or lightly cooked, is a useful salad ingredient, above all in winter when there isn't a great variety of fresh vegetables available. It soaks up flavours particularly effectively and benefits from anything sweet and sharp. This salad, which will go well with the Chicken sofrito (SEE PAGE 190) or with Grilled fish skewers with hawayej and parsley (SEE PAGE 226) is inspired by a recipe from a brilliant Australian chef and food writer, Karen Martini.

Preheat the oven to 220°C/200°C Fan/Gas Mark 7.

Mix the cauliflower with 3 tablespoons of the olive oil, ½ a teaspoon of salt and some black pepper. Spread out in a roasting tin and roast on the top oven shelf for 25–35 minutes, until the cauliflower is crisp and parts of it have turned golden brown. Transfer to a large mixing bowl and set aside to cool down.

Reduce the oven temperature to 170°C/150°C Fan/Gas Mark 3½. Spread the hazelnuts out on a baking tray lined with baking parchment and roast for 17 minutes.

Allow the nuts to cool a little, then roughly chop them and add to the cauliflower, along with the remaining oil and the rest of the ingredients. Stir, taste and season with salt and pepper accordingly. Serve at room temperature.

A'ja (bread fritters)

This Tripolitan version is one among endless kinds of vegetable or herb-based bread fritters and omelettes that are rife all over the city. This is convenience food at its best, ready to be stuffed inside a pita and put in a lunch box, or prepared as a quick 'solution' for a light meal using leftover bread and seasonal vegetables. It may not sound appetizing, but taste it once, and you will see what it's all about.

---

4 white bread slices, crusts removed (80g in total)
4 large free-range eggs
1½ tsp ground cumin
½ tsp sweet paprika
¼ tsp cayenne pepper
25g chives, chopped
25g flat-leaf parsley, chopped
10g tarragon, chopped
40g feta cheese, crumbled
sunflower oil, for frying
salt and freshly ground black pepper

You can add grated vegetables, such as courgette or sweet potato, to your A'ja, replacing the bread or adding to it. Feel free to play with the herbs and spices. Tunisians, for instance, add chopped mint and crushed garlic. Vegetable-based fritters are best served in a pita, warm or at room temperature, with Tahini sauce (SEE PAGE 298) *and sliced tomato and cucumber. This bread-based variety is nice on its own with a fresh salad* (SEE FATTOUSH, PAGE 29), *omitting the bread.*

Soak the bread in plenty of cold water for 1 minute, then squeeze well.

Crumble the soaked bread into a medium bowl then add the eggs, spices, ½ a teaspoon of salt and ¼ teaspoon of pepper and whisk well. Mix in the chopped herbs and feta.

Heat up 1 tablespoon of oil in a medium frying pan on a medium–high heat. Spoon about 3 tablespoons of the mixture into the centre of the pan and flatten it using the underside of the spoon; the fritters should be 2–3cm thick. Fry the fritter for 2–3 minutes on each side or until golden brown. Repeat with the remaining batter. You should get about 8 fritters.

Alternatively, you can fry all the batter at once, as you would a large omelette. Slice and serve warm or at room temperature.

Spicy carrot salad

Most typical mezze selections served in restaurants across the city have some variation on carrot salad, which must include cooked carrot, oil, garlic and lemon juice or vinegar. This is pretty much the standard. However, as is often the case, the devil is in the details and these vary substantially.

In our mind, the best carrot salads are found in North African kitchens, where a potent chilli and spice paste blends with the natural sweetness of the carrot and gives it some serious depth. Moroccans make a version where caraway seeds are added. Jews from Tripoli, Libya, a community with a rich and distinctive cuisine, make an array of chershi, which are piquant condiments. These are served at a Friday night dinner, along with pickles, next to the main course, stew, and couscous. The most typical is chershi kara'a, crushed pumpkin salad.

---

6 large carrots, peeled (about 700g in total)
3 tbsp sunflower oil
1 large onion, finely chopped (300g in total)
1 tbsp Pilpelchuma (see page 302) or 2 tbsp harissa (shop-bought or see page 301)
½ tsp ground cumin
½ tsp caraway seeds, freshly ground
½ tsp sugar
3 tbsp cider vinegar
30g rocket leaves
salt

This carrot salad is based on a recipe by Pascale Perez-Rubin, an illustrious food writer who has researched Tripolitan food in great detail. Rubin's pumpkin salad is very similar. You can substitute the carrot with cooked pumpkin or butternut squash and crush to create a beautiful, vibrant paste or dip. It is important to allow this salad to sit to let the flavours come together and mellow — at least 30 minutes. Harissa can substitute for the pilpelchuma — though pilpelchuma is the real deal — but you must assess how hot it is before adding.

Place the carrots in a large saucepan, cover with water and bring to a boil. Reduce the heat, cover and cook for about 20 minutes, until the carrots are just tender. Drain and, once cool enough to handle, cut into 5mm slices.

While the carrots are cooking, heat half the oil in a large frying pan. Add the onion and cook on a medium heat for 10 minutes, until golden brown.

Tip the fried onion into a large mixing bowl and add the pilpelchuma, cumin, caraway, ¾ of a teaspoon of salt, sugar, vinegar and remaining oil. Add the carrots and toss well. Leave aside for at least 20 minutes for the flavours to mature.

Arrange the salad on a large platter, dotting with rocket as you go.

Shakshuka

Shakshuka is originally a Tunisian dish but has become hugely popular in Jerusalem and all over Israel as substantial breakfast or lunch fare. Tunisian cuisine has a passionate love affair with eggs and this particular version of shakshuka is the seasonal variant for the summer and early autumn. Potatoes are used during the winter and aubergines in spring.

Having published recipes for shakshuka once or twice before, we are well aware of the risk of repeating ourselves. Still, we are happy to add another version of this splendid dish, seeing how popular it is and how convenient it is to prepare. This time the focus is on tomato and spice. But we encourage you to play around with different ingredients and adjust the amount of heat to your taste. Serve with good white bread and nothing else.

2 tbsp olive oil
2 tbsp Pilpelchuma
  (see page 302) or harissa
  paste (see page 301,
  or shop-bought)
2 tsp tomato purée
2 large red peppers, cut
  into 0.5cm dice
  (300g in total)
4 garlic cloves, finely
  chopped
1 tsp ground cumin
5 large, very ripe tomatoes,
  chopped (800g in total);
  tinned are also fine
4 medium free-range eggs
  plus 4 egg yolks
120g Labneh (see recipe
  page 302) or shop-
  bought, or thick yoghurt
salt

Heat the olive oil in a large frying pan over a medium heat and add the pilpelchuma or harissa, tomato purée, peppers, garlic, cumin and ¾ of a teaspoon of salt. Stir and cook on a moderate heat for about 8 minutes to allow the peppers to soften. Add the tomatoes, bring to a gentle simmer and cook for a further 10 minutes until you have quite a thick sauce. Taste for seasoning.

Make eight little dips in the sauce. Gently break the eggs and carefully pour each into its own dip. Do the same with the yolks. Use a fork to swirl the egg whites a little bit with the sauce, taking care not to break the yolks. Simmer gently for 8–10 minutes, until the egg whites are set but the yolks are still runny (you can cover the pan with a lid if you wish to hasten the process). Remove from the heat, leave for a couple of minutes to settle, then spoon into individual plates and serve with the labneh or yoghurt.

Butternut squash & tahini spread

1 very large butternut
  squash (about 1.2kg),
  peeled and cut into
  chunks (970g in total
  once peeled)
3 tbsp olive oil
1 tsp ground cinnamon
70g light tahini paste
120g Greek yoghurt
2 small garlic cloves,
  crushed
1 tsp mixed black and
  white sesame seeds
  (or just white, if you don't
  have black)
1½ tsp date syrup
2 tbsp chopped coriander
  (optional)
salt

Date syrup, which we use here to add intensity, is a popular natural sweetener with wonderful richness and treacly depth. Use it for salad and vegetable dressings, to sweeten stews or just drizzle over porridge in the morning. It is available from health food shops and Middle Eastern grocers but can be substituted with golden syrup, maple syrup or even treacle.

This dip seems to be fantastically popular with anyone who tries it. There is something about the magical combination of tahini and pumpkin or squash that we always tend to come back to (SEE ALSO ROASTED BUTTERNUT SQUASH, PAGE 36). *Serve as a starter with bread or as part of a mezze selection.*

Preheat the oven to 200°C/180°C Fan/Gas Mark 6.

Spread the squash out in a medium roasting tin. Pour over the olive oil and sprinkle on the cinnamon and ½ a teaspoon of salt. Mix together well, cover the tray tightly with foil and roast in the oven for 70 minutes, stirring once during the cooking. Remove from the oven and leave to cool.

Transfer the squash to a food processor bowl, along with the tahini, yoghurt and garlic. Roughly pulse so that everything is combined into a coarse paste, without the spread becoming smooth; you can also do this by hand using a fork or potato masher.

Spread the butternut in a wavy pattern over a flat plate and sprinkle with the sesame seeds, drizzle over the syrup and finish with the chopped coriander, if using.

Georgia

Walnuts, plums, beets, herbs, aubergines, pomegranates and grapes are some key ingredients of Georgian cuisine, which is influenced by Russian, Persian and Turkish cultures. Georgian legend tells that when God was handing out land to the peoples of the world, the Georgians were too busy eating, drinking and feasting. When they finally arrived it was too late and no land was left. The Georgians had told God they had been toasting his health and invited him to join them. He had such a good time at their table that he eventually decided to give them the land he had been saving for himself.

Jews from Georgia settled in Jerusalem in the late 19th century, just outside the old city walls, building a small neighbourhood near Damascus gate. They brought with them their rich and colourful food, which fitted perfectly with the local cuisine and produce available. Pkhali, a crushed walnut sauce that can be spooned over various vegetables such as aubergines, spinach and beets, bears a resemblance to muhammara, a local crushed walnut salad. Their beetroot salads were often similar to salatet banjar, the Palestinian version made up of sliced cooked beetroot, garlic, olive oil, lemon juice and chopped parsley. Sadly, as is too often the case in this city, this culinary brotherhood was not enough. The Georgian neighbourhood was completely decimated during the 1929 Palestinian revolt, the first of many uprisings protesting against the growing presence of Jewish settlers in Palestine. Still, Georgians managed to thrive in other parts of the city and over the years made their mark on the local food.

Spicy beetroot, leek & walnut salad

4 medium beetroots
   (600g in total after
   cooking and peeling)
4 medium leeks, cut into
   10cm segments
   (360g in total)
15g fresh coriander,
   roughly chopped
25g rocket
50g pomegranate seeds
   (optional)

DRESSING

100g walnuts, coarsely
   chopped
4 garlic cloves, finely
   chopped
¼ tsp chilli flakes
60ml cider vinegar
2 tbsp tamarind water
½ tsp walnut oil
2½ tbsp groundnut oil
1 tsp salt

This gutsy salad is inspired by Georgian cuisine (SEE PAGE 71). *The beetroot and leeks can be cooked well ahead of time, even a day in advance. We keep the two elements of the salad separate until serving, so the beetroot doesn't colour the leek red. This is not necessary if such an aesthetic consideration is not top of your priority list. Other colours of beetroot — golden, white or striped — are also good.*

Preheat the oven to 220°C/200°C Fan/Gas Mark 7.

Wrap the beetroots individually in tin foil and roast them in the oven for 60–90 minutes, depending on their size. Once cooked, you should be able to stick a small knife through to the centre easily. Remove from the oven and set aside to cool.

Once cool enough to handle, peel the beets, halve them and cut each half into wedges, 1cm thick at the base. Put in a medium bowl and set aside.

Place the leeks in a medium pan with salted water, bring to the boil and simmer for 10 minutes, until just cooked; it's important to simmer them gently and not to overcook them so they don't fall apart. Drain and refresh under cold water, then use a very sharp serrated knife to cut each segment into 3 smaller pieces and pat dry. Transfer to a bowl, separate from the beets, and set aside.

While the vegetables are cooking, mix all the dressing ingredients and leave to one side for at least 10 minutes for all the flavours to come together.

Divide the walnut dressing and the fresh coriander equally between the beets and the leeks and toss gently. Taste both and add more salt if needed.

To put the salad together, spread most of the beetroot on a serving platter, top with some rocket, then most of the leeks, then the remaining beetroot and finish with more leek and rocket. Sprinkle over the pomegranate seeds, if using, and serve.

Charred okra with tomato, garlic & preserved lemon

Okra in the Middle East is smaller and much less sinewy than the type we usually get in Britain. It is very popular in Jerusalem, where it is normally cooked with tomato, onion and garlic, often served with fresh coriander. Tamarind syrup and lemon juice are also popular accompaniments.

When okra was in season Sami's grandmother used to thread it, like a necklace, onto a long string, hang it in a cool place and leave it to dry. This would later be rehydrated when cooking it in yachne, a Palestinian meat and tomato stew, where it imparted a glorious flavour and thickened up the sauce.

300g baby or very small okra
2 tbsp olive oil, plus more if needed
4 garlic cloves, thinly sliced
20g preserved lemon skin, cut into 1cm wedges (see recipe page 303, or shop-bought)
3 small tomatoes (200g in total), cut into 8 wedges, or halved cherry tomatoes
½ tbsp chopped flat-leaf parsley
½ tbsp chopped coriander
1 tbsp lemon juice
Maldon sea salt and black pepper

For this quick stir-fry, a robust yet not too heavy starter, try to get small okra in markets or Asian grocers. Another alternative, available from some Middle Eastern shops or small supermarkets, is prepared frozen okra, usually from Egypt; it has great flavour and texture.

Trim the okra using a small, sharp fruit knife, removing the stems just above the pod, so as not to expose the seeds.

Place a large, heavy-based frying pan on a high heat and leave for a few minutes. Once almost red hot, throw in the okra in two batches and dry-cook, shaking the pan occasionally, for 4 minutes per batch. The okra pods should have the occasional dark blister.

Return all the charred okra to the pan, add the olive oil, garlic and preserved lemon. Stir-fry for 2 minutes, shaking the pan. Reduce the heat to medium then add the tomatoes, 2 tablespoons of water, the chopped herbs, lemon juice and ½ a teaspoon of salt and some black pepper. Stir everything together gently, so that the tomatoes do not break up, and continue to cook for 2–3 minutes, so that the tomatoes warm through. Transfer to a serving dish, drizzle with more olive oil and a sprinkle of salt and serve.

Baba ghanoush?

Burning an aubergine is probably the most effective tool of the Jerusalemite cook, as it is of many others throughout the region. Over the years we have cooked dozens of salads based on this super-popular technique. The aubergine pulp can be used in many contexts — stews, soups (SEE BURNT AUBERGINE AND MOGRABIEH SOUP, PAGE 141), with roasted meat or fish (SEE FISH AND CAPER KEBABS, PAGE 221) — but essentially it is in the department of salad and dips that it comes into its glorious own. The variations are numerous and depend on regions and cultures. You would think that everybody would live together in tolerant, yet smoky, harmony. Not quite.

Yotam recently went to talk and cook on a BBC radio programme about his baba ghanoush, a hugely popular Levantine dish that consists of burnt aubergine, mashed and mixed with various seasonings. To stir things up a bit, he was confronted with someone who had a very different idea about baba ghanoush. Rana Jawad, the courageous Lebanese BBC correspondent who went undercover in Tripoli during the final months of Gaddafi's reign, wasn't on the show to talk about food but was given a spoonful of the salad. She loved it but strongly protested against calling it baba ghanoush. 'If it doesn't have tahini in it, it isn't the real thing', she said. Yotam was happy to concede.

YOU WOULD THINK THAT EVERYBODY WOULD LIVE TOGETHER IN TOLERANT, YET SMOKY, HARMONY. NOT QUITE

We are not sure what Rana would have said had she seen the deconstructed baba ghanoush that the Jerusalemite chef Ezra Kedem cooked for Yotam, where he had beautifully spread out on a plate the flesh of a baby aubergine and dotted it with all the other salad elements, tahini included, but without stirring or mixing it. In any case, it seemed clear that everybody was agreed: baba ghanoush has to have tahini.

Then, another turn of events. When we went to talk to Nawal Abu Ghosh, an expert on Arab-Israeli food who has written a comprehensive book about it, she insisted that baba ghanoush has no tahini in it whatsoever — just cubed vegetables, lemon juice, garlic and olive oil — and that if you add tahini, it is just called aubergine salad. Go figure!

Burnt aubergine with garlic, lemon
& pomegranate seeds

4 large aubergines
  (1.5kg before cooking;
  550g after burning and
  draining the flesh)
2 garlic cloves, crushed
grated zest of 1 lemon and
  2 tbsp lemon juice
5 tbsp olive oil
2 tbsp chopped flat-leaf
  parsley
2 tbsp chopped mint
seeds of ½ a large
  pomegranate
  (80g in total)
salt and black pepper

*This salad has the most wonderful smoky aroma and works well with grilled meat or fish, as well as with other dips and salads to kick-start a passionate Levantine feast. But in order to get the full smoky flavour, you really need to stick to the instructions and allow the aubergines to burn well. If you want to turn it into a 'real' baba ghanoush, whatever that may be (*SEE PAGE 76*), drizzle on some light tahini paste at the end.*

If you have a gas hob, line the base with foil to protect it, keeping only the burners exposed. Place the aubergines directly on four separate moderate flames and roast for 15–18 minutes, until the skin is burnt and flaky and the flesh is soft. Use metal tongs to turn them around occasionally. Alternatively, score the aubergine with a knife in a few places, a couple of centimetres deep, and place on a baking sheet under a hot grill for about an hour. Turn them around every 20 minutes or so and continue to cook even if they burst and break.

Remove the aubergines from the heat and allow them to cool down slightly. Once cool enough to handle, cut an opening along each aubergine and scoop out the soft flesh, dividing it with your hands into long thin strips. Discard the skin. Drain the flesh in a colander for an hour at least, preferably longer to get rid of as much water as possible.

Place the aubergine in a medium bowl and add the garlic, lemon zest and juice, olive oil, ½ a teaspoon of salt and a good grind of black pepper. Stir and allow the aubergine to marinate at room temperature for at least an hour.

When you are ready to serve, mix in most of the herbs and taste for seasoning. Pile high on a serving plate, scatter on the pomegranate seeds and garnish with the remaining herbs.

Parsley & barley salad

We started off calling this 'Barley and feta tabbouleh', but the longer we spent with our recipes and sources the more we realized how strongly people feel about the names given to dishes. This is understandable in a place where so much is always at stake.

Still, this recipe is very much inspired by the concept of tabbouleh (SEE PAGE 85). It was first cooked for Yotam by Tami Rosenbaum, mother of Yoni, his childhood best friend. Tami is a fantastic cook. She comes from a Yekke family (German Jews), and had a 'proper', not particularly Middle Eastern, upbringing. Tami studied cookery at secondary school, again receiving traditional training. When Yotam used to visit Yoni as a child, it was the only home of any of his friends where bread rolls — sweet and savoury — were baked regularly; schnitzels were made from veal and stuffed with bacon, and all the children played musical instruments seriously. Just like back home in Germany. Despite all that, even Tami's food was not immune to local, Middle Eastern influences and many dishes she cooks today manage to fuse together the two worlds in a very delicious way.

'Serious' Jerusalem dishes — those substantial, slow-cooked ones that everybody adores but at the same time is also slightly terrified by, due to how heavy and sleep-inducing they can be (SEE CHICKEN WITH CARAMELIZED ONION AND CARDAMOM RICE, PAGE 184, OR TURNIP AND VEAL CAKE, PAGE 156) — *must always be accompanied by a sharp, fresh salad such as this one. The herbs and lemon juice cleanse the palate and give a certain sense of lightness, balancing out any overdose of carbs and unctuous meat. You can also serve it alongside other vegetable-based mezze dishes. Barley can be replaced with spelt, farro, or whole split wheat, with cooking times varying.*

40g pearl barley
150g feta
5½ tbsp olive oil
1 tsp za'atar
½ tsp coriander seeds, lightly toasted and crushed
¼ tsp ground cumin
80g flat-leaf parsley, leaves and fine stems
4 spring onions, finely chopped (40g in total)
2 garlic cloves, crushed
40g cashew nuts, lightly toasted and crushed roughly
1 green pepper, deseeded and cut into 1cm dice
½ tsp ground allspice
2 tbsp lemon juice
salt and black pepper

Place the pearl barley in a small saucepan, cover with plenty of water and boil for 30–35 minutes, or until tender but with a bite. Drain into a fine sieve, shake to remove all the water and transfer to a large bowl.

Break the feta into rough pieces, about 2cm in size, and mix in a small bowl with 1½ tablespoons of olive oil, za'atar, coriander seeds and cumin. Gently mix together and leave to marinate while you prepare the rest of the salad.

Chop the parsley finely and place in a bowl with the spring onion, garlic, cashew nuts, pepper, allspice, lemon juice, the remaining olive oil and cooked pearl barley. Mix together well and season to taste. To serve, divide the salad between four plates and top with the marinated feta.

Chunky courgette & tomato salad

8 pale green courgettes, or normal courgettes (about 1kg in total)
5 large, very ripe tomatoes (800g in total)
3 tbsp olive oil, plus extra to finish
300g Greek yoghurt
2 garlic cloves, crushed
2 red chillies, deseeded and chopped
grated zest of 1 medium lemon and 2 tbsp lemon juice
1 tbsp date syrup, plus extra to finish (see page 69)
200g walnuts, roughly chopped
2 tbsp chopped mint
20g flat-leaf parsley, chopped
salt and black pepper

This is a variation on mafghoussa, a popular Palestinian salad or spread. The vegetables for mafghoussa were traditionally grilled on the ambers in the tabun, the clay oven often found outdoors in village homes. The original recipe calls for grilled tomatoes and courgettes, garlic, buttermilk and chopped parsley. We added a bit of this and a bit of that so it is a little richer, a perfect meal opener, accompanied by bread. You can cook your vegetables on a barbecue, instead of a griddle pan.

Preheat the oven to 220°C/200°C Fan/Gas Mark 7 and place a ridged griddle pan on the hob over a high heat.

Trim the courgettes and cut them in half lengthways. Halve the tomatoes as well. Brush the courgettes and tomatoes with olive oil on the cut side and season with salt and pepper.

By now the griddle pan should be piping hot. Start with the courgettes. Place a few of them on the pan, cut-side down, and cook for 5 minutes; the courgettes should be nicely charred on one side. Now remove the courgettes and repeat the same process with the tomatoes. Place the vegetables in a roasting tin and put in the oven for about 20 minutes, until the courgettes are very tender.

Remove the tray from the oven and allow the vegetables to cool down slightly. Chop them roughly and leave to drain in a colander for 15 minutes.

Whisk the yoghurt, garlic, chilli, lemon zest and juice and the date syrup in a large mixing bowl. Add the chopped vegetables, walnuts, mint and most of the parsley and stir well. Season with ¾ of a teaspoon of salt and some pepper.

Transfer the salad to a large, shallow serving plate and spread it around. Garnish with the remaining parsley. Finally, drizzle over some date syrup and olive oil.

Tabbouleh

'If you want to find a good husband, you'd better learn how to chop your parsley properly,' Sami's mother sternly cautioned his sister when she was a teenager. Indeed tabbouleh, as is not always understood in the West, is all about parsley. It is a key ingredient — both in this salad and in Palestinian cuisine in general — and it must be treated with respect and great deftness, as implied by Sami's mum.

Tabbouleh probably hails from Lebanon and Syria, but has become such an essential part of the Palestinian heritage that nobody seems to remember any more. A good tabbouleh is based on plenty of fresh flat-leaf parsley and mint, carefully shredded by hand to prevent bruising, well seasoned and sharp, mixed with some tomato and *al dente* bulgar wheat. The exact proportions of parsley to bulgar vary. The Lebanese use the least amount of bulgar, just a tiny quantity of grain dotted sparingly among the parsley. The Palestinians add a little more. Other elements need to be very carefully added. Whichever way, this is, essentially, a parsley salad, not a bulgar salad.

30g fine bulgar wheat
2 large tomatoes, ripe but firm (300g in total)
1 shallot, finely chopped (30g in total)
3 tbsp lemon juice, plus a little extra to finish
4 large bunches of flat-leaf parsley (160g in total)
2 bunches of mint (30g in total)
2 tsp ground allspice
1 tsp baharat spice mix (shop-bought or see recipe, page 299)
80ml top-quality olive oil
seeds of about ½ a large pomegranate (70g in total), optional
salt and black pepper

If you can't get fine bulgar wheat or if the pack doesn't mention the grade, soak it in boiling water for 5 minutes, then drain and leave to dry in a fine sieve. Tabbouleh is traditionally eaten scooped up with small cos lettuce leaves. These can be arranged on a platter at the start of a meal and everybody helps themselves. It also goes well next to most meat and fish dishes.

Put the bulgar in a fine sieve and run under cold water until the water coming through looks clear and most of the starch has been removed. Transfer to a large mixing bowl.

Use a small serrated knife to cut the tomatoes into 0.5cm thick slices and then cut each slice into 0.5cm strips and then into dice. Add the tomatoes and their juices to the bowl, along with the shallot and lemon juice and stir well.

Take a few stalks of parsley and pack them together tightly. Use a large, very sharp knife to trim off most of the stems and discard. Now use the knife to move up the stems and leaves, gradually 'feeding' the knife in order to shred the parsley as finely as you can and trying to avoid cutting pieces wider than 1mm. Add to the bowl.

Pick the mint leaves off the stems, pack a few together tightly and shred them finely as you did the parsley; don't chop them up too much as they tend to discolour. Add to the bowl.

Finally add the allspice, baharat, olive oil, pomegranate, if using, and some salt and pepper. Taste, and add more salt and pepper if you like, possibly a little bit of lemon juice, and serve.

Roasted potatoes with caramel & prunes

This is our little tribute to Tzimmes, a common Polish Ashkenazi sweet stew of carrots and dried fruit that in most of its local manifestations, we have to admit, is pretty gross. However, when done properly, with beef flank pieces, marrow bones, goose fat, cinnamon, honey and lemon juice it is one of the most delectable wintery stews you can make. A lesser-known Lithuanian version is made with potatoes instead of carrots.

1kg floury potatoes, such as Maris Piper
120ml goose fat
150g whole soft Agen prunes, stones removed
90g caster sugar
50ml iced water
salt

We first published this recipe a few years back for a Guardian Christmas *booklet. It is perfectly suited to such seminal family feasts, where the eating carries on for hours, and the cooking isn't too much work. Serve it with roasted beef or chicken and Kohlrabi Salad* (SEE PAGE 46). *Vegetarians can substitute the goose fat with sunflower oil.*

Preheat the oven to 240°C/220°C Fan/Gas Mark 9.

Peel the potatoes, leave the small ones whole and halve the larger ones, so you end up with pieces of around 60g. Rinse under cold water then place the potatoes in a large pan with plenty of fresh cold water. Bring to the boil and then simmer for 8–10 minutes. Drain the potatoes well, then shake the colander to roughen their edges.

Place the goose fat in a roasting tin and heat in the oven until smoking, about 8 minutes. Carefully take the tin out of the oven and add the boiled potatoes to the hot fat with metal tongs, rolling them around in the fat as you do so. Gently place the tin on the highest shelf of the oven and cook for 50–65 minutes, or until the potatoes are golden and crunchy on the outside. Turn them over from time to time while they are cooking.

Once the potatoes are almost ready, take the tray out of the oven and tip it over a heatproof bowl to remove most of the fat. Add ½ a teaspoon of salt and the prunes and stir gently. Return to the oven for another 5 minutes.

During this time, make the caramel. Put the sugar in a clean heavy-based saucepan and place on a low heat. Without stirring watch the sugar turn a rich caramel colour. Make sure to keep your eyes on the sugar at all times. As soon as you reach this colour, remove the pan from the heat. Holding the pan at a safe distance from your face, quickly pour the water into the caramel to stop it from cooking. Return to the heat and stir to remove any sugar lumps.

Before serving, stir the caramel into the potatoes and prunes. Transfer to a serving bowl and eat at once.

Swiss chard with tahini, yoghurt & buttered pine nuts

1.3kg Swiss chard
40g unsalted butter
2 tbsp olive oil, plus extra
  to finish
40g pine nuts
2 small garlic cloves, sliced
  very thinly
60ml dry white wine
sweet paprika, to garnish
  (optional)
salt and black pepper

**TAHINI &
YOGHURT SAUCE**

50g light tahini paste
50g Greek yoghurt
2 tbsp lemon juice
1 garlic clove, crushed
2 tbsp water

Chard leaves are some of the most popular greens in Jerusalem. They have a fantastic sharp aroma and tend to hold their texture when cooked. We love stuffing them and sautéing them with herbs and various spices. Garlic is essential! Paired with tahini and yoghurt, they make a remarkable side dish — sharp, full of flavour and yet not too dominant to overshadow most main courses. Try it next to Mejadra (SEE PAGE 120) *or Lamb shawarma* (SEE PAGE 210).

Start with the sauce. Place all the ingredients in a medium bowl, add a pinch of salt and stir well with a small whisk until you get a smooth, semi-stiff paste. Set aside.

Use a sharp knife to separate the white chard stalks from the green leaves and cut both into 2cm wide slices, keeping them separate. Bring a large pan of salted water to the boil and add the chard stalks. Simmer for 2 minutes, add the leaves and cook for a further minute. Drain and rinse well under cold water. Allow the water to drain and then use your hands to squeeze the chard well until it is completely dry.

Put half the butter and the 2 tablespoons of olive oil in a large frying pan and place on a medium heat. Once hot, add the pine nuts and toss them in the pan until golden, about 2 minutes. Use a slotted spoon to remove them from the pan then throw in the garlic. Cook for about a minute, or until it starts to become golden. Carefully (it will spit!) pour in the wine. Leave for a minute or less, until it reduces to about a third. Add the chard and the rest of the butter and cook for 2–3 minutes, stirring occasionally, until the chard is completely warm. Season with ½ a teaspoon of salt and some black pepper.

Divide the chard into serving bowls, spoon some tahini sauce on top and scatter with the pine nuts. Finally, drizzle with olive oil and sprinkle with some paprika, if you like.

Sabih

This isn't a Jerusalem dish. It was developed by Iraqi Jews settling in the 1950s in the city of Ramat Gan, near Tel Aviv. It incorporates so many elements, though, that it perfectly epitomizes the jumble of cuisines of the region. The simply-fried aubergine slices are a mainstay of both Arab and Sephardi cooking. Tahini has a similar lineage. The zhoug (SEE PAGE 301) is a Jewish Yemeni chilli paste that has become the Israeli equivalent to ketchup. The savoury mango pickle the Iraqis brought with them is an Indian influence. Hard-boiled egg is another Sephardi basic and the chopped salad, well, that's as Arab and as Israeli as can be (SEE PAGE 29).

2 large aubergines (about 750g in total)
about 300ml sunflower oil
4 slices of good-quality white bread, toasted, or fresh and moist mini-pitas
⅔ recipe for Tahini sauce (see page 298)
4 medium free-range eggs, hard-boiled and cut into 1cm thick slices or quartered
about 4 tbsp Zhoug (see page 301)
amba or savoury mango pickle (optional)
salt and black pepper

CHOPPED SALAD

2 medium ripe tomatoes, cut into 1cm dice (200g in total)
2 mini cucumbers, cut into 1cm dice (120g in total)
2 spring onions, thinly sliced
1½ tbsp chopped flat-leaf parsley
2 tsp lemon juice
1½ tbsp olive oil

This mumbo-jumbo served in or on a pita is one of the most exciting street foods you can come across. If you can't get a thick, fresh pita from a Middle Eastern grocer, don't bother with the supermarket brands and use toasted bread instead. While you are there, get a savoury mango pickle if you can. Sweet mango pickles or mango chutneys are not really suitable.

Use a vegetable peeler to peel away strips of aubergine skin from top to bottom, leaving the aubergines with alternating strips of black skin and white flesh, zebra-like. Cut both aubergines widthways into 2.5cm thick slices. Sprinkle them with salt on both sides, then spread out on a tray for at least 30 minutes to remove some water. Use kitchen paper to wipe them.

Heat up the sunflower oil in a wide frying pan. Carefully — the oil spits — fry the aubergine in batches until nice and dark, turning once, about 6–8 minutes in total. Add oil if needed as you cook the batches. When done, the aubergine pieces should be completely tender in the centre. Remove from the pan and drain on kitchen paper.

Make the chopped salad by mixing together all the ingredients and seasoning with salt and pepper to taste.

Just before serving, place one slice of bread or pita on each plate. Spoon 1 tablespoon of the tahini sauce over each slice, then arrange the aubergine slices on top, overlapping. Drizzle over some more tahini without completely covering the aubergines. Season each egg slice with salt and pepper and arrange over the aubergine. Drizzle some more tahini on top and spoon over as much zhoug as you like; be careful, it's hot! Spoon over mango pickle as well, if you like. Serve the vegetable salad on the side, spooning some on top of every sabih if you like.

Latkes

600g peeled and grated
  Desiree potatoes
300g peeled and grated
  parsnips
30g chives, finely chopped
4 egg whites
2 tbsp cornflour
80g unsalted butter
100ml sunflower oil
salt and freshly ground
  black pepper
soured cream, to serve

We would like to thank our friend Helen Goh, a true perfectionist if ever there was one, for perfecting this Ashkenazi Hanukkah speciality for us. Don't save latkes just for holidays though, they are truly marvellous and a good way to start any meal, or to accompany simply roasted beef. Latkes are often also served sweet. To do this, remove the chive and reduce the salt. Serve warm with soured cream and sprinkled with caster sugar.

Rinse the potato in a large bowl of cold water. Drain in a colander, squeeze out any excess water and then spread the potato out on a clean kitchen towel to dry completely.

In a large bowl mix together the potato, parsnip, chives, egg whites, cornflour, 1 teaspoon of salt and plenty of black pepper.

Heat up half the butter and half the oil in a large frying pan over a medium–high heat. Use your hands to pick out portions of about 2 tablespoons of the latke mix, squeeze firmly to remove some of the liquid and shape into thin patties, about 1cm thick and 8cm wide. Carefully place as many latkes as you can comfortably fit in the pan, push them down gently and level with the back of a spoon and fry on a medium–high heat for 3 minutes on each side. The latkes need to be completely brown on the outside. Remove the fried latkes from the oil, place on kitchen paper then keep warm while you cook the rest. Add the remaining butter and oil as needed. Serve at once with soured cream on the side.

PULSES
& GRAINS

Falafel

Falafel and hummus are the ultimate daily grub in Muslim Jerusalem. As a little boy, Sami used to be sent out to the shops every morning to buy breakfast for his older brothers: hummus and freshly fried falafel balls. He'd take an empty plate to Abu Shukri, a famous hummus spot in the old city, and the man himself would spread the warm paste over the plate and, with much attention, garnish it with herbs, spices and pickled cucumber. The warm falafel and fresh pitas were carried alongside in a brown paper bag. Sami would charge his brothers 'a little something' for the task, which he always spent in the sweet shop.

And that was not the end of it. Fresh falafel was sold as a snack — stuffed into pita with hummus, tahini sauce, fiery red chilli sauce and chopped salad — throughout the day. Sami would often come back from school with a stained uniform and no appetite for lunch after slyly indulging in one on the way home. Na'ama wasn't happy.

Over on the west side of the city, Yotam had a pretty similar experience: school day end, a massive falafel sandwich, tahini-stained shirt, no appetite, angry mother.

In west Jerusalem, as in the rest of Israel, it was Yemeni Jews arriving in the country in the first half of the 20th century who set up falafel shops and introduced the street food to Jewish society for the first time. The iconic Israeli 'mana falafel', the pita pocket stuffed with falafel, potato chips, salad and other goodies, emerged when the Yemenis began to flavour falafel with hawayej (SEE PAGE 226) and zhoug (SEE PAGE 301).

Don't be alarmed about not boiling the chickpeas before they are blitzed into a falafel mix. This is part of the process. When frying falafel, it is important that they get just the right amount of time in the oil. If you don't have an appropriate thermometer, assess the temperature of the oil by frying one falafel ball as instructed, making sure it takes the specified amount of time to cook through completely but without burning on the outside. Serve hot with pita bread, Tahini sauce (SEE PAGE 298), chopped tomato and cucumber salad (SEE SPICED CHICKPEAS AND FRESH VEGETABLE SALAD, PAGE 56), Zhoug (SEE PAGE 301) and pickles (SEE PICKLED TURNIP AND BEETROOT, PAGE 307).

250g dried chickpeas
½ a medium onion, finely
   chopped (80g in total)
1 garlic clove, crushed
1 tbsp finely chopped
   flat-leaf parsley
2 tbsp finely chopped
   coriander
¼ tsp cayenne pepper
½ tsp ground cumin
½ tsp ground coriander
¼ tsp ground cardamom
½ tsp baking powder
1½ tbsp plain flour
about 750ml sunflower oil
   for deep-frying
½ tsp sesame seeds,
   for coating
salt

Place the chickpeas in a large bowl and cover with cold water at least twice their volume. Set aside to soak overnight.

The next day, drain the chickpeas well and combine them with the onion, garlic, parsley and coriander. For the best results, use a meat grinder for the next part. Put the chickpea mixture once through the machine, set to its finest setting, then pass it through the machine for a second time. If you don't have a meat grinder, use a food processor. Blitz the mix in batches, pulsing each for 30–40 seconds, until it is finely chopped, but not mushy or pasty, and holds itself together. Once processed, add the spices, baking powder, ¾ of a teaspoon of salt, flour, and 3 tablespoons of water. Mix well by hand until smooth and uniform. Cover the mixture and leave it in the fridge for 1 hour or until ready to use.

Fill a deep, heavy-based, medium saucepan with enough oil to come 7cm up the sides of the pan. Heat the oil to 180°C.

With wet hands, press 1 tablespoon of mixture in the palm of your hand to form a patty or a ball the size of a small walnut, about 25g (you can also use a wet ice-cream scoop for this). Press them well as they tend to crumble and break.

Sprinkle the balls with a tiny amount of sesame seeds and deep-fry them in batches for 4 minutes, or until well browned and cooked through. It is important they really dry out on the inside so make sure they get enough time in the oil. Drain in a colander lined with kitchen paper and serve at once.

Split wheat & Swiss chard with pomegranate molasses

This recipe was given to us with much love by our friend Anat Teitelbaum, a passionate Jerusalem cook who personifies some of the most wonderful things about this city. Anat does all her shopping in Machne Yehuda market, where she knows every street vendor and every restaurant owner. She is familiar with her ingredients and makes the most out of them, with great confidence and just in the right season. Just like us, she likes big flavours and simple cooking techniques, and she is happy to pick and choose from all the different cuisines around her. This dish, with its deep sweet and sour flavours and with its marvellous earthiness, is typical Anat and typical Jerusalem.

600g Swiss chard or
  rainbow chard
2 tbsp olive oil
1 tbsp unsalted butter
2 large leeks, white and
  pale-green parts, thinly
  sliced (350g in total)
2 tbsp light brown sugar
about 3 tbsp pomegranate
  molasses
200g split wheat
  or whole wheat
500ml chicken stock
salt and black pepper
Greek yoghurt, to serve

This potent dish is great eaten on its own as a light supper, or can be served with plainly cooked chicken or burgers (try it with the TURKEY AND COURGETTE BURGERS WITH SPRING ONION AND CUMIN, PAGE 200, *leaving out the sauce). Split wheat or whole wheat is available online or from Middle Eastern and Turkish grocers. Pearl barley is an okay substitute but doesn't take as long to cook so you won't get that deep flavour that comes from the caramelizing of the sugars. Brands of pomegranate molasses vary so we suggest assessing the flavour of the dish at the end and adding more if needed.*

Separate the chard's white stalks from the green leaves using a small, sharp knife. Slice the stalks into 1cm slices and the leaves into 2cm slices.

Heat the oil and butter in a large heavy-based pan. Add the leek and cook, stirring, for 3–4 minutes. Add the chard stalks and cook for 3 minutes, then add the leaves and cook for a further 3 minutes. Add the sugar, 3 tablespoons of pomegranate molasses and the wheat and mix well. Add the stock, ¾ teaspoon of salt and some black pepper, bring to a gentle simmer and cook on a low heat, covered, for 60–70 minutes. The wheat should be *al dente* at this point.

Remove the lid and, if needed, increase the heat and allow any remaining liquid to evaporate. The base of the pan should be dry and have a bit of burnt caramel on it. Remove from the heat.

Before serving, taste and add more molasses, salt and pepper if needed; you want it sharp and sweet so don't be shy with your molasses. Serve warm, with a dollop of Greek yoghurt.

Balilah

On the corner of the souk in the old city stood the very popular balilah man. He had large piles of freshly cooked chickpeas on his stall, steaming and beautifully decorated with parsley and lemon. Like a magician, he used to whip the balilah into a newspaper cone in a flash, and serve it to the eager customer.

Balilah is a popular Palestinian street food consisting of fresh chickpeas seasoned with cumin and lemon juice and it makes the most gratifying snack. Curiously, in the Jewish Orthodox neighbourhood of Me'ah She'arim they sell a cheap and cheerful snack, called arbes, which is just like balilah, only seasoned with black pepper instead of cumin. It, too, is highly popular.

200g dried chickpeas
1 tsp bicarbonate of soda
60g chopped flat-leaf parsley
2 spring onions, thinly sliced
1 large lemon
3 tbsp olive oil
2½ tsp ground cumin
salt and freshly ground black pepper

Balilah can be eaten warm, not hot, or at room temperature as a little between-meal snack. It is also delicious served next to grilled chicken or fish, or can be turned into a salad by adding some leaves, feta and diced tomatoes.

Start the night before by putting the chickpeas in a large bowl and filling it with enough water so that the chickpeas are covered by twice their height. Add the bicarbonate of soda and leave at room temperature to soak overnight.

Drain the chickpeas and place them in a large saucepan. Cover with plenty of cold water and place on a high heat. Bring to the boil, skim the surface of the water, then reduce the heat and simmer for 60–90 minutes, until the chickpeas are very soft but still retain their shape.

While the chickpeas are cooking, put the parsley and spring onion in a large mixing bowl. Peel the lemon by topping and tailing it, placing on a board and running a small sharp knife along its curves to remove the skin and white pith. Discard the skin, pith and pips and roughly chop the flesh. Add the flesh and all of the juices to the bowl.

Once the chickpeas are ready, drain and add them to the bowl while they are still hot. Add the olive oil, cumin, ¾ of a teaspoon of salt and a good grind of pepper. Mix well. Allow to cool down until just warm, taste for seasoning and serve.

Basmati rice & orzo

Just like the Palestinians (SEE PAGE 184), rice is the basic grain for most Sephardic communities, excluding North Africans. Though the cooking methods and accompanying ingredients vary greatly, with Iranians developing the most complex method and best texture, rice is an essential element in every Friday night dinner. Mixing chickpeas with rice (or bulgar) is common practice among Sephardim (SEE PAGE 106), as it makes the rice, served next to stews and long cooked dishes, more interesting in look and texture. Many other substantial elements — vermicelli (see below), potatoes, lentils, nuts — could also be included.

Bucharan Jews, a substantial community in Jerusalem, make a pilaf with plenty of spices (ginger, clove, cardamom, cinnamon), lots of mint, raisins and peas. It is a luxurious and rich dish, appropriate for a previously wealthy Jewish community that had built its own neighbourhood when its members started coming to Palestine in the late 19th and early 20th century, wearing unusual embroidered clothes, adorned with jewellery. Later on, after the Russian revolution, many lost their wealth and the neighbourhood lost much of its past glory but the food remains as spectacular and vibrant.

250g basmati rice
1 tbsp melted ghee or
  unsalted butter
1 tbsp sunflower oil
85g orzo
600ml chicken stock
1 tsp salt

Long grain rice, cooked simply with plain vermicelli noodles, is common all over the Levant and Turkey. Its neutral flavour and playful textures make an effective background for various stews, soups and salads. Our version uses orzo — tiny rice-like shaped pasta — but you can use vermicelli, just don't fry them as long as they burn very quickly. Do try this, you may not want to cook plain rice ever again.

Wash the basmati rice well, then place in a large bowl and cover with plenty of cold water. Allow it to soak for 30 minutes, then drain.

Heat the ghee or butter and oil on a medium–high heat in a medium heavy-based saucepan for which you have a lid. Add the orzo and sauté for 3–4 minutes, until the grains turn dark golden. Add the stock, bring to a boil and cook for 3 minutes. Add the drained rice and salt, bring to a gentle boil, stir once or twice, cover the pan and simmer on a very low heat for 15 minutes. Don't be tempted to uncover the pan; you'll need to allow the rice to steam properly.

Off the heat, remove the lid and quickly cover the pan with a clean tea towel. Place the lid back on top of the towel and leave for 10 minutes. Fluff the rice up with a fork before serving.

Saffron rice with barberries, pistachio & mixed herbs

This dish is inspired by shirin polo, a celebration rice dish of the Iranian Jewish community. The original includes candied orange peel, sour cherries, cranberries and almonds and is often served at weddings. We use barberries, an Iranian mainstay, to give a sweet and sour effect but our rice is by no means very sweet. You could easily add cranberries, sliced dried apricots, or even chopped dates if you want to emphasize the sweetness. This would be very much in line with the sensibilities of Iraqi, Iranian and North African Jews, who love mixing sweet with savoury.

Alternatively, make a simplified version of baghali polo, another inspired Iranian rice dish, by simply leaving out the barberries and pistachios and adding skinned, cooked broad beans.

40g unsalted butter
360g basmati rice, rinsed under cold water and drained well
560ml boiling water
1 tsp saffron threads, soaked for 30 minutes in 3 tbsp boiling water
40g dried barberries, soaked for a few minutes in freshly boiled water with a pinch of sugar
30g dill, roughly chopped
20g chervil, roughly chopped
10g tarragon, roughly chopped
60g slivered or crushed unsalted pistachios, lightly toasted
salt and freshly ground white pepper

Barberries are tiny, jewel-like dried sweet and sour Iranian berries which we have started using a bit obsessively recently. It is hard not to. Their intense sharpness accentuates the other flavours in the dish and adds wonderful 'drama'. They are available online, or from Iranian and some Middle Eastern grocers. If you can't get them, consider substituting with currants soaked in a little lemon juice. Serve this rice with roasted chicken or Turkey and courgette burgers with spring onion and cumin (SEE PAGE 200).

Melt the butter in a medium saucepan and stir in the rice, making sure the grains are well coated in butter. Add the boiling water, 1 teaspoon of salt and some white pepper. Mix well, cover with a tightly fitting lid and leave to cook on a very low heat for 15 minutes. Don't be tempted to uncover the pan; you'll need to allow the rice to steam properly.

Remove the rice pan from the heat — all the water will have been absorbed by the rice — and pour the saffron water over one side of the rice's surface, covering about a quarter of the surface and leaving the majority of it white. Cover the pan immediately with a tea towel and re-seal tightly with the lid. Set aside for 5–10 minutes.

Use a large spoon to remove the white part of the rice into a large mixing bowl and fluff it up with a fork. Drain the barberries and stir them in, followed by the herbs and most of the pistachios, leaving a few to garnish. Mix well. Fluff up the saffron rice with a fork and gently fold it into the white rice. Don't over-mix — you don't want the white grains to be stained by the yellow. Taste and adjust the seasoning. Transfer the rice to a shallow serving bowl and scatter the remaining pistachios on top. Serve warm or at room temperature.

Basmati & wild rice with chickpeas, currants & herbs

50g wild rice
2½ tbsp olive oil
220g basmati rice
330ml boiling water
2 tsp cumin seeds
1½ tsp curry powder
240g cooked chickpeas
    (tinned are fine),
    drained
180ml sunflower oil
1 medium onion, thinly
    sliced
½ tbsp plain flour
100g currants
2 tbsp chopped flat-leaf
    parsley
1 tbsp chopped coriander
1 tbsp chopped dill
salt and black pepper

This Sephari-inspired dish can be the centrepiece of a festive vegetarian meal, or served alongside Chicken sofrito (SEE PAGE 190) *or Pan-fried mackerel with golden beetroot and orange salsa* (SEE PAGE 222). *See more about combining rice with chickpeas on page 103.*

Start by putting the wild rice in a small saucepan, cover with plenty of water, boil and leave to simmer for about 40 minutes, or until the rice is cooked but still quite firm. Drain and set aside.

To cook the basmati rice, pour a tablespoon of the olive oil into a medium saucepan with a tightly fitting lid and place on a high heat. Add the rice and ¼ teaspoon of salt and stir as you warm up the rice. Carefully add the boiling water, reduce the heat to very low, cover the pan with the lid and leave to cook for 15 minutes.

Remove the pan from the heat, cover with a clean tea towel, then the lid and leave off the heat for 10 minutes.

While the rice is cooking prepare the chickpeas. Heat up the remaining olive oil in a small saucepan on a high heat. Add the cumin seeds and curry powder and after a couple of seconds add the chickpeas and ¼ teaspoon of salt; make sure you do this quickly or the spices may burn in the oil. Stir on the heat for a minute or two, just to heat up the chickpeas, then transfer to a large mixing bowl.

Wipe the saucepan clean, pour in the sunflower oil and place on a high heat. Make sure the oil is hot by throwing in a small piece of onion; it should sizzle vigorously. Use your hands to mix the onion with the flour to coat it slightly. Take some of the onion and carefully (it may spit!) place in the oil. Fry for 2–3 minutes, until golden brown, transfer to kitchen paper to drain and sprinkle with salt. Repeat in batches until all the onion is fried.

Finally, add both types of rice to the chickpeas, add the currants, herbs and fried onion. Stir, taste and add salt and pepper as you like. Serve warm or at room temperature.

Barley risotto with marinated feta

200g pearl barley
30g unsalted butter
90ml olive oil
2 small celery stalks, cut
 into 5mm dice
2 small shallots, cut into
 5mm dice
4 garlic cloves, cut into
 2mm dice
4 thyme sprigs
½ tsp smoked paprika
1 bay leaf
4 strips of lemon rind
¼ tsp chilli flakes
400g tin chopped tomatoes
700ml vegetable stock
300ml passata
1 tbsp caraway seeds
300g feta, broken roughly
 into 2cm pieces
1 tbsp fresh oregano leaves
salt

This vegetarian main course is a dish everybody loves, particularly children. Unlike the proper Italian risotto, ours does not require the exact precision and meticulous preparation, but still tastes sensational.

Rinse the pearl barley well under cold water and leave to drain.

Melt the butter and 2 tablespoons of the olive oil in a very large frying pan and cook the celery, shallot and garlic on a gentle heat for 5 minutes or until soft. Add the barley, thyme, paprika, bay leaf, lemon rind, chilli flakes, tomatoes, stock, passata and ½ a tablespoon of salt. Stir to combine. Bring the mixture to a boil, then reduce to a very gentle simmer and cook for 45 minutes, stirring frequently to make sure the risotto does not catch on the bottom of the pan. When ready, the barley should be tender and most of the liquid absorbed.

Meanwhile, toast the caraway seeds in a dry pan for a couple of minutes. Then lightly crush them so that some whole seeds remain. Add them to the feta with the remaining olive oil and gently mix to combine.

Once the risotto is ready, check the seasoning and then divide it between four shallow bowls. Top each with the marinated feta, including the oil, and a sprinkling of oregano leaves.

Conchiglie with yoghurt, peas & chilli

Cooking or serving pasta in hot yoghurt sauce may sound slightly out of the ordinary, but the Palestinian classic shishbarak — ravioli-like dumplings stuffed with meat — is prepared in just such a manner. Turkish and Armenian manti are similar examples. The yoghurt gives a delightful creaminess, without the heaviness of cream, and we urge you to try it as an alternative to the familiar Italian sauces.

500g Greek yoghurt
150ml olive oil
4 garlic cloves, crushed
500g fresh peas or frozen, de-frosted
500g conchiglie pasta
60g pine nuts
2 tsp Turkish or Syrian chilli flakes (or less, depending on how spicy the variety you use is)
40g basil leaves, roughly torn
240g feta, broken into chunks
salt and freshly crushed white pepper

Turkey and Syria produce many types of dried chilli flakes, known throughout the region, varying greatly in sweetness, acidity, smokiness, heat and earthiness. Each has its own unique aroma and identifiable tinge and we like playing around with them in flavouring many of our dishes. We particularly like Urfa chilli, dark purple and almost musky in flavour; Aleppo chilli, burgundy colour and fruity; or the more general Kirmizi biber, literally translating from Turkish as 'red pepper', which is easier to find and covers a range of Turkish products. Look out for all of them in Middle Eastern and Turkish shops, or online. If you can't get them, use regular chilli flakes with a tiny amount of smoked paprika.

Put the yoghurt, 90ml of the olive oil, garlic and 100g of the peas in a food processor. Blitz to a uniform pale-green sauce and transfer to a large mixing bowl.

Cook the pasta in plenty of salted boiling water until *al dente*. As the pasta cooks, heat up the remaining olive oil in a small frying pan on a medium heat. Add the pine nuts and chilli flakes and fry for 4 minutes until the nuts are golden and the oil deep red. Also, heat up the remaining peas in some boiling water, then drain.

Drain the cooked pasta into a colander, shake well to get rid of the water and add the pasta gradually to the yoghurt sauce; adding it all at once may cause the yoghurt to split. Add the warm peas, basil, feta, 1 teaspoon of salt and ½ a teaspoon of freshly crushed white pepper. Toss gently, transfer to serving bowls and spoon over the pine nuts and their oil.

Hummus wars

Political and nationalistic discussions about hummus — where it started and how; who was the first to crush chickpeas and mix them with sesame paste and when — are almost compulsive. No one enjoys them anymore, but no one is ready to concede either.

Generally, most people agree that it was Levantine or Egyptian Arabs who first made hummus, though even this is debatable. In an article published in a local paper the celebrated Jewish author Meir Shalev interpreted a certain biblical passage as evidence that Jews ate hummus in biblical times. But when push comes to shove, nobody seriously challenges the Palestinian hegemony in making hummus, even though both they and the Jews like calling it their own. The arguments never cease. And even if the question of authorship is somehow set aside, you are still left with who makes the best hummus now? And here we need to start again— is it Ta'ami in west Jerusalem or Lina in the old city? Pinati or Abu Hassan?

THE HUMMUSIA FETISH IS SO POWERFUL THAT EVEN THE BEST OF FRIENDS MAY EASILY TURN AGAINST EACH OTHER IF THEY SUDDENLY FIND THEMSELVES ON OPPOSITE HUMMUS CAMPS

Jews in particular, and even more specifically Jewish men, never tire from arguments about the absolute, the one and only, the most fantastic hummusia. A hummusia is a simple eatery specializing almost only in hummus, which is normally open for breakfast and until late afternoon. It is, like the English chippy, a savoured local treasure. Yet, typically, it carries with it much stronger sentiments. The hummusia fetish is so powerful that even the best of friends may easily turn against each other if they suddenly find themselves on opposite hummus camps. The discussions and lively arguments can carry on for hours, going into the minutest of details regarding consistency (some like it smooth and fluffy, others a little chunky and spicy), temperature (some like it warm, others ambient) and about the perfect condiments (cooked chickpeas, re-hydrated dried broad beans, spice paste, or nothing at all). Still, the hummus debate is fun.

As mentioned, it is also a source of identity — personal or national — which can easily turn into an issue of confused identity. A typical story is that of a hummusia in the Arab village of Abu Gosh, about 10km west of Jerusalem.

Abu Shukri was for years considered one of the best hummusia in the country, only rivalled by the famous Abu Hassan in Jaffa or Said's in Acre (or Akko). One day, across the unpaved dirt road, another hummusia opened, with a little sign hanging over the door saying 'We moved here. This is the real Abu Shukri.' The newcomer, believe it or not, was Abu Shukri's son-in-law, an ex-waiter. The outrage! The next day the old restaurant hung a sign on its door: 'We didn't move anywhere. This is the real Abu Shukri.' A large banner appeared across the road not long afterwards: 'The real real, one and only, original Abu Shukri.' You can probably imagine what followed. In the end, after years of fierce rivalry and many confused diners mistaking one Abu Shukri for the other, a big food corporation selling packed hummus in supermarkets decided to run a TV campaign to promote its own brand. It culminated in a big reconciliation event between the two Abu Shukris and was labelled 'The End of Hummus Wars'.

Basic hummus

250g dried chickpeas
1 tsp bicarbonate of soda
270g light tahini paste
4 tbsp lemon juice
4 garlic cloves, crushed
100ml ice cold water
salt

Our basic hummus recipe is super-smooth and rich in tahini, just as we like it, and can be kept in the fridge for up to three days and used simply spread over a plate, drizzled with olive oil and eaten with a pita or bread. However, the two recipes that follow it turn hummus into an altogether different thing, an exciting centrepiece of a seriously substantial meal, as it is mostly enjoyed in Jerusalem. If you prefer to stick to the basic recipe, you can vary it by folding in cooked and crushed chickpeas thus adding texture, adding some ground cumin and adjusting the amount of lemon juice and tahini to suit you.

Start a day before by washing the chickpeas well and placing them in a large bowl. Cover them with cold water, at least twice their volume, and leave to soak overnight.

The next day, drain the chickpeas. Place a medium saucepan on a high heat and add the drained chickpeas and the bicarbonate of soda. Cook for about 3 minutes, stirring constantly. Add 1.5 litres of fresh water and bring to a boil. Cook, skimming off any foam and any skins that float to the surface. The chickpeas can cook for anywhere between 20 and 40 minutes, depending on the type and freshness, sometimes even longer. Once done, they should be very tender, breaking up easily when pressed between your thumb and finger, almost but not quite mushy.

Drain the chickpeas. You should have roughly 600g now. Place the chickpeas in a food processor bowl. Process until you get a stiff paste; then, with the machine still running, add the tahini paste, lemon juice, garlic and 1½ teaspoons of salt. Finally, slowly drizzle in the iced water and allow it to mix until you get a very smooth and creamy paste, about 5 minutes. Transfer the hummus into a bowl, cover the surface with cling film and let it rest for at least 30 minutes. If not using straight away, refrigerate until needed. Make sure to take it out of the fridge at least 30 minutes before serving.

Hummus kawarma (lamb) with lemon sauce

1 quantity of Basic
  hummus (see page 114),
  reserving 4 tablespoons
  of the cooked chickpeas
  to garnish
2 tbsp pine nuts, toasted
  in the oven or fried in a
  little unsalted butter

KAWARMA

300g neck fillet of lamb,
  finely chopped by hand
¼ tsp ground black pepper
¼ tsp ground white pepper
1 tsp ground allspice
½ tsp ground cinnamon
good pinch of freshly
  grated nutmeg
1 tsp crushed dried za'atar
  or oregano leaves
1 tbsp white wine vinegar
1 tbsp chopped fresh mint
1 tbsp chopped flat-leaf
  parsley, plus extra to
  garnish
1 tsp salt
1 tbsp unsalted butter or
  ghee
1 tsp olive oil

LEMON SAUCE

10g flat-leaf parsley, finely
  chopped
1 green chilli, finely
  chopped
4 tbsp lemon juice
2 tbsp white wine vinegar
2 garlic cloves, crushed
¼ tsp salt

Hummus kawarma is the Lebanese name given to freshly made hummus, topped with fried chopped lamb. It is a small meal or a starter in a bowl and one of the most sensational things you can put in your mouth. Have it with Fattoush (SEE PAGE 29) or a similar salad and pita. Minced lamb can be used instead of chopping the meat by hand, but it won't have quite the same gratifying texture. This dish also works well without lamb altogether, just the hummus, chickpeas, lemon sauce and pine nuts.

To make the kawarma, place all the ingredients apart from the butter or ghee and oil in a medium bowl. Mix well, cover and allow the mixture to marinate in the fridge for 30 minutes.

Just before you intend on cooking the meat, place all the ingredients for the lemon sauce in a small bowl and stir well.

Heat the butter or ghee and the olive oil in a large frying pan over a medium–high heat. Add the meat in 2–3 batches and stir as you fry each batch for 2 minutes. The meat should be slightly pink in the middle.

Divide the hummus between 6 individual shallow serving bowls, leaving a slight hollow in the centre of each. Spoon the warm kawarma into the hollow and scatter with the reserved chickpeas. Drizzle generously with the lemon sauce and garnish with some chopped parsley and the pine nuts.

See picture on previous page

Musabaha (warm chickpeas with hummus) & toasted pita

250g dried chickpeas
1 tsp bicarbonate of soda
1 tbsp ground cumin
70g light tahini paste
3 tbsp lemon juice
1 garlic clove, crushed
2 tbsp iced water
4 small pitas (120g in total)
2 tbsp olive oil
2 tbsp chopped flat-leaf
  parsley
1 tsp sweet paprika
salt and black pepper

TAHINI SAUCE

75g light tahini paste
60ml water
1 tbsp lemon juice
½ a garlic clove, crushed

LEMON SAUCE

10g flat-leaf parsley, finely
  chopped
1 green chilli, finely
  chopped
4 tbsp lemon juice
2 tbsp white wine vinegar
2 garlic cloves, crushed
¼ tsp salt

Traditionally, this dish is served for breakfast along with various pickles, fresh radish and spring onion or white onion wedges. You can serve it for a weekend brunch. The dried pita is used to scoop the musabaha when eating.

Follow the Basic hummus recipe (SEE PAGE 114) for the method of soaking and cooking the chickpeas, just cook them a little less; they should have a little resistance left in them but still be completely cooked. Drain the cooked chickpeas, reserving 80ml of the cooking water, and weigh them. You should end up with roughly 600g of cooked chickpeas. Keep three quarters of these (450g) unprocessed, mixing them with the reserved cooking water, the cumin, ½ a teaspoon of salt and ¼ of a teaspoon of black pepper. Keep them somewhere warm.

Place the remaining chickpeas (150g) in a small food processor bowl and process until you get a stiff paste; then, with the machine still running, add the tahini paste, lemon juice, garlic and ½ a teaspoon of salt. Finally, slowly drizzle in the iced water and allow it to mix until you get a very smooth and creamy paste, about 3 minutes. Leave the hummus to one side.

While the chickpeas are cooking, you can prepare the other elements of the dish. For the tahini sauce, put all the ingredients and a pinch of salt in a small bowl. Mix well and add a little more water if needed to get a consistency slightly runnier than honey.

Next, simply mix together all of the lemon sauce ingredients and set aside.

Finally, open up the pitas, tearing the two sides apart. Place under a hot grill for 2 minutes or until golden and completely dry. Allow to cool down before breaking into odd shaped pieces.

Divide the hummus between four individual shallow serving bowls; don't level it or press it down, you want the height. Spoon over the warm chickpeas, followed by the tahini sauce, the lemon sauce and a drizzle of olive oil. Garnish with chopped parsley and a sprinkle of paprika. Arrange the toasted pita pieces around the musabaha and serve.

Mejadra

This ancient dish, popular throughout the Arab world, is also one of our most loved. The fried onion, with its sweet oiliness and slight crunch, is the secret. When Sami's family went out on a day trip to Jericho, it was a large pot of mejadra they used to take with them for the picnic. It was divided into small bowls and topped with a spoonful of fresh yoghurt sauce. Dessert was a huge watermelon that Sami's dad chilled in a small stream running into the Jordan River.

250g green or brown lentils
4 medium onions
  (700g before peeling)
3 tbsp plain flour
about 250ml sunflower oil
2 tsp cumin seeds
1½ tbsp coriander seeds
200g basmati rice
2 tbsp olive oil
½ tsp ground turmeric
1½ tsp ground allspice
1½ tsp ground cinnamon
1 tsp sugar
350ml water
salt and black pepper

The two of us can spend many pointless hours discussing what makes the best comfort food and why, but never seem to reach any kind of serious conclusion. Mejadra, however, is where the dispute ends. When served alongside Yoghurt with cucumber (SEE PAGE 299) *or just plain Greek yoghurt, the sweetly spiced rice and lentils strewn with soft, fried onion is as comforting as it gets in Jerusalem. It is best served warm but is also fine at room temperature.*

Place the lentils in a small saucepan, cover with plenty of water, bring to a boil and cook for 12–15 minutes or until the lentils have softened but still have a little bite, then drain.

Peel and slice the onions thinly. Place on a large flat plate, sprinkle with the flour and 1 teaspoon of salt and mix well with your hands. Heat up 250ml of sunflower oil in a medium heavy-based saucepan placed on a high heat. Make sure the oil is hot by throwing in a small piece of onion; it should sizzle vigorously. Reduce the heat to medium–high and carefully (it may spit!) add a third of the sliced onion. Fry for 5–7 minutes, stirring occasionally with a slotted spoon, until the onion takes on a nice golden-brown colour and turns crispy (adjust the temperature so the onion doesn't fry too quickly and burn). Use your spoon to transfer into a colander lined with kitchen paper and sprinkle with a little more salt. Do the same with the other two batches of onion; add a little extra oil if needed.

Wipe clean the saucepan in which you fried the onion and put in the cumin and coriander seeds. Place on a medium heat and toast the seeds for a minute or two. Add the rice, olive oil, turmeric, allspice, cinnamon, sugar, ½ a teaspoon of salt and plenty of black pepper. Stir to coat the rice with oil and then add the cooked lentils and the water. Bring to the boil, cover with a lid and simmer on a very low heat for 15 minutes.

Remove from the heat, lift off the lid and quickly cover the pan with a clean tea towel. Seal tightly with the lid and set aside for 10 minutes.

Finally, add half the fried onion to the rice and lentils and stir gently with a fork. Pile up in a shallow serving bowl and top with the rest of the onion.

One-pot wonders

Maqluba (SEE PAGE 127) is a one-pot meal of rice, vegetables and meat turned on its head. Literally translating to 'upside down', it is made with fried cauliflower or aubergine, often with carrots and potatoes, all of which are usually fried, and includes meat such as chicken, lamb, goat or beef. Sami's mum used to prepare this dish for dinner and at the same time she'd fry more vegetables than needed. The next day she would warm them up, add garlic and lemon and serve them for lunch with homemade flat bread, tahini and pickles. It's the nicest thing to have as a child — a sandwich of garlicky, lemony, warm fried vegetables.

Normally, women with children had their hands full with the general family requirements and the running of the house so the need to prepare a delicious and hearty meal that would feed an entire family inexpensively, with little fuss or washing up, is the general idea behind maqluba, as it is behind the Ashkenazi tchulnt, the Sephardi dafina and the Iraqi-Jewish tebit. While they may each be arranged differently in the pot, require specific cooking times and incorporate different combinations of meat, cereals, legumes and vegetables, essentially all of them feed many mouths from a single pot.

_____

THE FAMOUS, SLOW-COOKED DISHES OF BOTH ASHKENAZIM AND SEPHARDIM ARE FINE EXAMPLES OF NECESSITY CREATING CULINARY ARTISTRY

_____

In Jewish communities, this is also a solution to the Shabbat's challenges, where copious quantities of food have to be prepared by Friday afternoon and last the entire weekend. The famous, slow-cooked dishes of both Ashkenazim and Sephardim are fine examples of necessity creating culinary artistry. Their iconic standing in Jewish culture reflects the amount of love and thought put into them. The challenge is to make a dish that is appealing and diverse even though it has been cooked, or has started its cooking, many hours before. The solutions are so creative and varied that Israeli food writer Sherry Ansky has even dedicated a whole book to tchulnt or hamin as it is also called. Each community has managed to include its staple ingredients in the famous one-pot meal to uncanny degrees of harmony and deliciousness. Among others, chickpeas and all types of dried beans are included, wheat, rice or barley, kosher sausages, various fritters, all meat varieties, eggs, noodles, potatoes, courgettes and stuffed vegetables of any description.

Maqluba

2 medium aubergines
(650g in total),
cut into 0.5cm slices
320g basmati rice
6–8 boneless chicken
thighs, with the skin on,
about 800g in total
1 large onion, peeled and
quartered lengthways
10 black peppercorns
2 bay leaves
sunflower oil, for frying
1 medium cauliflower
(500g), divided into large
florets
melted butter, for greasing
the pan
3–4 medium ripe tomatoes
(350g in total), cut into
0.5-cm thick slices
4 large garlic cloves, halved
1 tsp ground turmeric
1 tsp ground cinnamon
1 tsp ground allspice
¼ tsp ground black pepper
1 tsp baharat spice mix
(shop-bought or see
recipe, page 299)
30g pine nuts, fried in 15g
of ghee or unsalted butter
until golden
1 quantity of Yoghurt with
cucumber (see page 299),
to serve
salt

*Even if this massive savoury cake doesn't manage to keep its shape
— and to assist with that, Sami swears, all members of the family
must place the palms of their hands on the inverted pot and wait the
specified three minutes — you are still in for a hearty celebration of
flavours. See more about maqluba on page 125.*

Place the aubergine slices on a piece of kitchen paper, sprinkle
with some salt on both sides and leave for 20 minutes to lose some
of the water.

Wash the rice and soak in plenty of cold water and 1 teaspoon of salt
for at least 30 minutes.

Meanwhile, heat up a large saucepan and sear the chicken over
a medium–high heat for 3–4 minutes on each side or until golden
brown (the chicken skin should produce enough oil to cook it; if
needed, add a little sunflower oil). Add the onion, peppercorns, bay
leaves and 900ml of water. Bring to a boil, then cover and cook on a
low heat for 20 minutes. Remove the chicken from the stock and set it
aside. Drain the stock and reserve for later, skimming the fat.

While the chicken is cooking, heat up a saucepan or casserole dish
over a medium–high heat, preferably non-stick, that is roughly 24cm
in diameter and 12cm high. Add enough sunflower oil to come about
2cm up the sides of the pan. When you start seeing little bubbles
surfacing, carefully (it may spit!) place some of the cauliflower florets
in the oil and fry until golden brown, up to 3 minutes. Use a slotted
spoon to remove the first batch onto kitchen paper and sprinkle with
salt. Repeat with the remaining cauliflower.

Pat-dry the aubergine slices with kitchen paper and fry them
similarly in batches.

Remove the oil from your pan and wipe it clean. If it isn't a non-stick
pan line the base with a circle of baking parchment cut to the exact
size and brush the sides with some melted butter. Now you are ready
to layer the maqluba.

Start by arranging the slices of tomato in one layer, overlapping,
followed by the aubergine slices. Next, arrange the cauliflower pieces
and chicken thighs. Drain the rice well and spread it over the final
layer and scatter the garlic pieces on top. Measure out 700ml of the
reserved chicken stock and mix in all the spices, plus 1 teaspoon of
salt. Pour this over the rice and then gently press it down with your
hands making sure all the rice is covered with stock. Add a little
extra stock or water if needed.

Recipe continued on next page

Put the pan on a medium heat and bring to a simmer; the stock doesn't need to simmer vigorously but you do need to make sure that it boils properly before covering the pan with a lid, reducing the heat to low and cooking on low heat for 30 minutes. Don't be tempted to uncover the pan; you'll need to allow the rice to steam properly. Remove the pot from the heat, take off the lid and quickly place a clean tea towel over the pot, then seal with the lid again. Leave to rest for 10 minutes.

Once ready, remove the lid and place a large round serving plate or platter over the open pan and carefully but quickly invert the pan holding both sides firmly. Leave the pot on the plate for 2–3 minutes then slowly and carefully lift it off. Garnish with the pine nuts and serve with the Yoghurt with cucumber (see page 299).

Couscous with tomato and onion

3 tbsp olive oil
1 medium onion, finely
  chopped (160g in total)
1 tbsp tomato purée
½ tsp sugar
2 very ripe tomatoes, cut
  into 0.5cm dice
  (320g in total)
150g couscous
220ml boiling chicken or
  vegetable stock
40g unsalted butter
salt and black pepper

This wonderfully comforting couscous is based on a dish Sami's mother cooked for him when he was a child (SEE PAGE 8). All we did was add a crust, similar to Iranian tadik, which is a famous rice dish cooked in such a way that a crispy crust forms at the bottom of the pot; this crunchy bit is everybody's favourite. Good-quality stock is important here. Serve with Grilled fish skewers with hawayej and parsley (SEE PAGE 226), Turkey and courgette burgers with spring onion and cumin (SEE PAGE 200), or just with salad as a light vegetarian meal.

Pour 2 tablespoons of the olive oil into a non-stick pan, about 22cm in diameter, and put on a medium heat. Add the onion and cook for 5 minutes, stirring often, until it has softened but not coloured. Stir in the tomato purée and sugar and cook for 1 minute. Add the tomatoes, ½ a teaspoon of salt and some black pepper and cook for 3 minutes.

Meanwhile, put the couscous in a shallow bowl, pour over the boiling stock and cover with cling film. Set aside for 10 minutes, then remove the cover and fluff up the couscous with a fork. Add the tomato sauce and stir well.

Wipe your pan clean and heat up the butter and remaining olive oil on a medium heat. When the butter has melted, spoon the couscous into the pan and use the back of the spoon to gently pat it down so it's all packed in snugly. Cover the pan, reduce the heat to its lowest setting and allow the couscous to steam for 10–12 minutes, until you can see a light brown colour around the edges. Use a palette or other knife to help you peer between the edge of the couscous and the side of the pan: you want a really crisp edge all over the base and sides.

Place a large plate on top of the pan and quickly turn the couscous on to the plate. Serve warm or at room temperature.

Pictured opposite

SOUPS

Watercress & chickpea soup with rose water & ras el hanout

2 medium carrots (250g in total), cut into 2cm dice
3 tbsp olive oil
¾ tbsp ras el hanout
½ tsp ground cinnamon
240g cooked chickpeas, fresh or tinned
1 medium onion, thinly sliced
15g finely chopped fresh root ginger
600ml vegetable stock
200g watercress
100g spinach leaves, washed
2 tsp caster sugar
1 tsp rose water
salt
Greek yoghurt, to serve (optional)

Ras el hanout is a spice blend brought to Jerusalem by North African Jews consisting of mainly sweet and hot spices, toasted and ground. There isn't one definitive recipe, every spice shop in North Africa (hanout means 'shop' in Arabic) has its own 'flagship' spice blend with a typical set of secret components. Home cooks buy the blend or try to emulate it themselves. In any case, the name stuck, signifying a sweet and heady mix. Commercial varieties available in the UK are fine but feel free to enhance them with your own additions. If your ras el hanout doesn't contain cinnamon, make sure you add some as we do here. If you don't like rose water, leave it out.

Preheat the oven to 220°C/200°C Fan/Gas Mark 7.

Mix the carrots with 1 tablespoon of the olive oil, the ras el hanout, cinnamon and a generous pinch of salt and spread flat in a roasting tin lined with baking parchment. Place in the oven for 15 minutes, then add half the chickpeas, stir well and cook for another 10 minutes or until the carrot softens but still has a bite.

Meanwhile, place the onion and ginger in a large saucepan. Sauté with the remaining olive oil for about 10 minutes on a medium heat, or until the onion is completely soft and golden. Add the remaining chickpeas, stock, watercress, spinach, sugar and ¾ of a teaspoon of salt, stir well and bring to the boil. Cook for a minute or two, just until the leaves wilt.

Using a food processor or blender blitz the soup until smooth. Add the rose water, stir, taste and add more salt or rose water if you like. Set aside until the carrot and chickpeas are ready, then reheat to serve.

To serve, divide the soup into four bowls and top with the hot carrot and chickpeas and, if you like, about 2 teaspoons of yoghurt per portion.

From top: Cannellini bean & lamb soup, hot yoghurt & barley soup, watercress & chickpea soup with rose water & ras el hanout

Hot yoghurt & barley soup

This is adapted from an Armenian recipe for warm rice and yoghurt soup, not dissimilar to Sephardi soups using rice, yoghurt, onion, herbs and lemon juice.

Armenians have lived in Jerusalem since the 4th century AD and their food assimilated many of the local cultures. They have a small quarter within the walls of the crowded old city — one of only four: Muslim, Jewish, Christian and Armenian — where they reside in relative isolation, speaking Armenian. The heart of the quarter is St James' cathedral and it has its own institutions — churches, schools and social clubs.

1.6 litres water
200g pearl barley
2 medium onions, finely chopped
1½ tsp dried mint
60g unsalted butter
2 medium eggs, beaten
400g Greek yoghurt
20g fresh mint, chopped
10g flat-leaf parsley, chopped
3 whole spring onions, thinly sliced
salt and black pepper

This soup is very comforting and quick to prepare. Save it for when you need to cook unexpectedly using storecupboard ingredients and whatever you have in the fridge. Omit or use other soft herbs if you wish.

Bring the water to the boil with the barley in a large saucepan, adding 1 teaspoon of salt, and simmer until the barley is cooked but still *al dente*, 15–20 minutes. Remove from the heat. Once cooked, you will need 1.1 litres of the cooking liquid for the soup; top the saucepan up with water if you are left with less due to evaporation.

While the barley is cooking, sauté the onion and dried mint over a medium heat in the butter until soft, about 15 minutes. Add this to the cooked barley.

Whisk the eggs and yoghurt in a large heatproof mixing bowl. Slowly mix in some of the barley and water, one ladle at a time, until the yoghurt has warmed. This will temper the yoghurt and eggs and stop them from splitting when added to the hot liquid. Add the yoghurt to the soup pot and return to a medium heat, stirring continuously, until the soup comes to a very light simmer. Remove from the heat, add the chopped herbs and spring onion and check the seasoning. Serve hot.

Pictured on page 133

Cannellini bean & lamb soup

1 tbsp sunflower oil

1 small onion (150g in
  total), finely chopped

¼ of a small head of
  celeriac, peeled and cut
  into 0.5cm dice
  (170g in total)

20 large garlic cloves,
  peeled

1 tsp ground cumin

500g stewing meat from
  lamb (or beef if you
  prefer), cut into 2cm
  cubes

1.75 litres water

100g dried cannellini
  or pinto beans, soaked
  overnight in plenty of
  cold water, then drained

7 cardamom pods, lightly
  crushed

½ tsp ground turmeric

2 tbsp tomato purée

1 tsp caster sugar

4 Charlotte potatoes,
  (about 250g), peeled and
  cut into 2cm cubes

salt and black pepper

bread, to serve

lemon juice, to serve

chopped coriander or
  Zhoug (see page 301)

Yemeni Jews, who set up simple eateries in Israel after settling there in the 1950s, are famous for their soups and stews, skilfully using bones, cheap cuts of meat and various spices to get a real intensity of flavour. This particular soup is what we would cook to brighten up a dreary winter's night. It is fantastic! If you like, consider adding ground cinnamon as Aleppian Jews do in a very similar soup. A few marrow bones won't go amiss either.

This soup can be served simply with wedges of lemon and sprinkled with fresh coriander but, really, it will taste best with a little Zhoug (SEE PAGE 301).

Heat the oil in a large frying pan and cook the onion and celeriac on a medium–high heat for 5 minutes, or until the onion starts to brown. Add the garlic cloves and cumin and cook for a further 2 minutes. Take off the heat and set aside.

Place the meat and water in a large saucepan or casserole over a medium–high heat, bring to a boil, lower the heat and simmer for 10 minutes, skimming the surface frequently until you get a clear broth. Add the onion and celeriac mix, the drained beans, cardamom, turmeric, tomato purée and sugar. Bring to the boil, cover and simmer gently for 1 hour, or until the meat is tender.

Add the potatoes to the soup and season with 1 teaspoon of salt and ½ a teaspoon of black pepper. Bring back to the boil, lower the heat and simmer, uncovered, for a further 20 minutes, or until the potatoes and beans are tender. The soup should be thick. Let it bubble away a bit longer, if needed, to reduce, or add some water. Taste and add more seasoning to your liking. Serve the soup with bread and some lemon juice and fresh chopped coriander, or Zhoug.

Pictured on page 133

Seafood & fennel soup

2 tbsp olive oil

4 garlic cloves, thinly sliced

2 fennel bulbs (300g in total), trimmed and cut into thin wedges

1 large waxy potato (200g in total), peeled and cut into 1.5cm cubes

700ml fish stock (or chicken or vegetable stock, if preferred)

½ a medium preserved lemon (15g in total), chopped (shop-bought or see page 303)

1 red chilli, sliced (optional)

6 tomatoes (400g in total), peeled and cut into quarters

1 tbsp sweet paprika

good pinch of saffron

4 tbsp finely chopped flat-leaf parsley

4 fillets of sea bass (about 300g in total), skin on, cut in half

14 mussels (about 220g in total)

15 clams (about 140g in total)

10 tiger prawns (about 220g in total), in their shells or peeled and deveined

3 tbsp arak, ouzo or Pernod

2 tsp chopped tarragon (optional)

salt and black pepper

You don't see lots of seafood in Jerusalem. The distance from the sea and kosher rules (SEE PAGE 231) make it a rare find. However, many of Jerusalem's culinary inventions aren't necessarily 'natural' to its surroundings or population. The restaurant Machenyuda, which became famous for its little Kilner jars of polenta topped with asparagus and truffle, is the current trend-setter. Just as influential in the 1990s was Occianus (Ocean), where Eyal Shani, the enfant terrible of Israeli cooking, made his name. Shani's prawns grilled over orange-tree charcoal and his ingredients foraged in the Judean mountains, combined with his fiery and eccentric ways, made him *the* voice of modern Israeli cuisine.

This is our interpretation of a Tunisian fish soup, with embellishments that take it way out of the realm of traditional, kosher cooking. Of all Jewish communities, it is the Tunisians who make the most extensive and creative use of fresh fish (SEE PAN-FRIED SEA BREAM WITH HARISSA AND ROSE, PAGE 219, AND FRICASSEE SALAD, PAGE 227). *Tunisian Jews traditionally had fish most days of the week and served it over couscous. This soup would, obviously, not appear on a traditional Tunisian Jewish table but it would still taste wonderful when spooned over couscous (just reduce the soup a little so it turns slightly thicker).*

Place the olive oil and garlic in a wide, low-rimmed frying pan and cook on a medium heat for 2 minutes without colouring the garlic. Stir in the fennel and potato and cook for a further 3–4 minutes. Add the stock and preserved lemon, season with ¼ teaspoon of salt and some black pepper, bring to a boil, then cover and cook on a low heat for 12–14 minutes or until the potatoes are cooked. Add the chilli, if using, tomatoes, spices and half the parsley and cook for a further 4–5 minutes.

Add up to another 300ml of water at this point, simply as much as is needed to be able just to cover the fish to poach it, and bring to a simmer again. Add the sea bass and seafood, cover the pan and allow to boil quite fiercely for 3–4 minutes or until the shellfish open and the prawns turn pink.

Using a slotted spoon, remove the fish and seafood from the soup. If it is still a bit watery, allow the soup to boil for a few more minutes to reduce. Add the arak and taste for seasoning.

Finally, return the seafood and fish to the soup to reheat them. Serve at once, garnished with the remainder of the parsley and the tarragon, if using.

Pistachio soup

¼ tsp saffron threads
200g shelled unsalted
  pistachios
30g unsalted butter
4 shallots, peeled and
  finely chopped
  (100g in total)
25g ginger, peeled and
  finely chopped
1 leek, finely chopped
  (150g in total)
2 tsp ground cumin
700ml chicken stock
80ml freshly squeezed
  orange juice
1 tbsp lemon juice
salt and black pepper
soured cream, to serve

Don't be too quick to judge. This soup, traditional of the Iranian Jewish community, only reveals its true glory at the very last stage, when fresh orange juice is stirred through it. Serve small portions; it's quite rich. If you don't want to skin the pistachios, don't, it will only affect the colour.

Preheat the oven to 180°C/160°C Fan/Gas Mark 4. Pour 2 tablespoons of boiling water over the saffron threads in a small cup and leave to infuse for 30 minutes.

To remove the pistachio skins, blanch them in boiling water for 1 minute, strain and while still hot remove the skins by pressing between your fingers. Not all the skins will come off as with almonds — this is fine as it won't affect the soup — but getting rid of some skin will improve the colour, making it a brighter green. Spread the pistachios out on a baking tray and roast in the oven for 8 minutes. Remove and leave to cool.

Heat the butter in a large saucepan and add the shallots, ginger, leek, cumin, ½ teaspoon of salt and some black pepper. Sauté on a medium heat for 10 minutes, stirring often, until the shallots are completely soft. Add the stock and half of the saffron liquid. Cover the pan, reduce the heat and let the soup simmer for 20 minutes.

Place all but one tablespoon of the pistachios in a large bowl along with half of the soup. Use a hand-held blender to blitz until smooth and then return this to the saucepan. Add the orange and lemon juice, reheat and taste to adjust the seasoning.

To serve, roughly chop up the reserved pistachios. Transfer the hot soup into bowls and top with a spoonful of soured cream. Sprinkle with pistachios and drizzle with saffron liquid.

Couscous & Co.

It is extremely characteristic of Jerusalem's position at the heart of so many Middle Eastern and North African cuisines that it is impossible to untangle and unravel the distinct name and characteristics of certain ingredients. Take little pasta balls — we are not even sure by what name to introduce them — most commonly known in the West as couscous.

Well, there is indeed couscous, tiny semolina balls that in the past were only freshly rolled by women, steamed and served with soups and tagines, and are now sold dried and packaged and are also used for making salads and as a general side dish. Couscous is relatively new to Jerusalem, gaining popularity mostly since the arrival of large numbers of North African Jews in the 1950s and 1960s, particularly from Morocco. Still, it had spread deep roots and is extremely popular in Jewish culture. Many Jerusalem women still roll their own couscous, which can be found in restaurants around the city.

The local Palestinian equivalent to couscous is called maftoul. Maftoul are less even in shape, larger than couscous and are also either made at home or sold dried. Similar to couscous, maftoul is served with stews and soups, often steamed, and reserved for special occasions (SEE ALSO PAGE 141).

Israeli couscous, ptitim, is another variation on the theme, made of wheat. This is also substantially larger than couscous and was thought up during the 1950s' food shortages by the then prime minister, David Ben-Gurion, as an industrial solution for feeding the vast number of newly arrived immigrants. It has taken root in Israeli culture and is particularly liked by children when cooked with onion and tomato (SEE PAGE 8).

The spread of 'Israeli couscous' in the West, from comfort food in its early years, to top chefs' latest trendy ingredient, caused some resentment among Palestinians, whose maftoul isn't very different from ptitim, and among Lebanese, whose mograbieh, or Lebanese couscous, is similar to and only a bit larger than ptitim. Mograbieh, which literally means 'from North Africa', clearly affirms its origin and source of inspiration through its name, while 'Israeli couscous', claim the critics, does the exact opposite.

Burnt aubergine & mograbieh soup

5 small aubergines
   (about 1.2kg in total)
sunflower oil, for frying
1 onion, sliced
   (125g in total)
1 tbsp cumin seeds,
   freshly ground
1½ tsp tomato purée
2 large tomatoes
   (350g in total), skinned
   and diced
350ml chicken
   or vegetable stock
400ml water
4 garlic cloves, crushed
2½ tsp sugar
2 tbsp lemon juice
100g mograbieh, or
   alternative, such as
   maftoul, fregola or giant
   couscous (see page 139)
2 tbsp shredded basil,
   or 1 tbsp chopped dill,
   whichever you prefer,
   optional
salt and black pepper

Mograbieh, and to a lesser degree maftoul, are available from some Middle Eastern grocers and online (SEE MORE ON MOGRABIEH AND MAFTOUL ON PAGE 139). *Giant or Israeli couscous are widely available and so is fregola, the Sardinian equivalent. Whichever you choose for making this wonderfully hefty soup, check the package for cooking times, making sure the little pasta balls are just* al dente. *Follow the soup with something light, like the Broad bean kuku* (SEE PAGE 39) *or Pan-fried mackerel with golden beetroot and orange salsa* (SEE PAGE 222).

Start by burning three of the aubergines. To do this, follow the instructions for Burnt aubergine with garlic, lemon and pomegranate seeds (PAGE 79).

Cut the remaining aubergines into 1.5cm dice. Heat about 150ml of oil in a large saucepan over a medium–high heat and, when it is hot, add the aubergine dice. Fry for 10–15 minutes, stirring often, until coloured all over; add a little more oil if needed so there is always some oil in the pan. Remove the aubergine, place in a colander to drain and sprinkle with salt.

Make sure you have about 1 tablespoon of oil left in the pan, then add the onion and cumin and sauté for about 7 minutes, stirring often. Add the tomato purée and cook for another minute before adding the tomatoes, stock, water, garlic, sugar, lemon juice, 1½ teaspoons of salt and some black pepper. Simmer gently for 15 minutes.

Meanwhile, bring a small saucepan of salted water to the boil and add the mograbieh or alternative. Cook until *al dente*; this will vary according to brand but should take about 15–18 minutes (check the packet). Drain and refresh under cold water.

Transfer the burnt aubergine flesh to the soup and blitz to a smooth liquid with a hand-held blender. Add the mograbieh and fried aubergine, keeping some to garnish at the end, and simmer for another 2 minutes. Taste and adjust the seasoning. Serve hot, with the reserved mograbieh and fried aubergine on top and garnished with basil or dill, if you like.

Tomato & sourdough soup

Yotam's mother, Ruth, who kindly gave us this recipe, is in many ways a typical Jewish Jerusalem cook. She was born to a Yekke family, German Jews who settled in the city just before the Second World War. Growing up, she spoke German at home and ate sweet-spiced red cabbage, potatoes and sausages. Outside, she would experience some Arab food — it tasted thoroughly exotic to her — and the food of various Jewish immigrants, particularly from Poland and Eastern Europe. She would also experience the beginnings of what later developed into a pretty defined Israeli cuisine, particularly as it was prepared in the Kibbutzim — the famous chopped cucumber and tomato salad, tahini sauce and olives.

Ruth married Michael, of Italian background, and so a whole new culinary world was opened up for her. She also got to travel a bit, mainly to Europe and the USA, and being an open person, she was always seeking new influences, new cuisines to try.

Growing up, Yotam remembers Ruth daringly trying all kinds of dishes. She made Spanish gazpachos, Italian zabagliones and Malaysian curries. She cooked boeuf bourguignon; roast beef, English-style; and sweet and sour chicken. She also cooked many specialities of her German heritage. What you could hardly find in her kitchen were many local, Palestinian ingredients. Yotam can't remember ever seeing a tub of tahini in the house or a bag of bulgar. Still, over the years, Arab food gained respectability in Israeli culture and people started daring to go beyond the obligatory visit to a Palestinian joint for a kebab skewer and a plate of hummus when visiting the old city. Ruth, like many other Israeli cooks, began to get to know what was happening in her neighbours' kitchens and what was laid on their tables. Instead of feeling exotic, ingredients like za'atar made their way into the daily food repertoire, until they felt like they had always been there.

Today, like many other Jewish cooks, Ruth is comfortable with her European culinary heritage but her style has changed and the ingredients she uses are much more local. In her larder you can now find freekeh and tahini sitting next to fusilli and a jar of rollmops. On her spice shelf are sumac, cumin and organic Swiss bouillon powder. And you can even catch her, once in a while, burning a little aubergine.

---

2 tbsp olive oil, plus extra to finish
1 large onion, chopped (250g in total)
1 tsp cumin seeds
2 garlic cloves, crushed
750ml vegetable stock
4 large ripe tomatoes, chopped (650g in total)
400g tin chopped Italian tomatoes
1 tbsp caster sugar
1 slice of sourdough bread (40g in total)
2 tbsp chopped coriander, plus extra to finish
salt and black pepper

This modest list of ingredients yields the most delicate soup. It is truly wonderful.

Heat the oil in a medium saucepan and add the onion. Sauté for about 5 minutes, stirring often, until the onion is translucent. Add the cumin and garlic and fry for 2 minutes. Pour in the stock, both types of tomato, sugar, 1 teaspoon of salt and a good grind of black pepper.

Bring the soup to a gentle simmer and cook for 20 minutes, adding the bread, torn into chunks, halfway through the cooking. Finally, add the coriander and then blitz, using a blender, in a few pulses so that the tomatoes break down but are still a little coarse and chunky. The soup should be quite thick; add a little water if it is too thick at this point. Serve, drizzled with oil and scattered with fresh coriander.

Clear chicken soup with knaidlach

Knaidlach, matzo meal dumplings served in chicken or beef broth, appear on most Jewish tables in Jerusalem and around the world at Pesach (Passover) and often also at Rosh Hashana. Believe it or not but Sami, with not a Jewish bone in his body, is renowned for his knaidlach. So much so, that he has personally disclosed to many respectable North London housewives his hush-hush tips for making this ultimate Ashkenazi festive delicacy that he has perfected over time.

Knaidlach need to be light, but not too fluffy, with just enough flavour to bring out the qualities of the broth, the real pride of the housewife.

Chicken soup is deeply engrained in Jewish culture, famous for its mythological healing qualities. It is the basis for the Ashkenazi Shabbat and holiday meals, with every woman having her own 'secret' recipe.

It is said that the former Israeli prime minister, Golda Meir, used to be a good cook and that even while she held the office in the 1970s, she never had a dedicated cook in the prime minister's residence, rather she did the cooking herself or it was done by one of only two staff members. Golda was a daring eater and would try whatever she was offered around the world. Still, at home it was a typical Ashkenazi affair. Her chicken soup with knaidlach was her grandchildren's favourite.

The knaidlach take a while to make so are better started a day in advance. You can stop at the batter stage, or once they are shaped, cooked and cooled. In both cases, keep in the fridge till the next day. The soup can also be made a day ahead and chilled.

You can opt for making the soup only. If you do, return the chicken meat to the finished soup to warm up, and serve the soup with the chicken pieces and some cooked egg vermicelli. If you do make the knaidlach, serve the chicken warm over well-seasoned cooked rice or bulgar wheat (but not during Pesach!) with a drizzle of olive oil and a sprinkle of toasted pine nuts, coarse sea salt, black pepper and chopped parsley.

1 free-range chicken, about 2kg, divided into quarters, with all the bones, plus giblets if you can get them and any extra wings or bones you can get from the butcher
1½ tsp sunflower oil
250ml dry white wine
2 carrots, peeled and cut into 2cm slices (250g in total)
4 celery sticks, cut into 6cm segments (300g in total)
2 medium onions, cut into 8 wedges (350g in total)
1 large turnip, peeled, trimmed and cut into 8 segments (200g in total)
50g bunch flat-leaf parsley
50g bunch coriander
5 thyme sprigs
1 small rosemary sprig
20g dill, plus extra to garnish
3 bay leaves
100g fresh root ginger, thinly sliced
20 whole black peppercorns
5 whole allspice berries
salt

KNAIDLACH
(MAKES 12–15)

2 large eggs
40g margarine or chicken fat, melted and allowed to cool a bit
2 tbsp finely chopped parsley
75g matzo meal
4 tbsp soda water
salt and freshly ground black pepper

To make the knaidlach, whisk the eggs in a medium bowl until frothy. Whisk in the melted margarine or fat, then ½ a teaspoon of salt, some black pepper and the parsley. Gradually, stir in the matzo meal, followed by the soda water, and stir to a uniform paste. Cover the bowl and chill the batter until cold and firm, at least an hour or two and up to 1 day ahead.

Line a baking sheet with cling film. Using your wet hands and a spoon, shape the batter into balls the size of small walnuts and place on the baking sheet.

Drop the matzo balls into a large pot of gently boiling salted water. Cover partially with a lid and reduce the heat to low. Simmer gently until tender, about 30 minutes.

Using a slotted spoon, transfer the knaidlach onto a clean baking sheet where they can cool down, and then be chilled for up to a day. Or, they can go straight into the hot soup.

For the soup, trim any excess fat off the chicken and discard. Pour the oil into a very large saucepan or casserole and sear the chicken pieces over a high heat on all sides, 3–4 minutes. Remove from the pan, discard the oil and wipe the pan. Add the wine and let it bubble away for a minute. Return the chicken, cover with water and bring to a very gentle simmer. Simmer for about 10 minutes, skimming away the scum. Add the carrot, celery, onion and turnip. Tie all the herbs into one bundle with string and add to the pot. Add the bay leaves, ginger, peppercorns, allspice and 1½ teaspoons of salt and then pour in enough water to cover everything well.

Bring the soup back to a very gentle simmer, cook for 1½ hours, skimming occasionally and adding water as needed to keep everything well covered. Lift the chicken from the soup and remove the meat from the bones. Keep the meat in a bowl with a little broth to keep it moist, and refrigerate. Return the bones to the pot and simmer for another hour, adding just enough water to keep the bones and vegetables covered. Strain the hot soup and discard the herbs, vegetables and bones. Warm the cooked knaidlach in the soup. Once they are hot, serve the soup and knaidlach in shallow bowls, sprinkled with dill.

Spicy freekeh soup with meatballs

MEATBALLS

400g minced beef, lamb or a combination of both
1 small onion (150g in total), finely diced
2 tbsp finely chopped flat-leaf parsley
½ tsp ground allspice
¼ tsp ground cinnamon
3 tbsp plain flour
2 tbsp olive oil
salt and black pepper

SOUP

2 tbsp olive oil
1 large onion (250g in total), chopped
3 garlic cloves, crushed
2 carrots (250g in total), peeled and cut into 1cm cubes
2 celery sticks (150g in total), cut into 1cm cubes
3 large tomatoes (350g in total), chopped
40g tomato purée
1 tbsp baharat spice mix (shop-bought or see recipe, page 299)
1 tbsp ground coriander
1 cinnamon stick
1 tbsp caster sugar
150g cracked freekeh
500ml beef stock
500ml chicken stock
10g coriander, chopped
1 lemon, cut into 6 wedges

Palestinians, like many others in the region, used to harvest some of their wheat while the grains were still green and not completely dry. These were then set on fire in order to burn the chaff and straw. The village women would then get together in large groups to beat the wheat and collect the green grains. The result of this process is freekeh, or green wheat, a highly popular cereal with a hint of smokiness. It imparts a brilliant aroma when added to soups or stews but can also be cooked like rice or bulgar.

Today, freekeh is produced and sold commercially, whole or cracked; when cracked, it looks like bulgar wheat but is green. We use it for making pilaffs, in salads and for serving with lamb or chicken (SEE POACHED CHICKEN WITH SWEET SPICED FREEKEH, PAGE 182). Its earthy flavour and slightly coarse texture go particularly well with sweet spices.

In our first book we published a recipe for the Moroccan soup harira, a traditional meal for breaking the Ramadan fast. It proved very popular with our readers who particularly mentioned the deep and comforting aromas, broken by a surprising sharpness of lemon juice and plenty of spices. This is a Palestinian version on the theme and it does the same job. It is warming, hearty, sweet and substantial. Look for freekeh online or in Middle Eastern grocers. Bulgar is an acceptable substitute; it wouldn't take as long to cook though, 20–25 minutes should be enough.

Start with the meatballs. In a large bowl mix together the minced meat, onion, parsley, allspice, cinnamon, ½ a teaspoon of salt and ¼ of a teaspoon of pepper. Using your hands, mix well then form the mixture into ping-pong-size balls and roll them in the flour; you will get about 15. Heat the olive oil in a large casserole and fry the meatballs on a medium heat for a few minutes, or until golden brown on all sides. Remove the meatballs and set aside.

Wipe out the pan with kitchen paper and add the olive oil for the soup. On a medium heat, fry the onion and garlic for 5 minutes. Stir in the carrot and celery and cook for 2 minutes. Add the tomatoes, tomato purée, spices, sugar, 2 teaspoons of salt and ½ teaspoon of pepper and cook for 1 more minute. Stir in the freekeh and cook for 2–3 minutes. Add the stocks, 800ml of hot water and the meatballs. Bring to a boil, reduce the heat and simmer very gently for a further 35–45 minutes, stirring occasionally, until the freekeh is plump and tender. The soup should be quite thick. Reduce or add a little water as needed. Finally, taste and adjust the seasoning.

Ladle the hot soup into serving bowls and sprinkle with the chopped coriander. Serve the lemon wedges on the side.

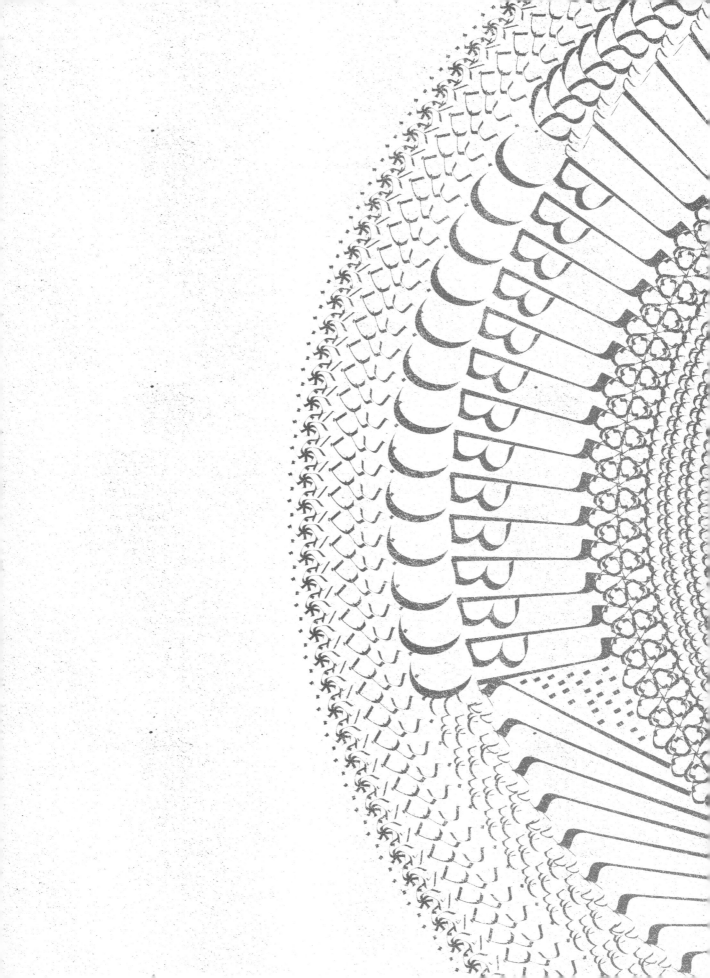

STUFFED

Stuffed

When Henry Kissinger visited Jerusalem in 1974 for one of his peace missions, the chef at the city's top restaurant at the time, Mishkenot Sha'ananim, prepared a special platter with six items, each representing a stop on the Secretary of State's tour: Morocco, Egypt, Syria, Jordan, Lebanon and Israel. Food writer Rina Valero, who recounts the story, mentions the six dishes on what became known as the 'Kissinger Platter': kubbeh, stuffed vine leaves, stuffed prunes wrapped in goose breast, filo stuffed with chicken liver and veal, cigars stuffed with foie gras and pears stuffed with walnuts and raisins. This selection reflects well the local fascination with all things stuffed. It is a unique phenomenon that doesn't only apply to top-end restaurants. Absolutely every single one of the city's numerous cultures has at least one major dish that involves stuffing, often many more, and a few cuisines, like the Kurdish Jewish, have become identified with a particular set of dishes that involve stuffing. Ma'amul cookies (SEE PAGE 288), much loved Palestinian staples, are based on a pastry shell stuffed with great deftness with a filling that is loaded with flavour. Numerous versions of mahshi, stuffed vegetables, can be found throughout the region and are much admired by everybody.

AUBERGINES, POTATOES, COURGETTES, BEETS, TOMATOES, ONIONS, PEPPERS, TURNIPS, CHARD, VINE AND CABBAGE LEAVES ARE AMONG THE POPULAR ONES. BUT ANYTHING GOES, REALLY

In the days before women went out to work, and still to a lesser degree today, groups of women, Jewish as well as Palestinian, would work together at home stuffing vegetables. This requires dexterity and patience, particularly hollowing out carrots and courgettes, for which there is a specialized tool, but they are made with much pride. The stuffing usually consists of seasoned rice either with or without the addition of minced meat, and the cooking liquid is either water or tomato-based. The Arab version is served with yoghurt and sometimes dried yoghurt (kishk) is added to the cooking liquid. Trotters or whole sheep's head can also be added to the pot for flavour.

Still seeing so many foods in Jerusalem being stuffed, filled or rolled today is a bit of a miracle. Stuffing is an activity suitable for old times, when people had more time and less money; when women spent hours at home but could afford much less. What stuffing does is stretch your meat or rice much further, with a result that is impressive to look at because of its complexity but is also very delicious. It also includes meat, veg and carb in one pot so saves the cook much cleaning up and having to flavour the separate components.

For Jews there is also the benefit of cooking for Shabbat. Their stuffed vegetables are slowly cooked on Friday and can be left on a warm platter or served cold. Sephardim also stuff vegetables for special events and holidays. The stuffed vegetables are sometimes dipped in egg, fried and then stewed on the stovetop or in the oven. Aubergines, potatoes, courgettes, beets, tomatoes, onions, peppers, turnips, chard, vine and cabbage leaves are among the popular ones. But anything goes, really. Dried apricots and other fruit can be added to the stuffing or the sauce — we've even seen apricot jam (!) — as well as tamarind. This mixture of sweet and sour is typical Jerusalem.

Polish Jews stuff cabbage, a result of the interaction during the 17th century with the Ottoman Empire. They stuff their cabbage with beef and rice and cook it in stock. Hungarian Jews stuff peppers and cook them in a sweet tomato and paprika sauce.

But stuffing doesn't end with vegetables. Shishbarak, little dumplings, a bit like tortellini, stuffed with meat and cooked in yoghurt, are an Arab speciality. The various Ashkenazi and Sephardic cuisines all have their own versions of dumplings that are still highly popular today.

Kubbeh — bulgar or semolina dumplings, normally stuffed with meat — are a mainstay of Palestinians (SEE PAGE 159), who fry them, and Kurdish Jews, who cook them in various soups (SEE KUBBEH HAMUSTA RECIPE, PAGE 162).

Hollowed-out carrots sold in a market ready to stuff

Lamb-stuffed quince with pomegranate & coriander

400g minced lamb
1 garlic clove, crushed
1 red chilli, chopped
20g coriander, chopped,
    plus 2 tbsp to garnish
50g breadcrumbs
1 tsp allspice
2 tbsp finely grated ginger
    (40g in total)
2 medium onions, peeled
    and finely chopped
    (220g in total)
1 medium free-range egg
4 quince (1.3kg in total)
½ a lemon, squeezed,
    plus 1 tbsp lemon juice
3 tbsp olive oil
8 cardamom pods
2 tsp pomegranate
    molasses
2 tsp sugar
500ml chicken stock
seeds of ½ a pomegranate
salt and black pepper

This is a stunning dish that we always go back to. We regularly teach a simplified version in our Saturday morning classes at Leiths cookery school in London. There, we don't stuff the quince but just dice it and cook it in the sauce with the meat filling shaped into meatballs. We recommend doing that if you don't have the time or the inclination to stuff the quince (it is a pretty hardy fruit!). You could use hard pears as an alternative. Another variation is based on a Persian dish, khoresht beh, which calls for lamb or beef cubes, chopped onion, cinnamon, nutmeg, sliced quince, lemon juice and sugar. All these are cooked together very slowly to make a sweet and sharp stew.

Place the lamb in a mixing bowl along with the garlic, chilli, coriander, breadcrumbs, allspice, half of the ginger, half of the onion, egg, ¾ teaspoon of salt and some pepper. Mix well with your hands and set aside.

Peel the quince and halve them lengthways. Keep them in a bowl of cold water with a squeezed half lemon so that they do not turn brown. Use a melon baller or small spoon to remove the pips and then hollow out the quince halves so that you are left with a 1.5cm shell. Keep the scooped-out flesh. Fill the hollows with the lamb mix, using your hands to push it down.

Heat up the olive oil in a large frying pan for which you have a lid. Place the reserved quince flesh in a food processor, blitz to chop well and then transfer this to the pan along with the remaining onion, ginger and cardamom pods. Sauté for 10–12 minutes, until the onion has softened, then add the molasses, 1 tablespoon of lemon juice, sugar, stock, ½ teaspoon of salt and some black pepper. Add the quince halves to the sauce, with the meat stuffing facing upwards, reduce the heat to a gentle simmer, cover the pan and cook for about 30 minutes. At the end the quince should be completely soft, the meat well cooked and the sauce thick. Lift the lid and simmer for a minute or two to reduce the sauce if needed.

Serve warm or at room temperature, sprinkled with the coriander and pomegranate seeds.

Turnip & veal 'cake'

300g basmati rice
400g minced veal, lamb
  or beef
30g chopped flat-leaf
  parsley
1½ tsp baharat spice mix
  (shop-bought or see
  recipe, page 299)
½ tsp ground cinnamon
½ tsp dried chilli flakes
2 tbsp olive oil
10–15 medium turnips
  (1.5kg in total)
about 400ml sunflower oil
300g chopped tomatoes,
  tinned are fine
1½ tbsp tamarind paste
200ml hot chicken stock
1½ tbsp caster sugar
2 thyme sprigs, leaves
  picked
salt and black pepper

After about an hour of serious struggling with various kitchen utensils and a host of small, sharp tools — and with turnip shells breaking up or cracking all over the place — we finally gave up trying to hollow out turnips for a popular Palestinian dish where they are stuffed with rice and cooked in tomato sauce. Instead, we came up with this layered dish that saves much hassle and time but also leaves us full of admiration and awe for generations of housewives and mothers who prepared these regularly and without a single grumble. Similar to Maqluba (SEE PAGE 127), *this is a meal in a pot. It is sweet and sour with a very clear aroma of all the spices. Turnips can be substituted with potatoes, if you prefer. Serve it with seasoned Greek yoghurt or Yoghurt with cucumber* (SEE PAGE 299).

Wash the rice and drain well. Place in a large mixing bowl and add the meat, parsley, baharat, cinnamon, 2 teaspoons of salt, ½ a teaspoon of pepper, chilli and olive oil. Mix well and set aside.

Peel the turnips and cut them into 1-cm thick slices. Heat up enough sunflower oil on a medium–high heat to come 2cm up the sides of a large frying pan. Fry the turnip slices in batches, 3–4 minutes, until golden. Transfer to a plate lined with kitchen paper, sprinkle with a little salt and allow to cool down.

Put the tomatoes, tamarind, stock, 250ml of water, sugar, 1 teaspoon of salt and ½ a teaspoon of pepper in a large mixing bowl. Whisk well. Pour about a third of this liquid into a medium, heavy-based saucepan (24cm in diameter). Arrange one third of the turnip slices inside. Add half the rice mixture and level. Arrange another layer of turnips, followed by the second half of the rice. Finish with the last of the turnips, pressing down softly with your hands. Pour the remaining tomato liquid over the turnip and rice layers and sprinkle with the thyme. Gently slide a spatula down the sides of the pot allowing the juices to flow to the base.

Place on a medium heat and bring to a boil. Reduce the heat to an absolute minimum, cover and simmer for 1 hour. Take off the heat, uncover and allow to rest for 10–15 minutes before serving. Unfortunately, it is impossible to invert the cake onto a plate as it doesn't hold its shape, so it must be spooned out.

Stuffed onions

4 large onions (900g in
    total, peeled weight)
about 400ml vegetable
    stock
1½ tbsp pomegranate
    molasses
salt and black pepper

STUFFING

1½ tbsp olive oil
150g finely chopped
    shallots
100g short grain rice
35g pine nuts, crushed
2 tbsp chopped fresh mint
2 tbsp chopped flat-leaf
    parsley
2 tsp dried mint
1 tsp ground cumin
⅛ tsp ground clove
¼ tsp ground allspice
¾ tsp salt
½ tsp black pepper
4 lemon wedges (optional)

*As a result of the long cooking and the sharp sweetness of the
pomegranate molasses, these onions have a surprisingly deep, yet fresh
flavour. Serve them at the start of a meat-centred meal, or alongside a
selection of small vegetable dishes, such as Charred okra with tomato,
garlic and preserved lemon (SEE PAGE 74) or Fried cauliflower with
tahini (SEE PAGE 60). Consider a variation based on a Syrian Jewish
dish: stuff the onions with minced beef flavoured with cinnamon and
allspice and braise in a sauce made with water, tamarind, lemon juice,
sugar and a little oil.*

Peel and cut about 0.5cm off the tops and tails of the onions, place
the trimmed onions in a large saucepan with plenty of water, bring
to a boil and cook for 15 minutes. Drain and set aside to cool down.

To prepare the stuffing, heat up the olive oil in a medium frying pan
over a medium–high heat and add the shallots. Sauté for 8 minutes,
stirring often, then add all of the remaining ingredients except the
lemon wedges. Turn the heat to low and continue to cook and stir
for 10 minutes.

Using a small knife, make a long cut from the top of the onion to
the bottom, running all the way to its centre, so that each layer of
onion has only one slit running through it. Start gently separating
the onion layers, one after another, until you reach the core. Don't
worry if some of the layers tear a little through the peeling; you can
still use them.

Hold a layer of onion in the cup of one hand and spoon about 1
tablespoon of the rice mixture into one half of the onion, placing
the filling near to one end of the opening. Don't be tempted to fill it
up more as it needs to be wrapped up nice and snug. Fold the empty
side of the onion over the stuffed side and roll it up tightly so the rice
is covered with a few layers of onion with no air in the middle. Place
in a medium frying pan for which you have a lid, seam-side down,
and continue with the remainder of the onion and rice mixture. Lay
the onions side-by-side in the pan, so that there is no space to move
about. Fill any spaces with parts of the onion that have not been
stuffed. Add enough stock so that the onions are three-quarters
covered, along with the pomegranate molasses, and season with ¼
of a teaspoon of salt.

Cover the pan and cook on the lowest possible simmer for 1½–2
hours, until the liquid has evaporated. Serve warm or at room
temperature, with lemon wedges if you like.

The capital of kibbeh

Jerusalem is the world capital of kibbeh; if not for quantity then definitely for variety. Most people would happily agree on that. The trouble is they'd find it much harder to agree on what that thing actually is. Food definitions can get terribly complicated in this city, but if you are happy to walk into this trap, it is fascinating. You'll find the most convoluted and intricate mixes when you look into Arabic cuisine and its counterpart, Sephardic cuisine of Jews of the Levant. And nowhere more so than when it comes to kibbeh.

Kibbeh, kubbeh or kobeba all mean 'the shape of a ball' in Arabic. Indeed, this is how they started. The most familiar variation in the West and in eastern Jerusalem is the Syrian and Lebanese national dish, where minced meat and bulgar wheat are mixed together to make a shell, stuffed with meat flavoured with sweet spices and pine nuts, shaped into balls or torpedoes and deep-fried. They are deliciously crisp and wholesome.

DAINTILY SHAPING THE CASES AS THINLY AS POSSIBLE, WITHOUT IT TEARING OR BREAKING, USED TO BE THE ULTIMATE INDICATOR OF FEMALE DEXTERITY AND GENERAL DOMESTIC APTITUDE

Daintily shaping the cases as thinly as possible, without them tearing or breaking, used to be the ultimate indicator of female dexterity and general domestic aptitude. For generations of Jewish and Arab women, being able to make nice kubbeh was considered one of the basic requirements of a 'good' domesticated woman; a test of their refinement and elegance. A less arduous version — why hasn't anyone told the poor women? — is kibbeh b'siniyah, where the casing and filling are layered in a dish to form a pie. And then there is the Lebanese kibbeh nayyeh, which is like steak tartare, using raw minced meat and bulgar — no trouble at all.

Jews from Iraq, Syria and Kurdistan have a range of kibbeh that are made with ground rice or semolina and cooked in soups or stews (as well as the fried kibbeh we described). These are unique to them but have come to be seen as the typical Jewish ethnic food of Jerusalem (SEE KUBBEH HAMUSTA, PAGE 162).

Open kibbeh

125g fine bulgar wheat
90ml olive oil
2 garlic cloves, crushed
2 medium onions, finely
    chopped
1 green chilli, finely
    chopped
350g minced lamb
1 tsp ground allspice
1 tsp ground cinnamon
1 tsp ground coriander
2 tbsp roughly chopped
    coriander
60g pine nuts
3 tbsp roughly chopped flat-
    leaf parsley
2 tbsp self-raising flour,
    plus a little extra if
    needed
50g light tahini paste
2 tsp lemon juice
1 tsp sumac
salt and black pepper

This variation of kibbeh (SEE PAGE 159) *is very untraditional. It is more of a layered savoury cake incorporating the essential elements — bulgar, minced meat, spices and pine nuts — plus the obligatory tahini dipping sauce, spread on top. Serve it warm or at room temperature as a light meal, alongside a sharp aromatic salad such as Tabbouleh or Fattoush* (SEE PAGES 85 AND 29).

Preheat the oven to 200°C/180°C Fan/Gas Mark 6. Line a 20cm loose-bottomed or spring-form cake tin with greaseproof paper.

Place the bulgar in a large bowl and cover it with 200ml of water. Leave for 30 minutes.

Meanwhile, heat 4 tablespoons of olive oil in a large frying pan. Sauté the garlic, onion and chilli on a medium–high heat until they are completely soft. Remove everything from the pan, return it to high heat and add the lamb. Cook for 5 minutes, stirring continuously, until brown.

Return the onion mixture to the pan and add the spices, coriander, ½ a teaspoon of salt, a generous grind of black pepper and most of the pine nuts and parsley, leaving some aside. Cook for a couple of minutes, remove from the heat, taste and adjust the seasoning.

Check the bulgar to see if all the water has been absorbed. Strain to remove any remaining liquid. Add the flour, 1 tablespoon of olive oil, ¼ teaspoon of salt and a pinch of black pepper and use your hands to work into a pliable mixture that just holds together; add a little bit more flour if the mixture is very sticky. Push firmly into the base of the tin so that it is compacted and levelled. Spread the lamb mixture evenly on top and press it down a little. Bake in the oven for about 20 minutes or until the meat is quite a dark brown and very hot.

While you wait, whisk together the tahini paste with the lemon juice, 50ml of water and a pinch of salt. You are after a very thick, yet pourable sauce. If needed, add a tiny amount of extra water.

Remove the kibbeh cake from the oven, spread the tahini sauce evenly on top, sprinkle with the reserved pine nuts and chopped parsley, and return to the oven immediately. Bake for 10–12 minutes until the tahini is just setting and has taken on a little bit of colour, and the pine nuts are golden.

Remove from the oven and leave to cool down until warm or at room temperature. Before serving, sprinkle the top with the sumac and a drizzle of olive oil. Carefully remove the sides of the tin and cut the kibbeh into slices. Lift them gently so they don't break.

Kubbeh hamusta

Friday lunchtime around Machne Yehuda market is all about kubbeh in soup, a tradition of Kurdish and other Jews from Iraq, Syria and Turkey that has caught on and become the ultimate local comfort food, served in simple dedicated restaurants around the market. Unlike the more familiar fried kibbeh using bulgar (SEE PAGE 160), these are normally made with semolina or ground rice, stuffed with meat and poached in a variety of soups. The principal three are tomato (and often okra), beetroot and the sour, green hamusta, the most popular soup, made with chard, celery, courgette, garlic and lemon juice. All are extremely potent and sharp, typical of Jerusalem.

For Syrian Jews, whose wonderful cuisine is world renowned, the ultimate Shabbat meal is a soup similar to hamusta. Chamot or hamud, is also made with celery and lemon, only they add meatballs instead of dumplings.

The story of the kubbeh soup is another example of necessity breeding culinary ingenuity. Back in Kurdistan, Jews could only afford to buy meat very rarely. When they did, they had to buy a whole animal and make the most of it. They cooked their meat for a very long time in vast chunks, adding celery towards the end. Then everything was minced and kept in a very dry place for up to a few months (!) and used sparingly to stuff the kubbeh dumplings and cook in a fresh soup.

Making the dumplings for this soup is not the kind of thing we'd embark on when in a hurry or without perfect peace of mind. It is a kind of meditative activity that one can take up on leisurely weekends or when cooking in company. However, there are less time-consuming alternatives that we urge you to try because this soup is quite spectacular. One option is to forget the dumplings and simply add diced potato, celeriac or both and cook them in the soup. Another is to make small and simple meatballs and poach them in the soup (USE THE RECIPE FOR BEEF MEATBALLS WITH BROAD BEANS AND LEMON, PAGE 196, BUT WITHOUT THE CAPERS). *This would be our preferred option for balancing work and flavour. If you still want the semolina casing in the soup, make little round balls and cook them next to the meatballs. The stuffed kubbeh can be cooked, chilled and then reheated in the soup.*

KUBBEH STUFFING

1½ tbsp sunflower oil
½ medium onion, very
    finely chopped (75g in
    total)
350g minced beef
½ tsp ground allspice
1 large garlic clove, crushed
2 pale celery stalks, very
    finely chopped, or an
    equal amount of chopped
    celery leaves (60g in total)
salt and black pepper

KUBBEH CASES

325g semolina
40g plain flour
220ml hot water

SOUP

4 garlic cloves, crushed
5 celery stalks, leaves
    picked and stalks cut on
    an angle into 1.5cm slices
    (230g in total)
300g Swiss chard leaves,
    green part only, cut into
    2cm strips
2 tbsp sunflower oil
1 large onion, roughly
    chopped (200g in total)
2 litres chicken stock
1 large courgette, cut into
    1cm cubes (200g in total)
100ml lemon juice, plus
    extra if needed
lemon wedges, to serve

First prepare the meat stuffing. Heat up the oil in a medium frying pan and add the onion. Cook on a medium heat until translucent, about 5 minutes. Add the minced beef, allspice, ¾ teaspoon of salt and a good grind of black pepper and stir as you cook for 3 minutes, just to brown. Reduce the heat to medium–low and allow the meat to cook slowly for about 20 minutes, until completely dry, stirring from time to time. At the end, add the garlic and celery, cook for another 3 minutes and remove from the heat. Taste and adjust the seasoning. Allow to cool down.

While the beef mix is cooking, prepare the kubbeh cases. Mix the semolina, flour and ¼ teaspoon of salt in a large mixing bowl. Gradually add the water, stirring with a wooden spoon and then your hands until you get a sticky dough. Cover with a damp cloth and set aside to rest for 15 minutes.

Knead the dough for a few minutes on a work surface. It must be supple and spreadable without cracking. Add a little water or flour if needed. To make the dumplings, get a bowl of water and wet your hands (make sure your hands are wet throughout the process to prevent sticking). Take a piece of dough weighing about 30g and flatten it in your palm — you're aiming for 10cm diameter discs. Place about 2 teaspoons of the stuffing in the centre. Fold the edges over the stuffing to cover and then seal it inside. Roll the kubbeh in between your hands to form a ball and then press it down into a round, flat shape, about 3cm thick. Place the dumplings on a tray covered in cling film and drizzled with a little water, and leave to one side.

For the soup, place the garlic, half the celery and half the chard in a food processor bowl and blitz to a coarse paste. Heat the oil in a large saucepan and sauté the onion on a medium heat for about 10 minutes, until pale golden. Add the celery and chard paste and cook for 3 minutes more. Add the stock, courgette, remaining celery and chard, the lemon juice, 1 teaspoon of salt and ½ a teaspoon of black pepper. Bring to a boil and cook for 10 minutes, then taste and adjust the seasoning. It needs to be sharp so add another tablespoon of lemon juice if you need to.

Finally, carefully add the kubbeh to the soup — a few at a time, so they don't stick to each other — and simmer gently for 20 minutes. Leave aside for a good half hour for them to settle and soften, then reheat and serve. Serve with a wedge of lemon for an extra lemony kick.

Ruth's stuffed Romano peppers

8 medium Romano
  peppers
1 large tomato, roughly
  chopped (170g in total)
2 medium onions, roughly
  chopped (250g in total)
about 500ml vegetable
  stock

STUFFING

140g basmati rice
1½ tbsp baharat spice
  mix (shop-bought or see
  recipe, page 299)
½ tsp ground cardamom
2 tbsp olive oil
1 large onion, finely
  chopped (200g in total)
400g minced lamb
2½ tbsp chopped flat-leaf
  parsley
2 tbsp chopped dill
1½ tbsp dried mint
1½ tsp sugar
salt and black pepper

This is Yotam's mother's recipe. It is mellow yet delectable and you don't need much else beside it. Serve with Kohlrabi salad (SEE PAGE 46) and you are sorted. Make sure you have a frying pan or pot wide enough to accommodate all the peppers snugly, in one layer; you can squash them together a little. Otherwise, consider cooking in two separate pans.

Start with the stuffing. Place the rice in a saucepan and cover with lightly salted water. Bring to the boil and then cook for 4 minutes. Drain, refresh under cold water and set aside.

Dry-fry the spices in a frying pan. Add the olive oil and onion and fry for about 7 minutes, stirring often, until the onion is soft. Pour this, along with the rice, meat, herbs, sugar and 1 teaspoon of salt into a large mixing bowl. Use your hands to mix everything together well.

Starting from the stalk end, use a small knife to cut lengthways three-quarters of the way down each pepper, without removing the stalk, creating a long opening. Without forcing the pepper open too much, remove the seeds and then stuff each with about 100g of the mixture.

Place the chopped tomato and onion in a very large frying pan for which you have a tight-fitting lid. Sit the peppers on top, close together, and pour in just enough stock so that it rises 1cm up the peppers. Season with ½ a teaspoon of salt and some black pepper. Cover the pan with a lid and simmer, on the lowest possible heat setting, for an hour. It is important that the filling is just steamed so the lid needs to fit tightly; make sure there is always a little bit of liquid at the bottom of the pan. Serve the peppers warm, not hot, or at room temperature.

Stuffed aubergine with lamb & pine nuts

Elran Shrefler is the youngest of Ezra and Rachela Shrefler's nine children, who run Azura, a restaurant in the heart of Machne Yehuda market that serves Jerusalemites traditional Kurdish recipes with a Turkish influence, the area from which Ezra hails. A member of the Slow Food movement, Elran starts work at four every morning and cooks all his food in massive pots on small oil-burning stoves (SEE PICTURE ON PAGES 122–3), just as his family has done for generations. His food, long-cooked stews and hearty soups, is ready for the first customers who arrive at around 8 a.m. (!). It is essentially real fast food — after the long hours of slow cooking, it takes seconds to plate and serve. Elran showed us how to make his stuffed aubergine, Turkish-style, which is our favourite dish at Azura. This is our interpretation.

In their book, *The Flavor of Jerusalem*, Joan Nathan and Judy Stacey Goldman give a slightly unorthodox recipe for stuffed aubergine with calves' liver and apples. This is the creation of Deacon William Gardiner-Scott who, in the 1970s, was head of St Andrew's, the only Presbyterian church in Jerusalem. The church was erected in 1927 to commemorate the capture of Jerusalem by the British during the First World War. This is one of only a few culinary marks the Brits have left behind.

4 medium aubergines (about 1.2kg), halved lengthways
6 tbsp olive oil
1½ tsp ground cumin
1½ tbsp sweet paprika
1 tbsp ground cinnamon
2 medium onions (340g in total), finely chopped
500g minced lamb
50g pine nuts
20g flat-leaf parsley, chopped
2 tsp tomato purée
3 tsp caster sugar
150ml water
1½ tbsp lemon juice
1 tsp tamarind paste
4 cinnamon sticks
salt and black pepper

These are deliciously hearty and best served with some bread or simple rice (SEE BASMATI RICE AND ORZO, PAGE 103) *and some pickles on the side* (SEE PICKLED TURNIP AND BEETROOT, PAGE 307).

Preheat the oven to 220°C/200°C Fan/Gas Mark 7.

Place the aubergine halves, skin-side down, in a roasting tin large enough to accommodate them snugly. Brush the flesh with 4 tablespoons of the olive oil and season with 1 teaspoon of salt and plenty of black pepper. Roast for about 20 minutes, until golden brown. Remove from the oven and allow to cool slightly.

While the aubergines are cooking, you can start making the stuffing by heating up the remaining olive oil in a large frying pan. Mix together the cumin, paprika and ground cinnamon and add half of this spice mix to the pan, along with the onion. Cook on a medium–high heat for about 8 minutes, stirring often, before adding the lamb, pine nuts, parsley, tomato purée, 1 teaspoon of the sugar, 1 teaspoon of salt and some black pepper. Continue to cook and stir for another 8 minutes, until the meat is cooked.

Place the remaining spice mix in a bowl and add the water, lemon juice, tamarind, remaining sugar, cinnamon sticks and ½ teaspoon of salt; mix well.

Reduce the oven temperature to 195°C/175°C Fan/Gas Mark 5½. Pour the spice mix into the bottom of the aubergine roasting tin. Spoon the lamb mixture on top of each aubergine. Cover the tin tightly with foil, return to the oven and roast for 1 hour 30 minutes, by which point the aubergines should be completely soft and the sauce thick; twice through the cooking, remove the foil and baste the aubergines with the sauce, adding some water if the sauce dries out. Serve warm, not hot, or at room temperature.

Stuffed potatoes

The cuisine of Libyan Jews, Tripolitans as they are known, is luxurious and complex and has made a clear mark on the local food culture. It is very much a North African cuisine with its love of sweet things, the use of semolina, long cooking and general vibrancy, but it is also influenced by Italian and Arab cuisines.

If you think stuffing vegetables is a time consuming and intricate activity at the best of times, Tripolitan cooks have managed to take it into completely new spheres. Their mafrum 'cakes' are highly popular, despite the fact that preparation is a lengthy affair. It involves peeling and slicing vegetables (normally potatoes), making a mincemeat filling and 'sandwiching' small portions of it between two layers of veg, dipping these in flour then egg and frying them, and finally cooking the sandwiches for a very long time in a fragrant tomato sauce.

Our stuffed potatoes are inspired by mafrum and the Aleppian medyas — hollowed-out potatoes stuffed with meat and cooked in tomato sauce. We also love the 'simple' versions — bastil (Tripoli), pastel (Morocco), bantash (Tunisia), kubbeh patata (Sephardi) — that involve mashing cooked potato to make a case, stuffing it with cooked meat and boiled egg, dipping it in flour and egg and frying. These are served plainly with just a lemon wedge. Ashkenazim make pirogen — potato cakes stuffed with a filling made from more potato, butter, egg yolk and soured cream, poached like gnocchi and served with fried onion.

500g minced beef
200g white breadcrumbs
1 medium onion, finely
    chopped (120g in total)
2 garlic cloves, crushed
20g flat-leaf parsley, finely
    chopped
2 tbsp thyme leaves,
    chopped
1½ tsp ground cinnamon
2 medium free-range eggs,
    beaten
1.5kg medium Charlotte
    or Nicola potatoes, about
    9cm x 6cm, peeled and
    halved lengthways
2 tbsp chopped coriander
salt and black pepper

TOMATO SAUCE

2 tbsp olive oil
5 garlic cloves, crushed
1 medium onion, finely
    chopped (120g in total)
1½ sticks of celery, finely
    chopped (80g in total)
1 small carrot, peeled and
    finely chopped
    (70g in total)
1 red chilli, finely chopped
1½ tsp ground cumin
1 tsp ground allspice
a pinch of smoked paprika
1½ tsp sweet paprika
1 tsp caraway seeds,
    crushed with a mortar
    and pestle or spice
    grinder
800g tinned chopped
    tomatoes
1 tbsp tamarind paste
1½ tsp caster sugar

Make this dish when you are in no hurry or working in partnership with someone else. The stuffed potatoes are fun to make and taste divine but they do require time and some patience. Choose pretty waxy potatoes that are relatively small but large enough to halve, hollow and stuff, so about 9cm x 6cm. Dipping the stuffed potatoes in flour and egg and then frying them in oil, prior to cooking in the sauce, is an optional additional stage that gives a nice, unctuous coating. If everything doesn't fit in one pan, consider using two smaller ones. All the excess raw potato can be chopped and used to make Latkes (SEE PAGE 92). Serve with couscous, rice, or rustic white bread.

Start with the tomato sauce. Heat up the olive oil in the widest frying pan you have; you will also need a lid for it. Add the garlic, onion, celery, carrot and chilli. Sauté over a low heat for 10 minutes or until the vegetables are soft. Add the spices, stir well and cook for 2–3 minutes. Pour in the chopped tomatoes, tamarind, sugar, ½ teaspoon of salt and some black pepper and bring to the boil. Remove from the heat.

To make the stuffed potatoes, place the beef, breadcrumbs, onion, garlic, parsley, thyme, cinnamon, 1 teaspoon of salt, some black pepper and the eggs in a mixing bowl. Use your hands to combine all the ingredients well.

Hollow out each potato half with a melon baller or a teaspoon, creating a 1.5-cm thick shell. Stuff the meat mixture into each cavity, using your hands to push it right down so that it fills up the potato completely. Carefully press all the potatoes down into the tomato sauce so that they are sitting close together, with the meat stuffing facing upwards. Add about 300ml of water, or just enough to almost cover the patties with sauce, bring to a light simmer, cover the pan with a lid and leave to cook slowly for at least 1 hour or even longer, until the sauce is thick and the potatoes very soft. If the sauce hasn't thickened enough, remove the lid and reduce for 5–10 minutes. Serve hot or warm, garnished with fresh coriander.

Stuffed artichokes with peas & dill

400g leeks, trimmed and
  cut into 0.5cm slices
250g minced beef
1 medium free-range egg
1 tsp ground allspice
1 tsp ground cinnamon
2 tsp dried mint
12 medium globe
  artichokes, or frozen
  artichoke bottoms
  (see introduction)
80ml olive oil
plain flour, for coating the
  artichokes
about 500ml chicken or
  vegetable stock
90ml lemon juice, plus
  extra if using fresh
  artichokes
200g frozen peas
10g dill, roughly chopped
salt and black pepper

Thrifty Jerusalem cooks make good use of the abundance in spring greens and preserve broad beans, young vine leaves and artichokes at the height of their season. The artichokes are trimmed and their hearts are frozen, ready to be used when needed (SEE PAGE 41). Increasingly, though, prepared frozen artichoke bases are available in supermarkets and they are pretty good. Look out for them in Middle Eastern shops and you will save yourself a lot of work. Serve these as a main course with Basmati rice and orzo (SEE PAGE 103).

Blanch the leeks in boiling water for 5 minutes. Drain, refresh and squeeze out the water. Roughly chop the leeks and place in a mixing bowl along with the meat, egg, spices, mint, 1 teaspoon of salt and plenty of pepper. Stir well.

If you are using fresh artichokes, prepare a bowl with water and the juice of half a lemon. Remove the stalk from the artichoke and pull off the tough outer leaves. Once you reach the softer, pale leaves, use a large sharp knife to cut across the flower so that you are left with the bottom quarter. Use a small sharp knife or a vegetable peeler to remove the outer layers of the artichoke until the base, or bottom, is exposed. Scrape out the hairy 'choke' and put the base in the acidulated water. Discard the rest then repeat with the other artichokes.

Heat up 2 tablespoons of the olive oil in a saucepan wide enough to hold the artichokes lying flat. Fill each artichoke bottom with 1–2 tablespoons of the beef mixture, pressing the filling in. Gently roll them in some flour, shaking off the excess, so they are lightly coated. Fry in the hot oil for 1½ minutes on each side over a medium heat. Wipe the pan clean and return the artichokes to the pan, sitting them flat and snugly side by side.

Mix the stock, lemon juice and remaining oil and season generously with salt and pepper. Ladle spoonfuls of the liquid over the artichokes until they are almost, but not completely, submerged; you may not need to use all the liquid. Place a piece of baking parchment over the artichokes, cover the pan with a lid and simmer on a low heat for 1 hour. When they're ready, about 4 tablespoons of the liquid should remain. If you need to, remove the lid and paper and reduce the sauce. Set the pan aside until the artichokes are just warm or at room temperature.

When ready to serve, blanch the peas for 2 minutes. Drain and add them and the dill to the pan with the artichokes, season to taste and mix everything together gently.

MEAT

Jerusalem mixed grill

Aside from the kugel (SEE PAGE 206), few dishes have gained the addition of 'Jerusalem' to their name. Despite the misleading name, Jerusalem artichokes aren't named after the city but are welcome here anyway. The me'orav Yerushalmi, literally translated as 'Jerusalem mixed grill', was invented on Agripas Street near Machne Yehuda market in the late 1960s. Several local steakhouses claim credit for the invention, but according to food writer Sherry Ansky, the original Jerusalem mixed grill was born at Makam steakhouse and almost overnight the chicken innards and onions, all fried in a particular spice mix, became one of the city's most iconic dishes. Today, many specialist steakhouses serve mixed grills to local clientele — mostly taxi drivers who flock there in the early evening or late at night for the offal delight.

Meanwhile, on the eastern side of Jerusalem, Palestinians have been making their version of the dish for centuries. They stuff the cooked innards in a pita and lightly season them with freshly squeezed lemon juice, hot chilli peppers, parsley and crushed cumin seeds. The dish, in either version, solves the issue of using the cheapest, unloved parts of Jerusalem's most loved meat, the chicken. We adore it.

300g chicken breast, cut into 2cm cubes
200g chicken hearts, cut in half lengthways (optional)
4 tbsp olive oil
250g chicken livers, diced
2 large onions, thinly sliced (about 500g in total)
1½ tsp ground turmeric
1 tbsp baharat spice mix (shop-bought or see recipe, page 299)
salt

Serve the mixed grill as a whole meal with fresh pita, savoury mango chutney, Tahini sauce (SEE PAGE 298) and pickles.

Put a large cast-iron or other heavy frying pan over a medium–high heat and leave for a few minutes, until nearly smoking. Add the chicken breast and leave for a minute, stir once, then cook until browned all over — about 2–3 minutes. Transfer the pieces to a bowl and set aside.

Put the hearts in the pan and cook, stirring occasionally, until browned but not cooked through, about 2–3 minutes. Add to the bowl.

Pour a teaspoon of the olive oil into the pan and add the livers. Cook for 2–3 minutes, stirring just once or twice, then remove from the pan.

Pour 2 tablespoons of olive oil into the pan and add half of the onions. Cook, stirring all the time, until the onions soften and slightly char but aren't completely limp, about 4–5 minutes. Add the remaining oil to the pan and repeat with the second half of the onions. Return the first batch to the pan, along with the spices and cooked chicken pieces, hearts and livers. Season with ¾ of a teaspoon of salt and continue to cook for about 3 minutes, scraping the pan as you cook, until the chicken is cooked through. Serve at once.

Braised quail with apricots, currants & tamarind

Tamarhindi, the Arab name for tamarind, literally translates to 'Indian date'. It arrived in the Levant somewhere around the 7th century, having made its way there from India via Persia, but it never really caught on to become a household staple in the region's cuisine. Apart from Jerusalem, that is, where it is mostly known in its ultra-sweet beverage form, sold cold under the scorching summer sun.

4 extra-large quails, about
   190g each, cut in half
   along the breastbone
   and back
¾ tsp dried chilli flakes
¾ tsp ground cumin
½ tsp fennel seeds, lightly
   crushed
1 tbsp olive oil
75ml white wine
80g dried apricots,
   thickly sliced
25g currants
1½ tbsp caster sugar
1½ tbsp tamarind paste
2 tbsp lemon juice
1 tsp picked thyme leaves
salt and black pepper
2 tbsp chopped mixed
   coriander and flat-leaf
   parsley, to garnish
   (optional)

With its sweet and sour combination of meat and dried fruit, this dish is typical of the Sephardi tradition of cooking. It is pretty special and can be placed in the middle of a festive dining table (Christmas, perhaps?) with great pride. Quail can be replaced with boneless chicken thighs. Serve with plain rice, sprinkled with toasted pine nuts or almonds.

Wipe the quails with kitchen paper and place in a mixing bowl. Sprinkle with the chilli flakes, cumin, fennel seeds, ½ a teaspoon of salt and some black pepper. Massage well with your hands, cover and leave to marinate in the fridge for at least 2 hours or overnight.

Heat the oil over a medium–high heat in a frying pan that is just large enough to accommodate the birds snugly and for which you have a lid. Brown the birds on all sides, for about 5 minutes, to get a nice golden-brown colour.

Remove the quails from the pan and discard most of the fat, leaving about half a tablespoon. Add 300ml of water, the wine, apricots, currants, sugar, tamarind, lemon juice, thyme, ½ a teaspoon of salt and some black pepper. Return the quails to the pan. They should be three-quarter-covered in liquid; if not, add more water. Bring to the boil, cover the pan and simmer very gently for 20–25 minutes, turning the quails over once or twice, until the birds are just cooked.

Lift the quails from the pan and onto a serving platter and keep warm. If the liquid isn't very thick, return it to a medium heat and simmer for a few minutes to reduce to a good sauce consistency. Spoon the sauce over the quails and garnish with the coriander and parsley, if using.

Roasted chicken with clementines & arak

100ml arak, ouzo or Pernod
4 tbsp olive oil
3 tbsp freshly squeezed
   orange juice
3 tbsp lemon juice
2 tbsp grain mustard
3 tbsp light brown sugar
2 medium fennel bulbs
   (500g in total)
1 large organic or free-
   range chicken, about
   1.3kg, divided into 8
   pieces, or the same weight
   in chicken thighs with the
   skin and on the bone
4 clementines, unpeeled
   (400g in total), sliced
   horizontally
   into 0.5cm slices
1 tbsp thyme leaves
2½ tsp fennel seeds, slightly
   crushed
salt and black pepper
chopped flat-leaf parsley, to
   garnish

All the intense flavours lavished on the poor chicken — arak, mustard, fennel, clementines with their skins, brown sugar — somehow manage to come together in a sweetly comforting dish you will always want to come back to. Serve it with plainly cooked rice or bulgar.

Put the first six ingredients in a large mixing bowl and add 2½ teaspoons of salt and 1½ teaspoons of black pepper. Whisk well and set aside.

Trim the fennel and cut each bulb in half lengthways. Cut each half into 4 wedges. Add the fennel to the liquids, along with the chicken pieces, clementine slices, thyme and fennel seeds. Stir well with your hands then leave to marinate in the fridge for a few hours or overnight (skipping the marinating stage is also fine, if you are pressed for time).

Preheat the oven to 220°C/200°C Fan/Gas Mark 7. Transfer the chicken and its marinade to a baking tray large enough to accommodate everything comfortably in a single layer (roughly a 30cm x 37cm tray); the chicken skin should be facing up. Once the oven is hot enough, put the tray in the oven and roast for 35–45 minutes, until the chicken is coloured and cooked through. Remove from the oven.

Lift the chicken, fennel and clementines from the tray and arrange on a serving plate; cover and keep warm. Pour the cooking liquids into a small saucepan, place on a medium–high heat, bring to a boil then simmer until the sauce is reduced by a third, so you are left with about 80ml. Pour the hot sauce over the chicken, garnish with some chopped parsley and serve.

Roasted chicken with Jerusalem artichoke & lemon

Jerusalem artichokes are well loved in the city but have actually got nothing to do with it; not officially anyway. The name is a distortion of the Italian name of this sunflower tuber, which has an artichoke-like flavour. From girasole articiocco to Jerusalem artichoke.

The combination of saffron and whole lemon slices does not only make for a beautiful-looking dish, it goes exceptionally well with the nutty earthiness of the artichokes. This is easy to prepare — you just need to plan ahead and leave it to marinate properly. Serve it with Mejadra (SEE PAGE 120).

450g Jerusalem artichokes, peeled and cut into six lengthways (1.5cm thick wedges)
3 tbsp lemon juice
8 chicken thighs, on the bone with the skin on, or a medium whole chicken, divided into four
12 banana shallots, peeled and halved lengthways
12 large garlic cloves, sliced
1 medium lemon, cut in half lengthways and then into very thin slices
1 tsp saffron threads
50ml olive oil
150ml cold water
1½ tbsp pink peppercorns, slightly crushed
10g fresh thyme leaves
40g tarragon leaves, chopped
2 tsp salt
½ tsp black pepper

Put the Jerusalem artichokes in a medium saucepan, cover with plenty of water and add half the lemon juice. Bring to the boil, reduce the heat and simmer for 10–20 minutes, until tender but not soft. Drain and leave to cool.

Place the Jerusalem artichokes and all the remaining ingredients, excluding the remaining lemon juice and half of the tarragon, in a large mixing bowl and use your hands to mix everything together well. Cover and leave to marinate in the fridge overnight, or for at least 2 hours.

Preheat the oven to 240°C/220°C Fan/Gas Mark 9. Arrange the chicken pieces, skin-side up, in the centre of a roasting tin and spread the remaining ingredients around the chicken. Roast for 30 minutes. Cover the tin with foil and cook for a further 15 minutes. At this point, the chicken should be completely cooked. Remove from the oven and add the reserved tarragon and lemon juice. Stir well, taste and add more salt if needed. Serve at once.

Poached chicken with sweet spiced freekeh

One of the most practical and fun ways of preparing meat and starch at the same time forms the basis of many fantastic Palestinian dishes. The technique involves poaching mutton or chicken in water, often flavoured with sweet spices, then using the stock to cook a grain — rice, bulgar, freekeh or maftoul (a kind of rough couscous). The meat is then served over the grain, topped with clarified butter and nuts, or served with yoghurt or tomato sauce.

When we filmed a documentary for the BBC about food in Jerusalem, a family from the neighbourhood of Atur, in the east of the city, cooked chicken and lamb together in this way and served it over maftoul with a simple yet delicious tomato and chickpea sauce. The incredible thing with all these is the intensity of flavour throughout the dish. Absolutely nothing is wasted.

Mansaf and kidreh are two festive examples, using lamb and saffron-flavoured rice, served lavishly in a large round platter. To cook kidreh, the rice and meat are arranged in layers in a special brass pot and topped with stock. As it requires long and slow cooking, these pots were often given to the local baker to put in his oven and cook for hours in the residual heat from the bread-baking. Maqluba (SEE PAGE 127) is a more everyday affair.

1 small free-range chicken, about 1.5kg
2 long cinnamon sticks
2 medium carrots, peeled and cut into 2cm thick slices
2 bay leaves
2 bunches of flat-leaf parsley (about 70g in total)
2 large onions
2 tbsp olive oil
300g cracked freekeh
½ tsp ground allspice
½ tsp ground coriander
40g unsalted butter
60g flaked almonds
salt and black pepper

This is a hearty dish that is easy to prepare and leaves everybody very satisfied. Serve it with Yoghurt with cucumber (SEE PAGE 299). *Freekeh is a wonderfully aromatic smoked green cracked wheat* (FOR MORE INFORMATION SEE PAGE 148); *you can find it in Middle Eastern grocers. Bulgar is a good substitute, just reduce the amount of stock by about 10 per cent and cook it for 5 minutes only.*

Place the chicken in a large pot, along with the cinnamon, carrots, bay leaves, 1 bunch of parsley and 1 teaspoon of salt. Quarter one of the onions and add to the pot. Add cold water to almost cover the chicken; bring to the boil and simmer, covered, for 1 hour. Occasionally, skim oil and froth away from the surface.

About half way through the cooking of the chicken, slice the second onion thinly and place it in a medium saucepan with the olive oil. Fry over a low–medium heat for 12–15 minutes, until the onion turns golden brown and soft. Add the freekeh, allspice, coriander, half a teaspoon of salt and some black pepper. Stir well and then add 600ml of the chicken broth. Turn the heat up to medium–high. As soon as the stock boils, cover the pan and reduce the heat. Simmer gently for 20 minutes, remove from the heat and leave covered for 20 minutes more.

Remove the leaves from the remaining parsley and chop them up, not too fine. Add most of the chopped parsley to the cooked freekeh, mixing it in with a fork.

Lift the chicken out of the broth and place it on a cutting board. Carefully carve off the breasts and slice them thinly at an angle; remove the meat from the legs and thighs. Keep the chicken and the freekeh warm.

When ready to serve, place the butter, almonds and some salt in a small frying pan and fry until golden. Spoon the freekeh onto individual serving dishes or one platter. Top with the leg and thigh meat then arrange the breast slices neatly on top. Finish with the almonds and butter and a sprinkle of parsley.

Chicken with caramelized onion
& cardamom rice

Although rice has never been grown locally, it has become a staple Palestinian grain and definitely the basic ingredient in all ceremonial meals (people of lesser means and from the countryside often had to make do with bulgar, which costs less).

Cooking meat with rice and water in one pot is a good way of introducing a good meaty flavour to the rice while keeping things relatively simple — no stock is needed and only one pot is used. Bukharan Jews (from Uzbekistan) have a more sophisticated version than the one below, called plov, which is at the centre of all Bukharan celebrations. There, the chicken and rice are layered more carefully so that when the pan is inverted at the end, the chicken is perfectly fried at the bottom, now the crown on top of the elaborate creation.

40g sugar
25g barberries
  (or currants; see page
  105)
4 tbsp olive oil
2 medium onions, finely
  sliced (250g in total)
1kg chicken thighs, with
  bone and skin, or 1 whole
  chicken divided into
  quarters
10 cardamom pods
⅓ tsp whole cloves
2 long cinnamon sticks,
  broken in two
300g basmati rice
550ml boiling water
5g parsley, chopped
5g dill, chopped
5g coriander, chopped
100g Greek yoghurt, mixed
  with 2 tablespoons of
  olive oil (optional)
salt and black pepper

This chicken and rice casserole is the definition of comfort food. For an Allepian variation, replace the chicken with 5cm pieces of good stewing beef. Boil it in some water with the spices until tender, 1–2 hours. Make the liquid up to 500ml before adding the rice and onion. At the end, you can also stir in some cooked and skinned broad beans.

Put the sugar in a small saucepan along with 40ml of water and heat until the sugar dissolves. Remove from the heat, add the barberries and set aside to soak. If using currants you do not need to soak them in this way.

Meanwhile, heat half the olive oil in a large sauté pan for which you have a lid, add the onion and cook over a medium heat for 10–15 minutes, stirring occasionally, until the onion has turned a deep golden brown. Transfer the onion to a small bowl and wipe the pan clean.

Place the chicken in a large mixing bowl and season with 1½ teaspoons of salt and black pepper. Add the remaining olive oil, cardamom, cloves and cinnamon and use your hands to mix everything together well. Heat your frying pan again and place the chicken and spices inside. Sear for 5 minutes on each side and remove from the pan (this is important as it part-cooks the chicken). The spices can stay in the pan but don't worry if they stick to the chicken. Remove most of the remaining oil as well, leaving just a millimetre at the bottom. Add the rice, caramelized onion, 1 teaspoon of salt and plenty of black pepper. Strain the barberries and add them as well. Stir well and return the seared chicken and push into the rice.

Pour the boiling water over the rice and chicken, cover the pan and cook on a very low heat for 30 minutes. Take the pan off the heat, remove the lid and quickly place a clean tea towel over the pan and seal again with the lid. Leave the dish undisturbed for another 10 minutes. Finally, add the herbs and use a fork to stir them in and fluff up the rice. Taste and add more salt and pepper if needed. Serve hot or warm with yoghurt if you like.

Chopped liver

'Liver-flavour aubergine' is a weird-sounding yet popular invention, which is probably one of the best products to expose the unique, often paradoxical, history of the city over the last 60 years.

During the days of rationing, in the 1950s, Ashkenazi Jews couldn't afford to make one of their most loved dishes, chopped liver, second only to gefilte fish in its iconic value. A creative solution was found using aubergines, a cheap and abundant local ingredient, that was 'made' to taste like the real thing. Still, over the years this dish, using an ingredient their Eastern European Ashkenazi ancestors would have thought was a UFO, has become a hit with many and is now sold everywhere, enjoying particular popularity in Orthodox neighbourhoods. The liver has turned into an aubergine within two generations, with the origins of the dish still carried on in the name.

Our 'real' chicken liver is a fantastic way to start a meal. Serve it with little toasts or with slices of good white bread.

100ml melted goose
   or duck fat
2 large onions, peeled
   and sliced (about 400g
   in total)
400g chicken livers,
   cleaned and broken down
   into roughly 3cm chunks
5 hard-boiled large
   free-range eggs
4 tbsp dessert wine
1 tsp salt
½ tsp coarse ground black
   pepper
2–3 spring onions,
   thinly sliced
1 tbsp chopped chives

Place two thirds of the goose fat in a large frying pan and fry the onions over a medium heat until dark brown, about 10–15 minutes, stirring occasionally. Remove the onions from the pan, pushing them down a little as you do so, so that you are left with some fat in the pan. Add a little fat if needed. Add the livers and cook them for up to 10 minutes, stirring from time to time, until they are properly cooked in the middle — no blood should be coming out at this stage.

Mix the livers with the onion before chopping them together. The best way to do this is with a meat grinder, processing the mixture twice to get the right texture. If you don't have a meat grinder a food processor is also fine. Blitz the onions and liver in two to three batches so the machine bowl isn't very full. Pulse for 20–30 seconds then check, making sure the liver and onions have turned into a uniformly smooth, yet still 'bumpy' paste. Transfer everything into a large mixing bowl.

Peel the eggs, then grate two of them roughly and another two finely and add them to the liver mixture. Add the remaining fat, the dessert wine and the salt and pepper and fold everything together gently. Transfer the mix into a non-metallic flat dish and cover the surface tightly with cling film. Leave it to cool down, then store in the fridge for at least 2 hours to firm up a little.

To serve, finely chop the remaining egg. Spoon some of the chopped liver into serving plates, garnish with the chopped egg and sprinkle with spring onion and chives.

Snow on high ground

Only Jaffa and Jericho oranges were sold in Jerusalem when we were growing up. The city sits at quite a high altitude and therefore gets very cold in winter, while its air is dry throughout the year — not good for oranges, which need shelter and warmer temperatures!

We Jerusalemites are blessed, or not, depending whom you ask, with a central European kind of climate: distinctly hot summers and cold winters. Only in Jerusalem we had central heating at homes and in classrooms, a completely foreign notion to most people in other parts of the country. Driving into Jericho or to Tel Aviv, you felt like you had arrived in a tropical land: humid air, lush vegetation and kids with no winter coats. Our perk, though, was snow.

GOSH, WE WERE OUT IN A NANOSECOND, THROWING SNOWBALLS, MAKING SNOWMEN AND CONSTRUCTING MAKESHIFT SLIDES; A VERY SMALL PRICE TO PAY FOR NO ORANGE ORCHARDS

Jerusalem is the only big city in Israel (though not in Palestine) to get snow. It didn't come every year, perhaps every other, and only settled occasionally but, boy, we loved it, and milked it. The night before a cold weather front was about to hit, we used to huddle around the radio and wait for the hugely anticipated news of 'snow on high ground'. And the cherry on this fluffy, white cake would be an announcement that schools were closed for the day. Gosh, we were out in a nanosecond, throwing snowballs, making snowmen and constructing makeshift slides; a very small price to pay for no orange orchards.

Saffron chicken & herb salad

1 orange
50g honey
½ tsp saffron threads
1 tbsp white wine vinegar
about 300ml water
1kg skinless chicken breast
4 tbsp olive oil
2 small fennel bulbs, thinly
    sliced
15g picked coriander leaves
15g picked basil leaves,
    torn
15 picked mint leaves, torn
2 tbsp lemon juice
1 red chilli, thinly sliced
1 garlic clove, crushed
salt and black pepper

This colourful salad is extraordinarily moist and refreshing. It was created by the chefs at Ottolenghi in Belgravia and is a big hit there. The trick — boiling a whole orange and blitzing it down to a paste — is very effective for many sauces, salsas and cakes. If you don't like fennel, replace it with a combination of spring onion and rocket.

Preheat the oven to 200°C/180°C Fan/Gas Mark 6. Trim and discard 1cm off the top and tail of the orange and cut it into 12 wedges, keeping the skin on. Remove any pips.

Place the wedges in a small saucepan with the honey, saffron, vinegar and just enough water to cover the orange wedges. Bring to the boil and simmer gently for about an hour. At the end you should be left with soft orange and about 3 tablespoons of thick syrup; add water during the cooking if the liquid gets very low. Use a food processor to blitz the orange and syrup into a smooth, runny paste; again, add a little water if needed.

Mix the chicken breast with half the olive oil and plenty of salt and pepper, and place on a very hot, ridged griddle pan. Sear for about 2 minutes on each side to get clear char marks all over. Transfer to a roasting tin and place in the oven for 15–20 minutes, or until just cooked.

Once the chicken is cool enough to handle, but still warm, tear it with your hands into rough and quite large pieces. Place in a large mixing bowl, pour over half the orange paste and stir well. (The other half you can keep in the fridge for a few days and would make a good addition for herb salsa to serve with oily fish such as mackerel or salmon.) Add the remaining ingredients to the salad, including the rest of the olive oil, and toss gently. Taste, add salt and pepper and, if needed, some more olive oil and lemon juice.

Chicken sofrito

Many of Jerusalem's most iconic dishes — and the most interesting, we dare say — are the result of necessity and straitened circumstances. The Palestinian population of the city and surrounding areas includes many comfortable city folk, but is mostly comprised of village people with very limited means. Of the Jews, the majority of 20th-century newcomers were poor in their countries of origin or, if not, became relatively poor in the first years after settling in the city. What all these people cooked, and still do to some extent, reflects the scarcity and costliness of many ingredients.

The Sephardi dish sofrito — actually more a cooking method than a dish — is a perfect example of how frugality yields some superb delicacies, and it became tremendously popular in Jerusalem. Originating from the Spanish verb *sofreír* (to fry lightly), it involves slowly cooking meat in a pot on the stovetop for a long time, with only oil and very little liquid. The slow braising and steaming of the meat, in its own juices, results in a very tender texture with a distinguishably comforting flavour. This slow cooking method — practised by Sephardim for centuries — meant that the dish could be made on a Friday for Shabbat and fitted perfectly with the lifestyle in Jerusalem, when, up until not too long ago, only cheap cuts of meat were realistically available, and other ingredients were expensive.

---

1 tbsp sunflower oil
1 small free-range chicken, about 1.5kg, butterflied or quartered
1 tsp sweet paprika
¼ tsp ground turmeric
¼ tsp sugar
2½ tbsp lemon juice
1 large onion, peeled and quartered
sunflower oil, for frying
750g Charlotte potatoes, peeled, washed and cut into 2cm dice
25 garlic cloves, unpeeled
salt and black pepper

We add potatoes to our sofrito, which isn't necessary, but trust us, you will never regret doing so because they take on the most gorgeous flavours from the bottom of the pan. If you have a wide enough pan to hold the whole chicken flat, butterfly it by cutting through the centre of the breast with a large knife, in between the two sides, until the bird opens up; you could also ask a butcher to do this for you. In the pan, press the bird down firmly so that it lies completely flat.

Pour the oil into a large, shallow pan or casserole dish and put over a medium heat. Place the chicken flat in the pan, skin-side down, and sear for 4–5 minutes, until golden brown. Season all over with the paprika, turmeric, sugar, ⅓ of a teaspoon of salt, a good grind of black pepper and 1½ tablespoons of the lemon juice. Turn the chicken over so that the skin faces up, add the onion to the pan and cover with a lid. Reduce the heat to low and cook for a total of about 1 hour 30 minutes; this includes the time the chicken is cooked with the potatoes. Lift the lid every now and then to check the amount of liquid in the bottom of the pan. The idea is for the chicken to cook and steam in its own juices but you may need to add a little bit of boiling water, just so that there is always 5mm of liquid at the bottom of the pan.

After the chicken has been cooking for about 30 minutes, pour enough sunflower oil into a medium saucepan so that it rises 3cm up the sides. Fry the potatoes and garlic together in a few batches, over a medium–high heat, for about 6 minutes, until they take on some colour and crisp up. Use a slotted spoon to lift each batch of potatoes and garlic away from the oil and onto a paper towel then sprinkle with salt.

After the chicken has been cooking for 1 hour, lift it from the pan and spoon in the fried potatoes and garlic, stirring them with the cooking juices. Return the chicken to the pan, placing it on top of the potatoes for the remainder of the cooking time, i.e. 30 minutes. The chicken should be falling off the bone and the potatoes should be soaked in the cooking liquid and completely soft. Drizzle with the remaining lemon juice when serving.

Meatballs

Together with cheesy pastries, pickled cucumbers and a plate of hummus, meatballs are one of the ubiquitous Jerusalem dishes, celebrated by absolutely everyone — traditional Jews, fervent Christians, Palestinian eateries and funky fusion chefs. But, like polpette al sugo (meatballs in tomato sauce) in Italy, they are essentially a 'Mama' food: something simple, basic and familiar, yet loaded with memories and associations, and every Jerusalemite will have his or her own version.

There are hundreds of varieties of meatballs — kofta (in Arabic) and ktsitsot (in Hebrew) — each with its own unique heritage and specific preparation technique. It is, really, as a result of necessity more than anything that meatballs became such an essential part of the local food fabric. In a place where serving whole cuts of meat was, for most of its history, considered a mad extravagance, meatballs, kebabs and stuffed vegetables (SEE PAGE 152) were a sensible alternative.

Meatballs can be made round, cigar-shaped or as small patties. They can have chopped up vegetables added to them (potato, courgette, onion, turnip), cracked wheat, rice, bread or couscous. They are sometimes cooked in sauces — tomato, lemon, tamarind, or stock-based — or left plain and served with a wedge of lemon or a light salsa.

In Palestinian culture the difference between kofta and kebab can cause some confusion to an outsider. Both are meatballs made from minced lamb, beef, veal, or a mixture of them. Often the meat is skilfully chopped by hand, using two large knives, along with the onion, garlic and parsley, and then seasoned. In the old city markets, kebab is sold on the street and in kebab shops, often served alongside pita, chopped salad, grilled onions and tahini sauce. Kebab is always cooked on long steel skewers, placed over coal. It is usually shaped into thick fingers.

Kofta, on the other hand, are normally cooked at home and can be made in any shape: flat patties, thin fingers or torpedoes. They can be wrapped in vine leaves or other leaves. They can be cooked on the hob in sauce, grilled or baked in the oven on a metal tray (a siniyah in Arabic), often with other elements: tahini, tomato or potato. Palestinian housewives sometimes get the butcher to mince their meat for their kofta together with parsley, garlic and onion saving them work and also ensuring the flavours and textures blend really well.

Kofta b'siniyah

150g light tahini paste
3 tbsp lemon juice
120ml water
1 medium garlic clove,
    crushed
2 tbsp sunflower oil
30g unsalted butter or
    ghee (optional)
sweet paprika, to garnish
salt

KOFTA

400g minced lamb
400g minced veal or beef
1 small onion (about 150g),
    finely chopped
2 large garlic cloves,
    crushed
50g toasted pine nuts,
    roughly chopped, plus
    extra whole ones to
    garnish
30g finely chopped flat-leaf
    parsley, plus extra to
    garnish
1 large medium-hot red
    chilli, deseeded and
    finely chopped
1½ tsp ground cinnamon
1½ tsp ground allspice
¾ tsp grated nutmeg
1½ tsp ground black
    pepper
1½ tsp salt

For these kofta, buy your meat freshly minced by your butcher, if you can. The lamb should be shoulder and the beef a good non-stewing cut. If you get the meat from a supermarket or another grocer, cook it through, just to be on the safe side. Finish the dish with butter only if you are serving it straight away and consuming it all at once. Otherwise, leave it out as it sets quickly, which isn't very nice. Serve with pita and cucumber and tomato salad (SEE SPICED CHICKPEAS WITH FRESH VEGETABLE SALAD, MINUS THE CHICKPEAS, PAGE 56).

Put all the kofta ingredients in a bowl and use your hands to mix everything together well. Now shape into long, torpedo-like fingers, roughly 8cm long (about 60g each). Press the mix to compress it and ensure the kofta is tight and keeps its shape. Arrange on a plate and chill until you are ready to cook them, for up to one day.

Preheat the oven to 220°C/200°C Fan/Gas Mark 7. In a medium bowl whisk together the tahini paste, lemon juice, water, garlic and ¼ teaspoon of salt. The sauce should be a bit runnier than honey; add 1 or 2 tablespoons of water if needed.

Heat the sunflower oil in a large frying pan and sear the kofta over a high heat; do this in batches so they are not cramped together. Sear them on all sides until golden brown, about 6 minutes for each batch. At this point they should be medium–rare. Lift out of the pan and arrange in an oven tray. If you want to cook them medium or well done, put the tray in the oven now for 2–4 minutes.

Spoon the tahini sauce around the kofta, so it covers the base of the tray. If you like, also drizzle some over the kofta but leave some of the meat exposed. Place in the oven for a minute or two, just to warm up the sauce a little.

Meanwhile, if you are using the butter, melt it in a small saucepan and allow it to brown a little, taking care that it doesn't burn. Spoon the butter over the kofta as soon as they come out of the oven. Scatter with pine nuts and parsley and finally sprinkle some paprika on top. Serve at once.

Beef meatballs with broad beans & lemon

4½ tbsp olive oil
350g broad beans, fresh
  or frozen
4 whole thyme sprigs
6 garlic cloves, sliced
8 spring onions, cut at an
  angle into 2cm segments
2½ tbsp lemon juice
500ml chicken stock
salt and black pepper

MEATBALLS

300g minced beef
150g minced lamb
1 medium onion, finely
  chopped
120g breadcrumbs
2 tbsp each chopped
  flat-leaf parsley, mint,
  dill and coriander, plus
  ½ tbsp extra of each to
  finish the dish
2 large garlic cloves,
  crushed
1 tbsp baharat spice mix
  (shop-bought or see
  recipe, page 299)
1 tbsp ground cumin
2 tsp capers, chopped
1 egg, beaten

Fresh, sharp and very, very tasty, these meatballs are our idea of the perfect spring supper dish. Serve them with Basmati rice and orzo (SEE PAGE 103) and there isn't need for much else. Whole blanched almonds would be a good addition, for texture. Add them to the pan along with the unshelled broad beans.

Place all of the meatball ingredients in a large mixing bowl. Add ¾ teaspoon of salt and plenty of black pepper and mix well with your hands. Form into balls about the same size as ping-pong balls. Heat 1 tablespoon of the olive oil in an extra-large frying pan for which you have a lid. Sear half the meatballs over a medium heat, turning them until they are brown all over, about 5 minutes. Remove, add another ½ tablespoon of olive oil to the pan and cook the other batch of meatballs. Remove from the pan and wipe it clean.

While the meatballs are cooking, throw the broad beans into a pot with plenty of salted boiling water and blanch for 2 minutes. Drain and refresh under cold water. Remove the skins from half the broad beans and discard the shells.

Heat the remaining olive oil in the same pan in which you seared the meatballs. Add the thyme, garlic and spring onion and sauté over a medium heat for 3 minutes. Add the unshelled broad beans, 1½ tablespoons of the lemon juice, 80ml of the stock, ¼ teaspoon of salt and plenty of black pepper. The beans should be almost covered with liquid. Cover the pan and cook over a low heat for 10 minutes.

Return the meatballs to the pan with the broad beans. Add the remaining stock, cover the pan and simmer gently for 25 minutes. Taste the sauce and adjust the seasoning. If it is very runny, remove the lid and reduce a little. Once the meatballs stop cooking they will soak up a lot of the juices so make sure there is still plenty of sauce at this point. You can leave the meatballs now, off the heat, until ready to serve.

Just before serving, reheat the meatballs and add a little water, if needed, to get enough sauce. Add the remaining herbs and tablespoon of lemon juice, the shelled broad beans and stir very gently. Serve immediately.

Lamb meatballs with barberries, yoghurt & herbs

750g minced lamb
2 medium onions, finely
    chopped
20g flat-leaf parsley, finely
    chopped
3 garlic cloves, crushed
¾ tsp ground allspice
¾ tsp ground cinnamon
60g barberries
1 medium free-range egg
100ml sunflower oil
700g banana shallots,
    peeled
200ml white wine
500ml chicken stock
2 bay leaves
2 thyme sprigs
2 tsp sugar
150g dried figs
200g Greek yoghurt
3 tbsp of mixed mint,
    coriander, dill and
    tarragon, torn roughly
salt and black pepper

The sweet and sour flavours of these meatballs are prominent yet tempered by the yoghurt, making this a very soothing main course, best served with couscous or rice. Barberries — small dried sour berries — are available online or from Middle Eastern and Iranian grocers. They can be substituted with cranberries. The figs get quite soggy through the long cooking but are essential for the flavour they add. You can remove and discard them at the end if you wish.

Place the lamb, onions, parsley, garlic, allspice, cinnamon, barberries, egg, 1 teaspoon of salt and ½ a teaspoon of black pepper in a large bowl. Mix with your hands and roll into balls, about the size of golf balls.

Heat one third of the oil in a large, heavy-based pot for which you have a tight-fitting lid. Put in a few meatballs at a time, cooking them over a medium heat and turning them around for a few minutes until they colour all over. Remove from the pot and set aside while you cook the remaining meatballs.

Wipe the pot clean and add the remaining oil. Add the shallots and cook them on a medium heat for 10 minutes, stirring frequently, until golden brown. Add the wine, leave to bubble for a minute or two, then add the chicken stock, bay leaves, thyme, sugar and some salt and pepper. Arrange the figs and meatballs amongst and on top of the shallots; the meatballs need to be almost covered in liquid. Bring to the boil, cover with the lid, reduce the heat to very low and leave to simmer for 30 minutes. Remove the lid and simmer for about another hour, until the sauce has reduced and intensified in flavour. Taste and add salt and pepper if needed.

Transfer to a large, deep serving dish. Whisk the yoghurt, pour on top and scatter with the herbs.

Turkey & courgette burgers with spring onion & cumin

500g minced turkey
1 large courgette,
   coarsely grated
   (about 200g in total)
40g spring onions, thinly
   sliced
1 medium free-range egg
2 tbsp chopped mint
2 tbsp chopped coriander
2 garlic cloves, crushed
1 tsp ground cumin
1 tsp salt
½ tsp coarse ground black
   pepper
½ tsp cayenne
about 100ml of sunflower
   oil for searing

SOURED CREAM
& SUMAC SAUCE

100g soured cream
150g Greek yoghurt
1 tsp grated lemon zest
1 tbsp lemon juice
1 small garlic clove,
   crushed
1½ tbsp olive oil
1 tbsp sumac
½ tsp salt
¼ tsp black pepper

The creamy sumac sauce served with these burgers is fantastically sharp and will go well with most non-red meats (CHICKEN SOFRITO, PAGE 190, FOR EXAMPLE) and also with grilled vegetables and fritters. You can make it in advance, or double the quantity, and keep it refrigerated. After a day the flavours will mellow so you may want to reinvigorate it by adding extra sumac and lemon juice. The burgers are very portable. You can have them as a snack from the fridge and they are also ideal for taking over to friends or in a lunchbox for work.

First make the soured cream sauce by placing all the ingredients in a small bowl. Stir well and set aside or chill until needed.

Preheat the oven to 220°C/200°C Fan/Gas Mark 7. In a large bowl mix together all the ingredients for the meatballs, bar the sunflower oil. Once evenly mixed, shape into burgers, weighing about 45g each and making about 18.

Pour enough sunflower oil into a large frying pan so you get a thin layer at the bottom, about 2mm thick. Heat well and sear the meatballs in batches over a medium heat on all sides. Cook them for about 4 minutes, adding oil as needed, until golden brown.

Carefully transfer the seared meatballs into an oven tray lined with greaseproof paper and place in the oven for 5–7 minutes, or until just cooked through. Serve warm or at room temperature, with the sauce spooned over or on the side.

Polpettone

On the Pesach (Passover) Seder table of Yotam's Nonna Luciana you could always count on finding a sliced meat loaf, beautifully presented, studded with pistachios and gherkins. It was served alongside other Jewish-Italian delicacies, such as fried courgettes in vinegar and artichokes fried in olive oil, a creation of the Jews of Rome.

Polpettone is a very old dish of Italian Jews. Claudia Roden gives a much more complicated version than Luciana's in *The Book of Jewish Food*, originating from Piedmonte. Hers is also cooked for Passover and it involves wrapping minced veal and turkey mixed with pistachios, egg, nutmeg and garlic in turkey skin, and poaching this in turkey stock made out of the carcass. Talk about thrift!

In Jerusalem, Jews from Aleppo cook koisat, a meat loaf simpler than Luciana's polpettone but also stuffed with pistachios (Aleppo is known for the best pistachios and the nut is often referred to as an Aleppine pistachio). Ashkenazi Jews cook klops, which is a baked meat loaf, typically a simple, some would even say bland, dish yet somehow it is highly popular.

---

3 medium free-range eggs
1 tbsp chopped flat-leaf
    parsley
2 tsp olive oil
500g minced beef
100g breadcrumbs,
    preferably fresh
60g shelled unsalted
    pistachios
80g gherkins, cut into 1cm
    pieces
200g cooked ox tongue
    (or ham), thinly sliced
1 large carrot, cut into
    chunks
2 celery stalks, cut into
    chunks
1 thyme sprig
2 bay leaves
½ onion, sliced
1 tsp powdered chicken
    stock
salt and black pepper

Okay, this is not your average Ottolenghi dish. It is slightly challenging technically, but it is highly impressive and loved by everybody. Make it in advance, when you have a bit of time, and serve as a starter. The salsina, diminutive for salsa (a grammatical form Yotam's dad enjoys using all the time), is a sharp yet luscious sauce that can also come in handy with plainly prepared chicken or lamb.

Start by making a flat omelette. Whisk together 2 eggs, the chopped parsley and a pinch of salt. Heat the olive oil in a large frying pan (about 28cm in diameter) and pour the eggs inside. Cook for 2–3 minutes on a medium heat, without stirring, until the eggs set into a thin omelette. Set aside to cool down.

In a large bowl mix together the beef, breadcrumbs, pistachios, gherkins, 1 egg, 1 teaspoon of salt and ½ a teaspoon of pepper. Take a large clean tea towel (you may want to use an old one you don't mind getting rid of; cleaning it will be a slight menace) and lay it over your work surface. Now take the meat mix and spread it on the towel, shaping it with your hands into a rectangular disc, 1cm thick, roughly 30cm x 25cm. Keep the edges of the cloth clear.

Cover the meat with tongue slices, leaving 2cm around the edge. Cut the omelette into four wide strips and spread them evenly over the tongue.

SALSINA VERDE

50g flat-leaf parsley, stalks and leaves
1 garlic clove, crushed
1 tbsp capers
1 tbsp lemon juice
1 tbsp white wine vinegar
1 hard-boiled medium free-range egg, peeled
150ml olive oil
3 tbsp breadcrumbs
salt and black pepper

Lift the cloth to help you start rolling the meat inwards from one of its wide sides. Continue rolling the meat into a large sausage shape, using the towel to assist you. In the end you want a tight, Swiss-roll-like loaf, with the beef mince on the outside and the omelette in the centre. Cover the loaf with the towel, wrapping it up well so it is sealed inside. Tie the ends with string and tuck any excess cloth underneath the log so you end up with a tightly bound bundle.

Place the bundle inside a large pan or casserole. Throw the carrot, celery, thyme, bay, onion and powdered stock around the loaf and pour over boiling water to almost cover it. Cover the pot with a lid and leave to simmer for 2 hours.

Remove the loaf from the pan and set it aside to allow some of the liquids to drain (the poaching stock would make a great soup base). After about half an hour place something heavy over it to remove more of the juices. Once it reaches room temperature put the meat loaf in the fridge, still covered in cloth, to chill thoroughly, about 3–4 hours.

For the sauce, put all the ingredients in a food processor and pulse to a coarse consistency (or, for a rustic look, chop the parsley, capers and egg by hand and stir together with the rest of the ingredients). Taste and adjust the seasoning.

To serve, remove the loaf from the tea towel, slice into 1cm thick pieces, layer on a serving plate and serve the sauce on the side.

Braised eggs with lamb, tahini & sumac

This concoction is Jerusalem fusion food at its very best. It incorporates traditional elements that are purely Palestinian with ingredients characteristic of various Jewish cuisines, and puts them all together in a completely non-traditional way. It was inspired by a very young classic, Hamshukah, signature dish at Machneyuda, the market restaurant that currently serves the most innovative food in town.

1 tbsp olive oil
1 large onion, finely chopped (200g in total)
6 garlic cloves, sliced thinly
300g minced lamb
2 tsp sumac, plus extra to finish
1 tsp ground cumin
50g toasted unsalted pistachios, crushed
50g toasted pine nuts
2 tsp harissa paste (shop-bought or see recipe, page 303)
1 tbsp finely chopped preserved lemon (shop-bought or see recipe, page 303)
200g cherry tomatoes
120ml chicken stock
4 medium free-range eggs
5g picked coriander leaves, or 1 tbsp zhoug (see recipe, page 301)
salt and black pepper

YOGHURT SAUCE

100g Greek yoghurt
25g tahini paste
2 tbsp lemon juice
1 tbsp water

This dish can be served at the centre of an informal supper. The flavours are intense and the contrasting colours and textures are also pretty dramatic, so you should really serve it on its own, with minimal distractions and just a piece of bread. The list of ingredients isn't set in stone. Other typical Jerusalem ingredients — roasted aubergine, red pepper strips, Swiss chard, cooked chickpeas, chopped almonds, za'atar — can be added or used as substitutes. The various components can be prepared in advance and cooked together at the very last minute.

Heat up the olive oil in a medium, heavy-based frying pan for which you have a tight-fitting lid. Add the onion and garlic and sauté on a medium–high heat for 6 minutes to soften and colour a bit. Add the minced lamb and brown well, 5–6 minutes, on a high heat. Season with the sumac, cumin, ¾ teaspoon of salt and some black pepper and cook for another minute. Off the heat, stir in the nuts, harissa and preserved lemon and set aside.

While the onion is cooking, heat up a separate small cast-iron or other heavy pan. Once piping hot, add the cherry tomatoes and char on a high heat for 4–6 minutes, tossing the pan occasionally, until slightly blackened on the outside. Set aside.

Prepare the yoghurt sauce by simply whisking together all the ingredients with a pinch of salt. It needs to be thick and rich, but you may need to add a splash of water if it is stiff.

You can leave the meat, tomatoes and sauce at this stage for up to an hour. When you are ready to serve, reheat the meat, add the chicken stock and bring to the boil. Make 4 small wells in the mix and break an egg into each. Cover the pan with a lid and cook the eggs on a low heat for 3 minutes. Place the tomatoes on top, avoiding the yolks, cover again and cook for 5 minutes, until the egg whites are cooked but the yolks are still runny.

Remove from the heat and dot with dollops of yoghurt sauce, sprinkle with sumac and finish with picked coriander or zhoug. Serve at once.

Slow cooked veal with prunes & leek

A unique piece of Jerusalem food is the cuisine of some Sephardic Jews, also referred to as 'Spanioli', a proud community that has lived in the city for many generations, long before the advent of Zionism. As many of them arrived from Spain after the Jewish expulsion of 1492, either directly or via other countries, their dishes are a real fusion of old Spanish food, elements picked up along the route, plus local Arab traditions and influences of the Ashkenazi Jews of the city. The result is the most fascinating mishmash, including, among others, albóndigas (Spanish meatballs), stuffed savoury pastries from Turkey and the Balkans, many of the iconic Palestinian mezzes and kugel — noodles and caramel slowly cooked in a pot overnight — an Ashkenazi staple to which the Sephardim added tons of black pepper (we are more than happy to skip this one if offered it).

The combination of meat and dried fruit, as in this dish, is a clear mark of most Sephardic traditions. This differentiates their cuisine clearly from Palestinian cooking, which never mixes sweet and savoury despite many other obvious similarities.

110ml sunflower oil
4 large osso buco steaks, on the bone (about 1kg in total)
2 large onions, finely chopped (500g in total)
3 garlic cloves, crushed
100ml dry white wine
250ml chicken or beef stock
400g tin chopped tomatoes
5 thyme sprigs, leaves finely chopped
2 bay leaves
shaved strips of rind of an orange
2 small cinnamon sticks
½ tsp ground allspice
2 star anise
6 large leeks, white part only (800g in total), washed and cut into 1½ cm slices
200g soft prunes, pitted
salt and black pepper

TO SERVE

120g Greek yoghurt
2 tbsp finely chopped flat-leaf parsley
2 tbsp grated lemon zest
2 garlic cloves, crushed

This dish takes about four hours to cook and is fairly complex, but the result is quite spectacular. Instead of osso buco steaks, which aren't always easy to get and are expensive, 1.5kg of oxtail can be used here. You'd need to work just a little bit harder getting the meat off the bones, but the flavour is as good. Serve with Mejadra (SEE PAGE 120) *or plain rice.*

Preheat the oven to 180°C/160°C Fan/Gas Mark 4.

Heat 2 tablespoons of the oil in a large, heavy-based pan. Fry the pieces of veal on a high heat for 2 minutes on each side, browning the meat well. Transfer to a colander to drain while you prepare the tomato sauce.

Remove most of the fat from the pan, add 2 more tablespoons of oil and add the onions and garlic. Return to a medium–high heat and sauté, stirring occasionally and scraping the base of the pan with a wooden spoon, for about 10 minutes, until the onions are soft and golden. Add the wine, bring to a boil and simmer vigorously for 3 minutes until most of it has evaporated. Add half the stock, the tomatoes, thyme, bay, orange rind, cinnamon, allspice, star anise, 1 teaspoon of salt and some black pepper. Stir well and bring to the boil. Add the veal pieces to the sauce and stir to coat.

Transfer the veal and sauce into a deep baking tray, roughly 33cm x 24cm, and spread it around evenly. Cover with tin foil and place in the oven for 2½ hours. Check a couple of times throughout the cooking that the sauce isn't turning too thick and burning around the sides; you'll probably need to add a little water to prevent this. The meat is ready when it comes away easily from the bone. Lift the veal from the sauce and place it in a large bowl. When it is cool enough to handle, pick all the meat from the bones and scrape out all the bone marrow using a small knife. Discard the bones.

Heat the remaining oil in a separate frying pan and brown the leeks well over a high heat for about 3 minutes, stirring occasionally. Spoon them over the tomato sauce. Next, in the pan in which you made the tomato sauce, mix together the prunes, remaining stock, pulled meat and bone marrow and spoon this over the leeks. Re-cover with the tin foil and continue to cook for another hour. Once out of the oven, taste and season with salt and more black pepper, if needed.

Serve hot, with cold yoghurt spooned on top, sprinkled with a mixture of the parsley, lemon zest and garlic.

Lamb

Before chicken, lamb and mutton were the key meats in the Palestinian diet. Shepherds were prevalent all around the hills of Jerusalem when we were children, and still are now, although to a lesser extent. Lamb is slaughtered on special occasions and is a sign of celebration — births, weddings, return of a family member — and religious holidays, such as Easter and Eid al-Adha (Festival of Sacrifice or 'Greater Eid'). Lamb and mutton are in many ways the essence of Palestinian cooking. The best-quality lamb is sold by Palestinian butchers, a fact recognized by many chefs in Tel Aviv who regularly get their supply from them.

THE BEST-QUALITY LAMB IS SOLD BY PALESTINIAN BUTCHERS, A FACT RECOGNIZED BY MANY CHEFS IN TEL AVIV WHO REGULARLY GET THEIR SUPPLY FROM THEM

On the subject of lamb, in their book *The Flavor of Jerusalem*, Joan Nathan and Judy Stacey Goldman mention a recipe they found in the 1970s in the Anglican Church's school in Jerusalem. It consists of lamb, potatoes, peas and mint, a very English-sounding recipe but made quite local by the fact that the peas and mint are added shortly before serving, keeping it bright and fresh.

The Anglican Church of Christ in Jerusalem is the oldest Anglican church in the Middle East and was built in the 1840s. The bishop of the church in Jerusalem at the time was a converted Jew, Michael Solomon Alexander. One of his missions was to convert local Jews to Anglicanism. He built a house that supplied free food to the city's poor. Not many came. Only when he started serving kosher soups and bread did his mission start to pick up some speed.

Lamb shawarma

Jerusalem proudly boasts its own indigenous Hebrew vocabulary, made up of random words that substitute the common names for words like liquorice, piggyback, lollypop and others. The flatbread referred to in the city as 'esh tanur' (burning furnace) is the carb of choice for encasing shawarma, slices of spiced meat and fat arranged on a large spit that rotates continuously near a hot grill, regularly 'shaved' with a large knife for passing customers. As well as meat, the flatbread includes chopped salad, tahini, fries, pickles and amba, a mango and fenugreek sauce originally from India that has been adopted into the Jewish version of shawarma via Iraqi immigrants.

Sami remembers that when he was growing up going for shawarma was a bit of a luxury, as it was quite expensive. In Arab shops it was sold in a pita with a condiment of onion marinated with salt and sumac. The fries had to be good!

This is hardly a proper shawarma recipe. But then again, we wouldn't expect most readers to have a vertical rotating skewer at home. Still, the marinated lamb leg ends up tasting close enough to the real thing, which is as common and popular in Jerusalem as it is anywhere else in the Middle East.

The first 11 ingredients, also known as Lebanese spice mix (SIMILAR TO THE YEMENITE HAWAYEJ ON PAGE 226), *make a versatile mixture that can be used to marinate fish, meat or root vegetables before roasting or grilling. You can double their quantity and keep half in a sealed jar for up to three weeks. If you don't have a spice grinder you can use a pestle and mortar to make this mix, but you would need to substitute ground cinnamon for cinnamon sticks, cardamom powder for pods and leave out the star anise.*

Always serve the shawarma with fresh cucumber and tomato salad, dressed with lemon juice, olive oil, garlic and chopped parsley or coriander. It really needs the freshness and moisture. On top of that, you can serve rice or bulgar and/or Tahini sauce (SEE PAGE 298). *If you wish, you can add some peeled waxy potatoes to the roasting tin about 90 minutes before the lamb is ready, and toss them in the cooking liquids every now and then.*

2 tsp black peppercorns
5 cloves
½ tsp cardamom pods
¼ tsp fenugreek seeds
1 tsp fennel seeds
1 tbsp cumin seeds
1 star anise
½ a cinnamon stick
½ a nutmeg, grated
¼ tsp ground ginger
1 tbsp sweet paprika
1 tbsp sumac
¾ tbsp Maldon sea salt
25g fresh ginger, grated
3 garlic cloves, crushed
40g chopped coriander,
    stems and leaves
60ml lemon juice
120ml groundnut oil
1 leg of lamb, with the
    bone, about 2.5–3kg

Put the first 8 ingredients in a cast-iron pan and dry-roast on medium–high heat for a minute or two, until the spices begin to pop and release their aromas. Take care not to burn them. Add the nutmeg, ginger and paprika, toss for a few more seconds, just to heat them, then transfer to a spice grinder. Process the spices to a uniform powder. Transfer to a medium bowl and stir in all the remaining ingredients, apart from the lamb.

Use a small sharp knife to score the leg of lamb in a few places, making 1.5cm deep slits through the fat and meat to allow the marinade to seep in. Place in a large roasting tin and rub the marinade all over the lamb; use your hands to massage the meat well. Cover the tin with foil and leave aside for at least a couple of hours or, preferably, chill overnight.

Preheat the oven to 170°C/150°C Fan/Gas Mark 3½.

Put the lamb in the oven with its fatty side facing up and roast for a total of about 4.5 hours, until the meat is completely tender. After 30 minutes of roasting add about a cup of boiling water to the pan and use this liquid to baste the meat every hour or so. Add more water, as needed, making sure there is always about half a centimetre in the bottom of the tin. For the last 3 hours, cover the lamb with foil to prevent the spices from burning. Once done, remove the lamb from the oven and leave to rest for 10 minutes before carving and serving.

The best way to serve this, in our mind, is inspired by Israel's most renowned shakshuka eatery (SEE RECIPE, PAGE 66) – Dr Shakshuka, in Jaffa, owned by Bino Gabso. Take six individual pita pockets and brush them liberally inside with a spread made by mixing together 120g chopped tinned tomatoes, 20g harissa paste, 20g tomato paste, 1 tablespoon olive oil and some salt and pepper. When the lamb is ready, warm up the pitas in a hot, ridged griddle pan until they get nice char marks on both sides. Slice the warm lamb and cut the slices into 1.5cm strips. Pile them high over each warm pita, spoon over some of the roasting liquids from the pan, reduced, and finish with chopped onion, chopped parsley and a sprinkle of sumac. And don't forget the fresh cucumber and tomato. It's a heavenly dish.

See picture on the following page

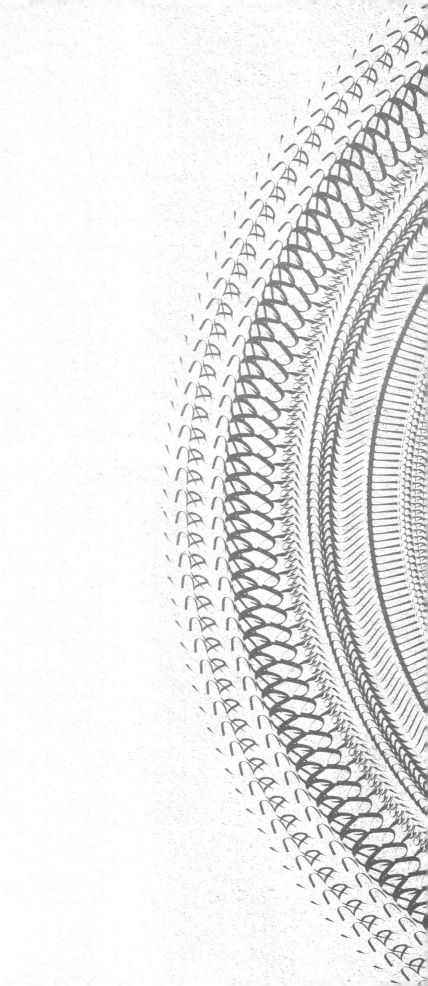

Fish in Jerusalem

Jerusalem is not a city of fish. Situated on the verge of the Judean desert, and with no substantial water source nearby, fish dishes were never a culinary focal point. As a kid, Sami can only remember one fish shop in the whole of the old city; as opposed to dozens of butchers.

Still, 20th-century immigration and technology brought fish onto the tables of many Jerusalemites, particularly Jewish immigrants who brought with them old traditions and cooking methods. In Machne Yehuda market and in some supermarkets, fish tanks, full of live carp, were a highlight. The person in charge would lift one out with a small net, hit it on the head, clean it and wrap it in newspaper. For a city child, it was a mesmerizing experience, as close as one gets to an African safari.

On the subject of fish, or lack thereof, in their book *The Flavor of Jerusalem*, Joan Nathan and Judy Stacey Goldman tell this story: as a result of Jerusalem's division in 1948, between 1948 and 1967 a barbed wire crossed Beit Tsafafa in the middle, dividing this Arab village located in the south-west of Jerusalem, between Jordan and Israel. Families were separated and neighbours and relatives divided. Residents of the Jordanian side of Beit Tsafafa were also cut off from the Mediterranean and its fish. To deal with the situation their ingenious relatives got busy inventing all sorts of creative ways to distract the soldiers and sneak some beautiful fresh fish across the barbed wire.

...INGENIOUS RELATIVES GOT BUSY INVENTING ALL SORTS OF CREATIVE WAYS TO DISTRACT THE SOLDIERS AND SNEAK SOME BEAUTIFUL FRESH FISH ACROSS THE BARBED WIRE

Pan-fried sea bream with harissa & rose

3 tbsp harissa paste (shop-bought or see page 301)

1 tsp ground cumin

4 sea bream or bass fillets, about 450g in total, pin bones removed

plain flour, for dusting

2 tbsp olive oil

2 medium onions, finely chopped

100ml red wine vinegar

1 tsp ground cinnamon

1½ tbsp honey

1 tbsp rosewater

60g currants (optional)

2 tbsp roughly chopped coriander (optional)

2 tsp small dried edible rose petals

salt and black pepper

This dish originates from Bizerte, the northernmost city in Africa. It is sweet and spicy and beautifully aromatic. It is adapted from a recipe kindly given to us by Rafram Hadad (SEE MORE ON HADAD ON PAGE 244). *Serve it as a main course with some plain rice or couscous and something green, like sautéed spinach or Swiss chard. Dried rose petals are available in Middle Eastern shops and also online.*

First marinate the fish. Mix together half the harissa paste, the ground cumin and ½ a teaspoon of salt in a small bowl. Rub the paste all over the fish fillets and leave them to marinate for 2 hours in the fridge.

Dust the fillets with a little flour and shake off the excess. Heat the olive oil in a wide frying pan, placed on a medium–high heat, and fry the fillets for 2 minutes on each side. You may need to do this in two batches. Set the fish aside, leave the oil in the pan and add the onions. Stir as you cook for about 8 minutes until the onions are golden.

Add the remaining harissa, vinegar, cinnamon, ½ a teaspoon of salt and plenty of black pepper. Pour in 200ml of water, reduce the heat and let the sauce simmer away gently for 10–15 minutes until quite thick.

Add the honey and rosewater to the pan along with the currants, if using, and simmer gently for a couple more minutes. Taste to adjust the seasoning and then return the fish fillets to the pan; you can slightly overlap them if they don't quite fit. Spoon the sauce over the fish and leave them to warm up in the simmering sauce for 3 minutes; you may need to add a few tablespoons of water if the sauce is very thick. Serve warm, or at room temperature, sprinkled with the coriander, if using, and rose petals.

Fish & caper kebabs with burnt aubergine & lemon pickle

Capers are not widely used in any of the local cuisines but the plants are abundant in the city. They are extremely hardy and grow out of cracks in stone walls. In fact, the Wailing Wall is covered with small caper bushes. The buds must be picked and pickled before the bush flowers, quite beautifully, around April/May.

---

2 medium aubergines (about 750g in total)
2 tbsp Greek yoghurt
1 garlic clove, crushed
2 tbsp chopped flat-leaf parsley
sunflower oil for frying, about 2 tbsp
2 dessertspoons Quick Pickled Lemons (page 303)
salt and black pepper

FISH KEBABS

400g haddock fillet, or any other white fish, skinless and boneless
30g fresh breadcrumbs
½ a medium free-range egg, beaten
20g capers, chopped
20g dill, chopped
2 spring onions, finely chopped
grated zest of 1 lemon
1 tbsp lemon juice
¾ tsp ground cumin
½ tsp ground turmeric
½ tsp salt
¼ tsp ground white pepper

The combination of the kebabs with the aubergine and pickled lemon makes a wonderfully rich main course; serve it with plain rice or bulgar. The lemon and aubergine condiments, however, are not necessary. You can easily serve the kebabs as a starter with just a squeeze of lemon and a small green salad.

Start with the aubergines. Burn, peel and drain the aubergine flesh following the instructions in the Burnt aubergine with garlic, lemon and pomegranate seeds recipe (SEE PAGE 79). Once well drained, roughly chop the flesh and place in a mixing bowl. Add the yoghurt, garlic, parsley, 1 teaspoon of salt and plenty of black pepper. Set aside.

Cut the fish into very thin slices, only a couple of millimetres thick, then cut these into tiny dice and put in a medium mixing bowl. Add the remaining ingredients and stir well. Slightly wet your hands and shape the mixture into 12 patties or fingers, about 45g each. Arrange on a plate, cover with cling film and leave in the fridge for at least 30 minutes.

Pour a small amount of oil into a frying pan so you have a thin layer, only about 1mm deep. Cook the kebabs in batches over a medium–high heat, 4–6 minutes for each batch, turning until coloured on all sides and cooked through.

Serve the kebabs while still hot, three per portion, alongside the burnt aubergine and a small amount of pickled lemon (careful, the lemons tend to dominate).

Pan-fried mackerel with golden beetroot & orange salsa

Although oranges aren't grown in Jerusalem, the famous Jaffa oranges, cultivated along the coast, have made their mark on the city's skyline, sort of.

In 1860, during the Ottoman rule, a complex of buildings was erected in Jerusalem by the Russian Tsar to serve the increasing number of Russian Christian pilgrims arriving in the city during Christmas and Easter. This included hostels, a hospital, a bathhouse and a church that were later used as the British headquarters during their mandate. The whole area became known as Migrash Harussim, or the Russian Compound.

In 1964, Israel signed a rental agreement with the Soviet Union for the right to use this property. The deal became known as 'the oranges deal', as nearly half the sum was paid out in exported Jaffa oranges.

1 tbsp harissa paste (shop-bought or see recipe, page 301)
1 tsp ground cumin
4 mackerel fillets, with skin (about 260g in total)
1 medium golden beetroot (100g in total)
1 medium orange
1 small lemon, halved widthways
30g pitted Kalamata olives, quartered lengthways
½ small red onion, finely chopped (40g in total)
15g chopped flat-leaf parsley
½ tsp coriander seeds, toasted and crushed
¾ tsp cumin seeds, toasted and crushed
½ tsp sweet paprika
½ tsp chilli flakes
1 tbsp hazelnut or walnut oil
½ tsp olive oil
salt

The salsa for the fish is inspired by a Moroccan orange and olive salad. You can add some bitter leaves and make it into a salad. Regular beetroot can be used instead of golden.

Mix together the harissa paste, ground cumin and a pinch of salt and rub this into the mackerel fillets. Set aside in the fridge until ready to cook.

Boil the beetroot in plenty of water for about 20 minutes (it may take much longer depending on the variety), or until a skewer inserted in it goes in smoothly. Allow to cool down, then peel, cut into 5mm dice and place in a mixing bowl.

Peel the orange and one lemon half, getting rid of all the outer pith, and cut them into quarters. Remove the middle pith and any seeds and cut the flesh into 5mm dice. Add to the beetroot, along with the olives, red onion and parsley.

In a separate bowl, mix the spices, juice of the remaining lemon half and the nut oil. Pour this onto the beetroot and orange mix, stir and season with salt to taste. It's best to allow the salsa to stand at room temperature for at least 10 minutes to allow all the flavours to mingle.

Just before serving, heat the olive oil in a large non-stick frying pan. Place the mackerel fillets inside, skin-side down, and cook the fillets on a medium heat for about 3 minutes, depending on size, turning once. Transfer to serving plates and spoon the salsa on top.

Cod cakes in tomato sauce

3 slices white bread,
  crusts removed
  (about 60g in total)
600g cod (sustainably
  sourced), halibut, hake
  or pollock fillet, skinless
  and boneless
1 medium onion, finely
  chopped (about 150g
  in total)
4 garlic cloves, crushed
30g flat-leaf parsley, finely
  chopped
30g coriander, finely
  chopped
1 tbsp ground cumin
1½ tsp salt
2 large free-range eggs,
  beaten
4 tbsp olive oil

TOMATO SAUCE

2½ tbsp olive oil
1½ tsp ground cumin
½ tsp sweet paprika
1 tsp ground coriander
1 medium onion, chopped
125ml white wine
400g tin chopped
  tomatoes
1 red chilli, deseeded and
  finely chopped
1 garlic clove, crushed
2 tsp caster sugar
2 tbsp mint leaves,
  roughly chopped
salt and black pepper

With their sweet and slightly sharp sauce these fish cakes, typical of Syrian Jews, manage to capture much of the spirit of Sephardi food. They are delicate, almost brittle and thus very comforting and very popular, perfect for a large family gathering where there are many, often fussy, diners to please. The cakes are almost better the day after they are cooked; just remember to bring them back to room temperature or warm them up before serving. Serve with bulgar, rice, couscous or bread, alongside sautéed spinach or Swiss chard.

First make the tomato sauce. Heat the olive oil in a very large frying pan for which you have a lid and add the spices and onion. Cook for 8–10 minutes, until the onion is completely soft. Add the wine and simmer for 3 minutes. Add the tomatoes, chilli, garlic, sugar, ½ a teaspoon of salt and some black pepper. Simmer for about 15 minutes, until quite thick, taste to adjust the seasoning and set aside.

While the sauce is cooking make the fish cakes. Place the bread in a food processor and blitz to form breadcrumbs. Chop up the fish very finely and place in a bowl along with the bread and everything else, apart from the olive oil. Mix together well and then, using your hands, shape the mixture into compact cakes that are about 2cm thick and 8cm wide. The mixture should make 8 cakes. If they are very soft, refrigerate for 30 minutes to firm up. (You can also add some dried breadcrumbs to the mix, though do this sparingly; the cakes need to be quite wet.)

Heat up half the olive oil in a frying pan and sear the cakes for 3 minutes on each side, so that they colour well on both sides. Add the remaining oil as you fry the cakes.

Place the seared cakes gently, side by side, in the tomato sauce; you can squeeze them a bit so they all fit. Add just enough water to partially cover the cakes, about 200ml. Cover the pan with the lid and simmer on a very low heat for 15–20 minutes. Turn off the heat and leave the cakes to settle, uncovered, for at least 10 minutes before serving warm or at room temperature, sprinkled with mint.

Grilled fish skewers with hawayej & parsley

1kg firm white fish, such
  as monkfish or halibut,
  skinless, boneless,
  cleaned and cut into
  2.5cm cubes
50g finely chopped flat-leaf
  parsley
2 large garlic cloves,
  crushed
½ tsp chilli flakes
1 tbsp lemon juice
2 tbsp olive oil
salt
lemon wedges, to serve

15–18 long bamboo
  skewers, soaked in water
  for 1 hour

HAWAYEJ SPICE MIX

1 tsp black peppercorns
1 tsp coriander seeds
1½ tsp cumin seeds
4 whole cloves
½ tsp ground cardamom
1½ tsp ground turmeric

Hawayej is a high-potency Yemeni spice mix used to flavour hearty soups and stews. Here we apply it to fish, which it lifts and spices up tremendously well. Cook this on a grill or a barbecue and serve alongside Balilah (SEE PAGE 102), *Fattoush* (SEE PAGE 29), *Yoghurt with cucumber* (SEE RECIPE PAGE 299), *or a simple diced tomato and red onion salad with vinegar and olive oil.*

Start with the hawayej mix. Place the peppercorns, coriander, cumin and cloves in a spice grinder or pestle and mortar and work until finely ground. Add the ground cardamom and turmeric, stir well and transfer to a large mixing bowl.

Place the fish, parsley, garlic, chilli flakes, lemon juice and 1 teaspoon of salt in the bowl with the hawayej spices. Mix well with your hands, massaging the fish in the spice mixture until all pieces are well coated. Cover the bowl and, ideally, leave to marinate in the fridge for 6–12 hours. If you can't spare that time, don't worry, an hour should also be fine.

Place a ridged griddle pan on a high heat and leave for about 4 minutes until hot. Meanwhile, thread the fish chunks onto the skewers, 5–6 pieces on each, making sure to leave gaps in between the pieces. Gently brush the fish with a little olive oil and place the skewers on the hot griddle in 3–4 batches so they aren't too close together. Grill for about 1½ minutes on each side, or until the fish is just cooked through. Alternatively, cook them on a barbecue or under a preheated grill, where they will take about 2 minutes on each side to cook.

Serve immediately with the lemon wedges.

Fricassee salad

This salad is a deconstruction of Tunisian fricassee: a fried bun stuffed with tuna, harissa, olives, anchovies, a spicy pumpkin relish, pickled lemon, cooked potato and hard-boiled egg. We are not quite sure how it got to signify something so different from the common French term 'fricassée', which is a type of meat stew, but the resemblance to another French classic, Niçoise salad, is no coincidence and is evidence of the interaction between French and Tunisian cuisines during the years of French occupation. The fried buns arrived in Jerusalem in the mid-20th century with Tunisian immigrants, and joined a long list of favourite fast foods.

Here we confit fresh tuna, a method of preservation that gives the fish both a rich flavour and a wonderful texture. Use olive oil of the best quality and reuse it later for preparing other fish and seafood dishes. You can, however, skip the long process of preservation by getting a good tinned tuna. We like Ortiz the best, though it is expensive. Turn this into a sandwich by halving the amount of potato and sticking everything inside a hearty baguette.

4 rosemary sprigs
4 bay leaves
3 tbsp black peppercorns
about 400ml extra virgin olive oil
300g tuna steak, in one piece or two
600g Desiree potatoes, peeled and cut into 2cm pieces
½ tsp ground turmeric
20g anchovies, roughly chopped
3 tbsp harissa paste (shop-bought or see recipe, page 301)
4 tbsp capers
2 tsp preserved lemon skin, finely chopped
60g black olives, pitted and halved
2 tbsp lemon juice
140g preserved piquillo peppers, torn into rough strips
4 medium free-range eggs, hard-boiled, peeled and quartered
2 baby gem lettuces (about 140g in total), leaves removed and torn
20g flat-leaf parsley, leaves picked and torn
salt

To prepare the tuna, put the rosemary, bay leaves and peppercorns in a small saucepan and add the olive oil. Heat the oil until it is just below boiling point, when tiny bubbles begin to surface. Carefully add the tuna (the tuna must be completely covered; if not, heat up some more oil and add to the pan). Remove from the heat and leave aside for a couple of hours, uncovered, then cover the pan and refrigerate for at least 24 hours in the pan.

Cook the potatoes with the turmeric in plenty of salted boiling water for 10–12 minutes, until cooked. Drain carefully, making sure none of the turmeric water spills (the stains are a pain to remove!). Place the potatoes in a large mixing bowl and while still hot, add the anchovies, harissa, capers, preserved lemon and olives, along with 90ml of the tuna preserving oil and some of the peppercorns. Mix gently and leave to cool.

Lift the tuna from the oil, break it up into bite-size chunks and add to the salad. Add the lemon juice, peppers, eggs, lettuce and parsley. Toss gently, taste, add salt if it needs it, possibly more oil, and serve.

See the following pages for pictures of raw and confit tuna

Keeping kosher

Kosher rules and the deviation from them were a source of illicit excitement for Yotam in his teens. Though the Ottolenghi household was always blatantly non-kosher, the vast majority of Jews in Jerusalem felt, and still feel, inclined to observe at least some of the Jewish dietary laws; very un-cool in a teenager's eyes. Yotam felt particularly proud that his mother would buy pork 'under the counter' from a local butcher and prepare ham sandwiches for his lunchbox, a fact that he was sworn to keep 'discreet'. It all felt terribly special and brave.

Youths' vanity aside, the observance of kashrut rules is a divisive issue in the city as it is in the rest of Israel. Your identity is to some degree determined by how strict you are: whether or not you fast on Yom Kippur, how far you try to keep meat and dairy separate, whether you eat in a non-kosher friend's home, whether you'd consume bread over Passover and a dozen other questions, big and small. The way you answer those questions is taken as an indication as to how traditional you are, how cosmopolitan, how nationalistic.

What made eating non-kosher food especially thrilling in the 1970s and '80s was that it was hardly ever consumed in public places. This is probably one of the reasons why Yotam was almost obsessive about Sea Dolphin, a restaurant in east Jerusalem serving prawns, squid, lobster and other forbidden creatures. His idea of the perfect birthday present was their famous plate of prawns with butter and garlic (and we are talking about a 10-year-old!).

The story of Sea Dolphin reflects much of the city's spirit and its taboos. It was set up in 1967 by Shraga Rosenzweig, son of a German-Jewish family who settled in Jerusalem in the 1930s, just like Yotam's mother's family. The Rosenzweigs opened a small fish shop in Machne Yehuda market and have run it successfully for years, despite the difficulties in transporting fresh fish from the ports on the Mediterranean during periods of war and the city's division. After the 1967 war, Shraga decided to start a restaurant and teamed up with a Palestinian partner to open Sea Dolphin in east Jerusalem. The place was a huge hit with Jews, Arabs and international guests, and became a small Mecca for all seafood lovers. Naturally, it also drew a fair amount of hostility. At some point, it was blown up and had to be closed down and revamped.

In the late 1980s the first intifada broke out, east Jerusalem became dangerous, and the Jewish customers all but disappeared. Shraga relocated the restaurant to Tel Aviv, marking an end to the Palestinian partnership. During the '90s the restaurant moved back to Jerusalem, to its current location in the west part of the city, still serving fish and seafood and basking in over 40 years of culinary glory.

Prawns, scallops & clams with tomato & feta

250ml white wine

1kg clams, cleaned

3 garlic cloves, thinly sliced

3 tbsp olive oil, plus extra to finish

600g peeled and chopped Italian plum tomatoes (fresh or tinned)

1 tsp caster sugar

2 tbsp chopped oregano

1 lemon

200g raw tiger prawns, peeled and deveined

200g large scallops, cleaned; if they are very big, cut them in half horizontally

120g feta, broken into 2cm chunks

3 spring onions, thinly sliced

salt and black pepper

This unusual combination of seafood and cheese deserves a place of honour on Ottolenghi's catering menu, making regular appearances for over 10 years and always hailed by our customers as 'unexpectedly delicious'. It works especially well in dinner-party situations, where you can cook everything in advance up to the stage when the prawns and scallops are added, chill the cooked clams and then reheat and put everything together at the very last minute. To save time and work, or if clams are not available, this dish can be done without them, just add white wine after cooking the garlic, reduce and continue as usual but without the clams. Add some chilli flakes to the sauce if you like some heat. Serve with rice, couscous or bread.

Place the wine in a medium saucepan and boil to reduce until you are left with a quarter of the quantity. Add the clams, cover immediately with a lid, and cook on a high heat for about 2 minutes, shaking occasionally, until the clams open. Transfer to a fine sieve to drain, keeping the cooking juices. Discard any clams that don't open then remove the remainder from their shells, leaving a few with their shells to finish the dish, if you like.

Preheat the oven to 240°C/220°C Fan/Gas Mark 9.

In a large frying pan cook the garlic in the olive oil on a medium–high heat for about a minute, until golden. Carefully add the tomatoes, clam liquid, sugar, oregano and some salt and pepper. Shave off three lemon peel strips, add them and simmer gently until the sauce thickens well, about 20–25 minutes. Taste and add salt and pepper accordingly. Discard the lemon peel.

Add the prawns and scallops, stir gently and cook for just a minute or two. Fold in the shelled clams and transfer everything to a small ovenproof dish. Sink feta pieces into the sauce and sprinkle with spring onion. Top with some clams in their shells, if you like, and place in the oven for 3–5 minutes, until the top colours a little and the prawns and scallops are just cooked. Remove the dish from the oven, squeeze a little lemon juice on top and finish with a drizzle of olive oil.

Salmon steaks in chraimeh sauce

In Jerusalem, just as famous as gefilte fish is chraimeh, the 'queen' of all dishes for Tripolitan (Libyan) Jews. It is a must-feature for many Sephardim, just like its Ashkenazi counterpart, on Rosh Hashanah, Passover and often on Shabbat meal tables. Despite the obvious differences — gefilte is beige and sweet, chraimeh is red, hot and spicy — they are similar in one essential element. In both dishes the flavour of the fish is really irrelevant, it is merely a vehicle for the flavours of the sauce or condiment, be it sweet, sharp or hot. Families pride themselves on their particular chraimeh recipe. It showcases the true skills of the Tripolitan cook — and, with variations on this theme, of other North African cooks — evident in the texture of the sauce, its colour, piquancy and heat.

Claudia Roden tells of the Jews of Livorno, Italy, and a similar traditional dish of a whole fish cooked in a sweet tomato sauce. The Marranos, Jews descending from Portugal and Spain that arrived in Italy in the 17th century, were among the first to introduce tomatoes to Italy and, as many of the Livornese Jewish merchants maintained a presence throughout the Mediterranean, Tripoli included, it is likely these culinary traditions travelled with them.

110ml sunflower oil

3 tbsp plain flour

4 salmon steaks, on the bone, about 950g

6 garlic cloves, roughly chopped

2 tsp sweet paprika

1 tbsp caraway seeds, dry-toasted and freshly ground

1½ tsp ground cumin

⅓ tsp cayenne

⅓ tsp ground cinnamon

1 green chilli, roughly chopped

150ml water

3 tbsp tomato purée

2 tsp caster sugar

1 lemon, cut into four wedges, plus 2 tbsp lemon juice

2 tbsp roughly chopped coriander

salt and black pepper

Chraimeh is commonly made using greater amberjack steaks, on the bone, but can be prepared with any other type of white fish. We use salmon here because these are the most widely available as steaks. If you find a large sea bass, that would be the best. White fish, off the bone, is another acceptable compromise.

Chraimeh is served as a starter, warm or at room temperature, with challa (you can use any good white bread) for dipping, a slice of lemon and a jug of water, to calm the heat. It is easily reheated and the sauce is so tasty you could double the amount if you wanted and just have more in which to dip the bread. Serve with couscous or rice.

Heat 2 tablespoons of the sunflower oil in a large frying pan for which you have a lid. Place the flour in a shallow bowl, season generously with salt and pepper then toss the fish in it. Shake off the excess flour and sear on a high heat for a minute or two on each side, until golden. Remove the fish and wipe the pan clean.

Place the garlic, spices, chilli and 2 tablespoons of sunflower oil in a food processor and blitz to form a thick paste. You might need to add a little bit more of the oil to bring everything together.

Pour the remaining oil into the frying pan, heat well and add the spice paste. Stir and fry it for just 30 seconds, so that the spices don't burn. Quickly but carefully (it may spit!), add the water and tomato purée to stop the spices cooking. Bring to a simmer and add the sugar, lemon juice, ¾ of a teaspoon of salt and some pepper. Taste for seasoning.

Put the fish in the sauce, bring to a gentle simmer, cover the pan and cook for 7–11 minutes, depending on the size of the fish, until it is just done. Remove the pan from the heat, take off the lid and leave to cool down. Serve the fish just warm or at room temperature, garnished with coriander and a wedge of lemon.

Cold fish

'Gefilte fish' is the answer you normally get when you ask someone what Jewish food is. Well, not in Jerusalem, at least not for everyone. Sami, needless to say, didn't have it until the age of 18. But he isn't Jewish. Yotam's first memory of this dish is from the age of 10, when the school initiated an evening of culinary exchange and asked every child to bring food representing his community — something typical of the country his parents or grandparents came from. Luckily for Yotam he could bring a pizza made by his dad and so quadrupled his popularity swiftly and effortlessly. Others were less fortunate. They brought gefilte fish.

_____

SWEET, GREY AND SMEARED WITH GELATINOUS GUNK, GEFILTE FISH WAS PERCEIVED AS A TYPICAL REMNANT OF THE OLD ASHKENAZI WORLD THAT WAS BEST LEFT BEHIND IN EASTERN EUROPE

_____

In our childhoods, gefilte fish, a poached mix of ground fish shaped into flat cakes, was plainly abhorred by almost everyone. Sweet, grey and smeared with gelatinous gunk, it was perceived as a typical remnant of the old Ashkenazi world that was best left behind in Eastern Europe. Compared alongside the sexy falafel or Yotam's mouth-watering pizza, it did indeed pale.

Still, despite everything, Yotam did develop a taste for gefilte fish, especially when liberally doused with chrein, the obligatory horseradish and beetroot sauce that makes all the difference.

Cold fish, sweetened or pickled, can actually be a real delicacy and is common in both Ashkenazi and Sephardi cooking. As Jews often didn't have access to fresh fish, and needed to cook them in advance for Shabbat, all sorts of preserving methods were developed in order to serve them cold, at the same time satisfying the Jewish love for all things sweet.

Apart from salting and pickling — as with the famous herring — many dishes involve coating fish in egg or batter, frying it and leaving it to cool down, often dipping it in a sugar-and-vinegar-based marinade. The Sephardi version is normally called Escabèche and is popular with North African Jews. The Roman Jews used pine nuts and raisins. These were mixed with olive oil, vinegar and sugar and spooned over red mullet; it was baked, not fried.

Marinated sweet & sour fish

3 tbsp olive oil
2 medium onions, peeled
   and cut into 1cm slices
   (350g in total)
1 tbsp coriander seeds
2 peppers (1 red and 1
   yellow), deseeded and
   cut into 1cm slices
   (300g in total)
2 garlic cloves, crushed
3 bay leaves
1½ tbsp curry powder
3 tomatoes, chopped
   (320g in total)
2½ tbsp sugar
5 tbsp cider vinegar
500g pollack fillet —
   or another white fish
   such as cod (sustainably
   sourced), haddock or
   halibut — divided into
   4 pieces
seasoned flour, for dusting
2 large eggs, beaten
20g chopped coriander
salt and black pepper

This dish is best served at room temperature, preferably after marinating it for a day or two in the fridge, with a chunk of bread. It makes a substantial starter or can be served at the centre of a light meal. Small whole fish are also good here: red mullet, sardines or small mackerel, scaled and gutted. We would like to thank Danielle Postma for this recipe.

Preheat the oven to 190°C/170°C Fan/Gas Mark 5.

Heat 2 tablespoons of the olive oil in a large frying pan or casserole that fits in the oven. Add the onions and coriander seeds and cook on a medium heat for 5 minutes, stirring often. Add the peppers and cook for a further 10 minutes before adding the garlic, bay leaves, curry powder and tomatoes. Cook for another 8 minutes, stirring occasionally. Add the sugar, vinegar, 1½ teaspoons of salt and some black pepper and continue to cook for another 5 minutes.

Meanwhile, heat the remaining oil in a separate frying pan. Sprinkle the fish with some salt, dip in flour, then in egg and fry for about 3 minutes, turning once. Dry on a paper towel and add to the pan with the peppers and onion, pushing the vegetables aside so the fish sits on the bottom of the pan. Add about 250ml of water so that the fish is just immersed in the vegetables and liquid.

Place the pan in the oven for 10–12 minutes, until the fish is cooked. Remove and leave to come to room temperature. The fish can be served then but is actually better after a day or two in the fridge. Before serving, taste and add salt and pepper, if needed, and garnish with coriander.

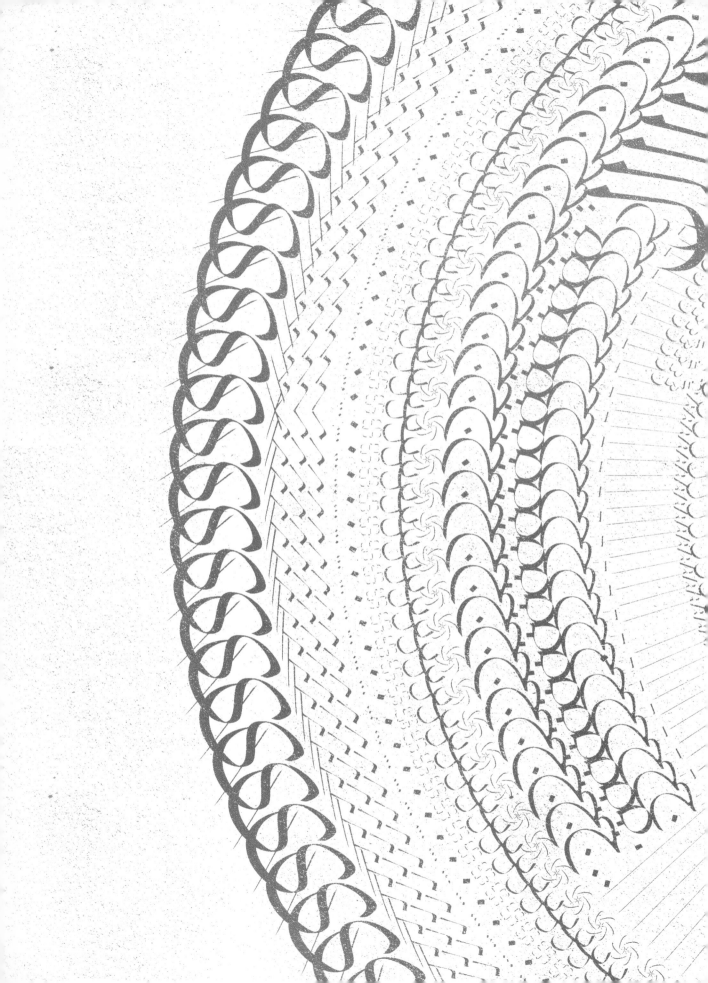

SAVOURY PASTRIES

Red pepper & baked egg galettes

Sit in any Arab restaurant in Jerusalem and before you know it the table fills up with tons of little salady mezzes of every consistency and colour (we always wonder how anyone manages to stomach anything after this but once the famous grilled meat skewers arrive, it is plainly obvious, in a very practical way). Roasted red peppers are very respectable members of the mezze clan. They are sweet (everybody loves sweet in Jerusalem), juicy and wonderfully colourful.

The contrast of the red peppers and the egg yolk make these snacky pastries stunning to look at. They are quite easy to make and taste brilliant; kids in particular love them. The egg can be substituted with feta, or any other young and salty white cheese (check if there's a Turkish grocer in your neighbourhood), which is ideal if you are not eating the galettes straight away.

4 medium red peppers, halved, deseeded and cut into 1cm wide strips
3 small onions, halved and cut into 2cm wide wedges
4 thyme sprigs, leaves picked and chopped
1 tsp ground coriander
1½ tsp ground cumin
6 tbsp olive oil, plus extra to finish
1½ tbsp flat-leaf parsley leaves, roughly chopped
1½ tbsp coriander leaves, roughly chopped
250g best-quality, all-butter puff pastry
30g soured cream
4 medium free-range eggs (or 160g feta cheese, crumbled), plus 1 lightly beaten
salt and cracked black pepper

Preheat the oven to 210°C/190°C Fan/Gas Mark 6½. In a large bowl, mix together the peppers and onions with the thyme leaves, ground spices, olive oil and a good pinch of salt. Spread out in a roasting tin and roast for 35 minutes, stirring a couple of times during the cooking. The vegetables should be soft and sweet but not too crisp or brown as they will get further cooking. Remove from the oven and stir in half of the fresh herbs. Taste for seasoning and set aside. Turn the oven up to 220°C/200°C Fan/Gas Mark 7.

On a lightly floured surface, roll out the puff pastry to about 3mm thick and cut out four 15 x 15cm squares. Prick all over with a fork and place the squares, spaced well apart, on a baking sheet lined with baking parchment. Leave to rest in the fridge for at least 30 minutes.

Remove the pastry from the fridge and brush the top and sides with beaten egg. Using a palette knife or the back of a spoon, spread half a tablespoon of soured cream over the pastry squares, leaving a 0.5cm border around the edges. Arrange three tablespoons of the pepper and onion mixture on top of the soured cream, leaving the borders clear to rise. It should be spread fairly evenly but leave a shallow well in the middle to break an egg into later on.

Bake the galettes for 14 minutes. Take the baking sheet out of the oven and carefully crack a whole egg into the well in the centre of each pastry. Return to the oven and cook for another 7 minutes, until the eggs are just set. Sprinkle with cracked black pepper and the remaining herbs and drizzle with oil. Serve at once.

Brick

We were given this recipe by Rafram Hadad, a very colourful character. Hadad was born in Djerba, a Tunisian island with a Jewish minority that settled there over 2500 years ago, and arrived in Israel with his family in the 1970s. The main Tunisian community in Jerusalem, which arrived earlier — in the 1950s and '60s — was very small so was 'annexed' to the much larger Moroccan community and lost some of its unique heritage. Hadad, however, is extremely proud of his unique Tunisian food heritage. He still has some family in Tunisia and he returns on a regular basis guiding culinary trips. He is also the Slow Food movement coordinator in Israel, an artist, a political activist and a food writer. He is one of those people that surfs life's waves, taking it all in as part of an adventure. In 2010 he got mixed up in an ordeal that resulted in him being kept in solitary confinement in a Libyan prison for five months. He was arrested after having been seen wandering in Tripoli taking photographs of the city and was released following a major diplomatic effort involving, among others, Tony Blair, Vladimir Putin and Silvio Berlusconi.

---

about 250ml sunflower oil
2 circles feuilles de brick pastry, 25–30cm in diameter
3 tbsp chopped flat-leaf parsley
1½ tbsp chopped spring onion, both green and white parts
2 medium free-range eggs
salt and black pepper

Brick is the commercial name given to a paper-thin type of pastry, not too dissimilar to filo only sturdier and crunchier (spring roll wrappers make a good substitute). It gets its name from a popular Tunisian street snack, also called brick. The snack has only a few ingredients, but tastes surprisingly complex and delicious. Other Tunisian staples can be added, such as crushed cooked potato seasoned with cinnamon, fried onion, minced meat, black olives, harissa paste or tinned tuna.

This recipe is all about timing. You will need to have the ingredients for the brick filling ready so that once your oil is at the right temperature you can assemble the parcels quickly and fry them as soon as they're made. The parcels won't hold together well if you don't fry them straight away.

Pour the sunflower oil into a medium saucepan; it should come about 2cm up the sides of the pan. Place on a medium heat and leave until the oil is hot. You don't want it too hot or the pastry will burn before the egg is cooked; tiny bubbles will start to surface when it reaches the right temperature.

Place one of the brick circles inside a shallow bowl. (You can use a larger piece if you don't want to waste much pastry and fill it up more.) You will need to work quickly so that the pastry does not dry out and become stiff. Put half the parsley in the centre of one round and sprinkle with half the spring onion. Create a little nest in which to sit an egg then carefully crack one in. Sprinkle generously with salt and pepper and fold in the sides of the pastry to create a parcel. The four folds will overlap so that the egg is sealed in; you can't seal the pastry but a neat fold should keep the egg in.

Carefully turn the parcel over and gently place in the oil, seal-side down. Cook for 60–90 seconds on each side by which time the pastry should be golden brown and the egg semi-cooked, with the yolk still runny. Lift the cooked parcel from the oil and place between two sheets of kitchen paper to soak up the excess oil. Keep warm while you repeat the process with the other piece of pastry and serve both parcels at once.

Sfiha or Lahm Bi'ajeen

Only a few decades ago, when many Palestinian families didn't have ovens at home, housewives used to bring a risen dough and lamb topping to their nearby bakery. The baker would deftly shape the dough for them, scatter over the minced lamb and bake in his wood-fired oven. His payment came in the form of a little gastronomic return: a couple of sfiha pastries.

Sfiha or Lahm Bi'ajeen, a Levantine lamb-topped dough, is a bit like a pizza and is as popular as its Italian cousin. The lamb is either flavoured with tahini or with tomato, but there are variations. Sami's mother used to make special small individual sfihas for her kids, that she would top, once baked, with heaps of fresh ingredients: parsley, radish, mint, spring onion and lemon juice. The little ones folded them into portable sandwiches that they gobbled in seconds.

These little savoury pastries can easily be taken to work, where they can be heated up, or served as they are, with a squeeze of lemon. The dough is quite wet and sloppy when you first mix it. Once you start kneading it, however, it should be fine, so don't be tempted to add much more flour.

Start with the dough. Put the flour, milk powder, salt, yeast, baking powder and sugar in a large mixing bowl. Stir well to mix then make a well in the centre. Put the sunflower oil and egg into the well then stir as you add the water. When the dough comes together, remove it from the bowl and knead for 3 minutes on a work surface until elastic and uniform. Put in a bowl, brush with some olive oil, cover with a towel and leave somewhere warm for 1 hour, at which point the dough should have risen a little.

In a separate bowl, use your hands to mix all of the topping ingredients, apart from the pine nuts and lemon wedges, and set aside.

Preheat the oven to 230°C/210°C Fan/Gas Mark 8 and line a large baking sheet with baking parchment.

Divide the risen dough into 30g balls, you should get about 14, and roll each into a thin disc, about 2mm thick and 12cm in diameter. Brush each disc lightly with olive oil on both sides and place on the baking sheet. Cover and leave to rise for 15 minutes.

Use a spoon to divide the filling between the pastries and spread it evenly so it covers the dough fully. Sprinkle with pine nuts. Set aside to rise for another 15 minutes then put in the oven for about 15 minutes or until just cooked. You want to make sure the pastry is just baked, not over-baked; the topping can be slightly pink inside and the pastry golden when you look underneath. Remove from the oven and serve warm or at room temperature, with a lemon wedge.

TOPPING

250g minced lamb
1 large onion, finely
  chopped (180g in total)
2 medium tomatoes, finely
  chopped (250g in total)
3 tbsp light tahini paste
1¼ tsp salt
1 tsp ground cinnamon
1 tsp ground allspice
⅛ tsp cayenne pepper
25g flat-leaf parsley,
  chopped
1 tbsp lemon juice
1 tbsp pomegranate
  molasses
1 tbsp sumac
25g pine nuts
2 lemons, divided into
  wedges

DOUGH

230g strong white flour
1½ tbsp milk powder
½ tbsp salt
1½ tsp fast-action dried
  yeast
½ tsp baking powder
1 tbsp sugar
125ml sunflower oil
1 medium free-range egg
110ml lukewarm water
olive oil, for brushing

Abadi cookies

Sold in iconic red printed bags carrying the founding father's portrait, Abadi's savoury cookies, ka'ach bilmalch, are dangerously addictive and immediately recognizable by generations of Jerusalemites. It was the pleasant crunch, hard crumble and roasted sesame seed topping that made the ring-shaped cookies so popular when they first burst onto the scene back in 1838.

It all began in Aleppo, when one of the family's ancestors set up a small neighbourhood bakery. In 1926 the family moved to Palestine carried on donkeys' backs and settled in Jerusalem, where they ran a tiny bakery from their house near Machne Yehuda market. Yosef, the son, who was born in Jerusalem, joined the bakery at the age of 13, and worked there for years perfecting his trade.

In 1949 Yosef and his wife, Simcha, extended the bakery and, based on Simcha's idea, the famous ring-shaped cookies were now made much smaller. Those proved tremendously popular the business expanded and so the manual cart used to make deliveries made way for a bike, then motorcycles, until finally, in the '60s, they could afford delivery trucks. Eventually, word got out and the cookies outgrew the city. Nowadays, they are sold nationally in supermarkets, but the artisanal, small-scale image has stuck and they are still wonderful.

Variations on Abadi's hard and short savoury biscuits appear all over the Arab and Sephardic worlds, normally shaped as rings and sprinkled with sesame seeds. Moroccans and Tripolitans make a similar cookie and serve it with black coffee. The ancient Sephardi community of Jerusalem call them biskochos salados and often shape them as sticks. However, it is the Allepian Jews' version that has the richest flavour, often containing lots of aromatic 'surprises' like anise seeds, mahleb (the ground stones of St Lucie cherries), coriander seeds and cumin seeds.

Recipe on next page

Ka'ach bilmalch

500g plain flour, sifted
100ml sunflower oil
100g unsalted butter,
    diced and left to soften
1 tsp fast-action dried
    yeast
1 tsp baking powder
1 tsp sugar
1½ tsp salt
½ tsp ground cumin
1½ tbsp fennel seeds,
    toasted and very lightly
    crushed
about 100ml water
1 medium free-range egg,
    whisked
2 tsp white and black
    sesame seeds

DIPPING SAUCE

35g flat-leaf parsley
    (stems and leaves)
1 garlic clove, crushed
25g light tahini paste
125g Greek yoghurt
25ml lemon juice
pinch of salt

These simple savoury cookies are normally kept at home in a jar, ready to be snacked on at any moment (Yotam's dad tends to sneak into the kitchen in the middle of the night and devour a couple — without anyone noticing, of course). They aren't very rich so will go well with a cheese dip or on their own with a glass of cold beer, arak on ice or black coffee. The dipping sauce given here is completely optional; make it if you want to upgrade them to a pre-dinner party appetizer.

Preheat the oven to 200°C/180°C Fan/Gas Mark 6. Place the sifted flour in a large bowl and make a well in the centre. Pour the oil into the well, add the butter, yeast, baking powder, sugar, salt and spices and stir together well until a dough is formed. Add the water gradually while stirring until the dough is smooth. Knead for a couple of minutes.

Line a baking sheet with baking parchment. Pinch pieces of the dough into small balls, about 25g each. On a clean surface, roll the balls into long snakes, around 1cm thick and 12–13cm long. Form each snake into a closed ring and arrange on the baking sheet spaced about 2cm apart. Brush each ring with the whisked egg and sprinkle lightly with sesame seeds. Leave to prove for 30 minutes.

Bake the biscuits in the oven for 22 minutes, until golden brown. Allow to cool down before storing them in a clean jar or an airtight container. They keep for up to 10 days.

To make the dipping sauce, just blitz all the ingredients together to get a uniformly green sauce. Add a tablespoon or so of water if the sauce is very thick; you want a nice coating consistency.

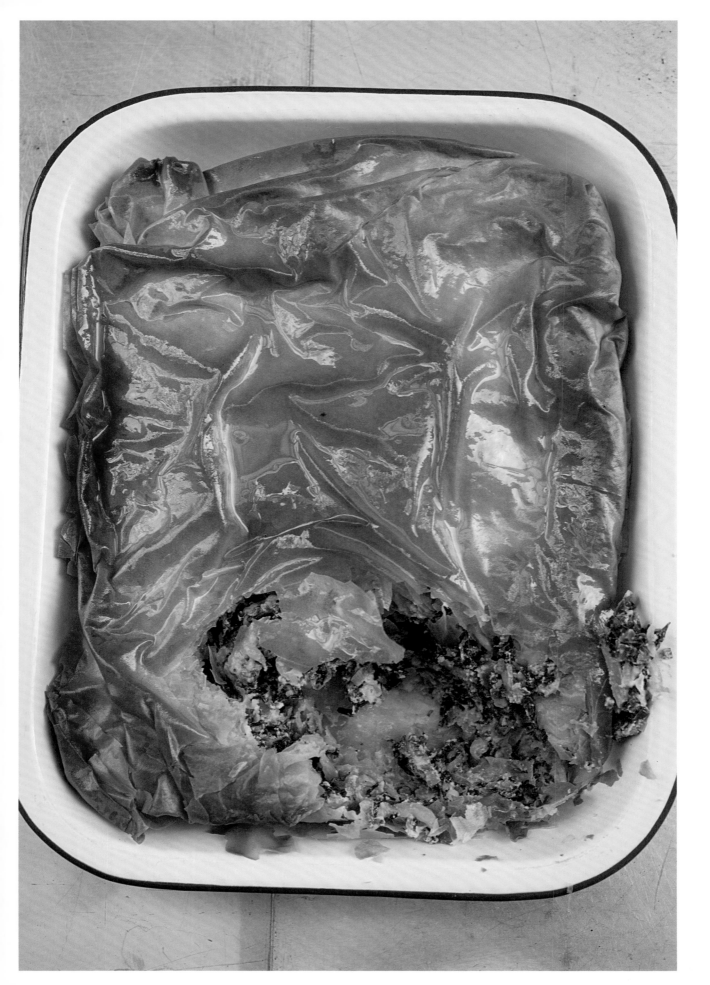

Herb pie

The extravagant use of herbs in our cooking is definitely to be blamed on Jerusalem. Herbs are sold there, quite literally, by the bucketload. Fallahat, Palestinian peasant women, come into the city with baskets and sacks brimming with fresh produce from the surrounding countryside to sell on the curbside. They used to carry the sacks of produce on their heads with amazing acts of graceful balance. Herbs are always there — particularly mint, parsley, za'atar, coriander, sage and dill — but also plenty of other vegetables and fruit in season. Housewives buy liberal quantities ready to go into salads, aromatic pastes, vegetable stuffings and most other dishes as well. It seems almost ironic that it is Israeli and Palestinian herbs which fill the miserly bags of fresh herbs sold in most UK supermarkets today, given that no sane cook there would consider buying anything less than five times this amount.

This pie, inspired by all kinds of Sephardi pastries from Turkey and the Balkans, can happily sit at the centre of a light vegetarian meal. Serve it after the Burnt aubergine and mograbieh soup (SEE PAGE 141).

2 tbsp olive oil, plus extra for brushing the pastry
1 large onion, diced
500g Swiss chard, stems and leaves thinly shredded but kept separate
150g celery, thinly sliced
50g spring onion, chopped
50g rocket
30g flat-leaf parsley, chopped
30g mint, chopped
20g dill, chopped
120g anari or ricotta cheese, crumbled
100g mature Cheddar, grated
60g feta, crumbled
grated zest of 1 lemon
2 medium free-range eggs
⅓ tsp salt
½ tsp coarsely ground black pepper
½ tsp caster sugar
250g filo pastry

Preheat the oven to 200°C/180°C Fan/Gas Mark 6. Pour 2 tablespoons of olive oil into a large, deep frying pan. Add the onion and sauté for 8 minutes over a medium heat without browning. Add the chard stems and the celery and continue cooking for 4 minutes, stirring occasionally. Add the chard leaves, increase the heat to medium–high and stir as you cook for 4 minutes until the leaves wilt. Add the spring onion, rocket and herbs and cook for 2 minutes more. Remove from the heat and transfer to a colander to cool.

Once the mixture is cool, squeeze out as much water as you can and transfer to a mixing bowl. Add the three cheeses, lemon zest, eggs, salt, pepper and sugar and mix well.

Lay out a sheet of filo pastry and brush it with some olive oil. Cover with another sheet and continue in the same manner until you have five layers of filo brushed with oil, all covering an area large enough to line the sides and base of a 22cm pie dish, plus extra to hang over the rim. Line the pie dish with the pastry, fill with the herb mix and fold the excess pastry over the edge of the filling, trimming the pastry as necessary to create a 2cm border.

Make another set of five layers of filo brushed with oil and place them over the pie. Scrunch up the pastry a little to create a wavy, uneven top and trim the edges so it just covers the pie. Brush generously with olive oil and bake in the oven for 40 minutes or until the filo turns a nice golden brown. Remove from the oven and serve warm or at room temperature.

Acharuli khachapuri

With its endless affinity for all things freshly baked, Jerusalem boasts the highest ratio of bakeries to residents in Israel. Naturally, it didn't take long before locals adopted another way of enjoying the seductive combination of baked dough and cheese, to add to their fascination with burekas (SEE PAGE 254).

Tango Shavit, a Jerusalemite of Georgian origins, is the man behind the Khachapuriah, a small bakery that opened several years ago near Machne Yehuda market, specializing in the traditional Georgian cheese-stuffed khachapuri, the recipes for which have been passed down through his mother's side of the family. The acharuli — a boat-shaped khachapuri baked with an egg on top — is one of the dishes most readily associated with the city's Georgian Jewish community (SEE ALSO PAGE 71).

The acharuli is also another product of the 'eating on the run' culture, an attitude, possibly a way of life, that has been taken to new heights in Jerusalem. In a place where manners and decorum are at the absolute bottom of the priority heap, all that is really required of you is to avert disaster. Hence the awkward, often comical, angular eating postures that have been developed in order to avoid anything edible landing on one's shoes or clothes: a cheesy egg yolk from a khachapuri, some tahini gathered at the bottom of a pita with falafel, amba (mango pickle) seasoning, the shawarma (SEE PAGE 210) that's been carved and folded into flatbread, or the tomato purée threatening to run loose from a quivering hot burekas.

These are like bread rolls that are stuffed and baked with lots of cheese inside. Serve them as a snack or a simple meal, alongside a fresh salad. The acharulis are fun to make but require a little bit of confidence with dough. The tricky part is shaping them with a large enough cavity to hold an egg inside. If you are not feeling up to this challenge just leave out the eggs, but they do add a wonderfully rich creaminess so we urge you to be daring.

DOUGH

250g strong white flour
**1½ tsp fast-action dried
  yeast**
**1 medium free-range egg,
  beaten**
110g Greek yoghurt
½ tsp salt

FILLING

**40g halloumi cheese,
  cut into 0.5cm cubes**
20g feta, crumbled
60g ricotta
**¼ tsp crushed black
  pepper**
⅛ tsp salt
**½ tbsp chopped thyme,
  plus extra to sprinkle**
½ tbsp za'atar
grated zest of ½ a lemon
6 medium free-range eggs
olive oil, to serve

Start with the dough. Sift the flour into a large mixing bowl and add the yeast. Mix lightly. Create a well in the centre and pour in half the egg (keep the other half to brush the rolls later), yoghurt and 60ml of lukewarm water. Sprinkle the salt around the well.

Begin stirring the mix, adding a fraction more water if needed (not much, this dough should be dry), until everything comes together to a rough dough. Transfer to a work surface and knead by hand for 10 minutes, until you have a soft and elastic dough that isn't sticky. Return to the bowl, cover with a tea towel and let it rise at room temperature until it doubles in size, about 1–1½ hours.

Knead again to knock out the air. Divide the dough into six parts and roll them into balls. Place on a lightly floured surface, cover with a towel and let rise at room temperature for 30 minutes.

To prepare the filling, combine all the ingredients, apart from the eggs and olive oil, and stir well. Preheat the oven to 220°C/200°C Fan/Gas Mark 7 with a baking tray inside.

On a well-floured surface roll the dough balls into flat circles, 16cm in diameter and about 2mm thick. You can do this with a rolling pin or just by stretching it with your hands.

Spoon roughly 20g of the cheese filling onto the centre of each circle and spread it slightly to the left and to the right so it almost reaches the two edges of the circle. Take the right and left sides in between your fingers and pinch them as you stretch the dough a little to create an elongated, boat-shaped pastry with the cheese in the centre. Straighten the side walls and try to make them at least 3cm high and wide, so that there is enough space in the centre to hold the cheese as well as a whole egg that is added in later. Pinch the ends again so they don't open up during the cooking.

Brush the rolls with the remaining half egg and put them on a piece of baking parchment the size of your baking tray. Sprinkle over some thyme leaves. Remove the baking tray from the oven, quickly place the baking parchment and rolls on the tray and put straight back in the oven. Bake for 15 minutes, until the edges have a golden tan.

Remove the baking tray from the oven and break an egg into a small cup. Gently lift the yolk with your fingers without breaking it and place in the centre of one of the rolls. Pour in as much of the white as will fit inside and repeat with the remaining eggs and rolls of dough. Don't worry if some egg white spills over, it's all part of the rustic charm. Return to the oven and bake for 5 minutes. The egg white should be done while the yolk should remain runny. Allow to cool for 5 minutes before you drizzle with olive oil, sprinkle with salt and serve.

Burekas

Opened in 1959, Burekas Mussa on Jaffa Street is the city's most popular burekas joint. It is easily recognizable; you simply follow the long queue of hungry mouths waiting patiently (by Israeli standards, that is) for their order of the incredibly greasy flaky pastry filled with a hard-boiled egg, spicy tomato or tahini sauce (SEE PAGE 298), with an equally legendary side dish of pickled cucumber (SEE PAGE 304).

Burekas — the large, Turkish variety — is a major contender for the title of a national dish, at least on the Jewish side. Best served freshly baked and still warm from the oven, sliced open and stuffed with goodies like a Christmas stocking, it makes for an indulgent meal and often comes under fire for the role it plays in the nation's expanding waistline.

The name burekas is a general term given to a vast array of flaky pastries made from either puff pastry, shortcrust pastry or filo and stuffed with a savoury filling, such as cheese (the most popular), mashed potato, seasoned ground meat, and cooked spinach, with a system of distinctive shapes to indicate the type of filling inside. Available in both small and large versions; industrially or handcrafted; in the frozen goods section of a supermarket or grocer's or freshly made at a specialist; burekas was brought over by Jewish immigrants from Turkey, Greece and the Balkans and was wholeheartedly adopted by all Jerusalemites. It has taken such a strong hold in the national culture that, similar to Spaghetti Westerns in the 1970s, Israeli B-movies were even named after it.

500g all-butter puff pastry

1 medium free-range egg, beaten

RICOTTA FILLING

60g cottage cheese

60g ricotta

90 feta, crumbled

10g melted unsalted butter

PECORINO FILLING

50g ricotta

70g mature pecorino, grated

50g mature Cheddar, grated

1 leek, cut into 5cm segments, blanched until tender and finely chopped (80g in total)

1 tbsp chopped flat-leaf parsley

½ tsp black pepper

SEEDS

1 tsp nigella seeds

1 tsp sesame seeds

1 tsp yellow mustard seeds

1 tsp caraway seeds

½ tsp chilli flakes

Our small bite-size burekas can be made larger if you like. You can serve them as a snack or as a modest meal, particularly if you slice them horizontally after they are baked and stuff them with all the wonderful additions we mention opposite.

We offer you two cheese fillings for your burekas, the second being the stronger and more potent. You can try both but you can also save yourself work by choosing only one of the fillings and just doubling its quantity if you are using the full 500g of pastry.

Roll out the pastry into two squares — 30cm wide and 3mm thick. Place the pastry sheets on a parchment-lined baking sheet — they can rest on top of one another, with a sheet of parchment in between — and leave in the fridge for one hour.

Place each set of filling ingredients in a separate bowl. Mix and set aside. Mix all the seeds together in a bowl and set aside.

Cut each sheet of pastry into 10cm squares; you should get 18 in total. Spoon about 20g of the first cheese filling into the centre of half the squares. Brush two edges of a corner of each square with egg and then fold along the centre placing the un-brushed corner directly over the brushed corner to create a triangle. Push out any air and pinch the sides together firmly. You want to press the edges very well so they don't open in the cooking. Repeat with the remaining pastries and the second filling. Place the burekas on a parchment-lined baking tray and chill in the fridge for at least 15 minutes to firm up. Preheat the oven to 220°C/200°C Fan/Gas Mark 7.

Brush the two short edges of every bureka with egg and dip these in the seed mix; a tiny amount of seeds, just 2mm wide, is required as they are quite dominant. Brush the top of each bureka with some egg as well, avoiding the seeds.

Make sure the burekas are spaced well apart, about 3cm, and bake for 15–17 minutes until golden brown all over. Serve warm or at room temperature. If some of the filling spills out of the pastry during the baking, just gently stuff it back in when the burekas are cool enough to handle.

SWEETS & DESSERTS

Sweet filo cigars

There was a time when you couldn't go to a bar mitzvah or Jewish wedding in Jerusalem without getting at least one type of 'cigar' pastry — filo stuffed and rolled, usually with a spiced meat filling, sometimes cheese. They were the heritage of various Sephardi communities, particularly Moroccan, one of the largest in the city. Luckily, those days are mostly over. Not so much because it is a bad idea, but mostly due to the poor quality of the execution and due to overexposure, a bit like the British prawn cocktail, a relic of the same era.

In actual fact, cigars can be completely wonderful. Iraqi Jews have a version with chopped chicken, onion and parsley. The famous Moroccan ones are stuffed with minced beef, sautéed onion, sweet spices, lemon juice and parsley. We particularly like the sweet varieties that are found throughout the region, in various configurations, the difference being whether they are baked or deep-fried and whether they are soaked in sweet syrup or just sprinkled with icing sugar.

80g flaked almonds
60g shelled unsalted
   pistachios, plus extra,
   crushed, to garnish
80g vanilla sugar
1 medium free-range egg,
   separated, white beaten
1 tbsp lemon zest
filo pastry, cut into 12
   squares, roughly
   18cm x 18cm
peanut oil, for frying
180g good-quality honey
1 tbsp water

These cigars, stuffed with almonds and pistachios, are a traditional Tunisian Jewish sweet served at Purim. They are wonderful served with black coffee as a snack or after a meal. Stored in an airtight container they keep for up to three days. The recipe was kindly given to us by Rafram Hadad.

In a food processor, bring the almond and pistachio together into a fine paste. Place the ground nuts in a frying pan and add 4 tablespoons of water and the sugar. Cook over a very low heat until the sugar has dissolved, about 4 minutes. Remove the pan from the heat and add the egg yolk and lemon zest, stirring them into the mixture.

Put one sheet of pastry on a clean surface. Spread about 1 tablespoon of the nut mixture in a thin strip along the edge closest to you, leaving 2cm clear on the left and right sides. Fold the two sides over the paste to hold it in at both ends and roll away from you to create a compact cigar. Tuck the top edge in and seal it with a little bit of the beaten egg white. Repeat with the pastry and filling.

Pour enough oil in a frying pan to come 2cm up the sides. Heat the oil well and fry the cigars over a medium–high heat for 10 seconds on each side or until golden.

Place the cigars on a plate lined with kitchen paper and allow to cool. While the cigars are cooling, place the honey and 1 tablespoon of water in a small saucepan and bring to a boil. When the honey and water are hot, lightly dip the fried cigars in the syrup for a minute and stir gently until well coated. Remove and arrange on a serving plate. Sprinkle with the crushed pistachio and leave to cool.

Ghraybeh

One of Yotam's oldest memories of the old city — it stands out clearly from all others — is a confectionery shop near David Street selling yellowish shortbread cookies with the most delectable melting texture. The flavour is one of those childhood sensations that cannot be replicated. They were sweet, almost sandy in texture, disappearing as soon as they hit the mouth, with the most wonderful aroma of rose water. These were, most probably, ghraybeh cookies.

Ghraybeh, meaning 'swoon' in Arabic, are to be found in Palestine, Syria, Lebanon and other countries in the region. They can be made in various shapes, either as a thin bracelet with a nut 'cementing' the two ends together, as a diamond with a nut in the middle, or as a round cake as we make them here.

200g ghee or clarified butter, from the fridge so it is solid
70g icing sugar
370g plain flour, sifted
½ tsp salt
1¼ tbsp orange blossom water
¾ tbsp rose water
30g whole shelled unsalted pistachios

Tripolitan Jews sometimes add semolina to their ghraybeh. Some Sephardi Jews use margarine or oil, which makes them both kosher and shorter. Jews from Aden (Yemen) make similar cookies called nayem — they have ground cardamom and each cookie is studded with a clove. All these are possible variations.

The flavours of orange blossom and rose water are quite intense here. Reduce them if you like. Serve the ghraybeh with black coffee or tea.

Place the ghee and icing sugar in the bowl of a food mixer and use a whisk to cream together for 5 minutes until fluffy, creamy and pale. Replace the whisk with a beater, add the flour, salt, orange blossom and rose waters and mix for a good 3–4 minutes, until you have a uniform and smooth dough. Wrap the dough in cling film and chill for an hour.

Preheat the oven to 180°C/160°C Fan/Gas Mark 4. Pinch a piece of dough, weighing about 15g, and roll it into a ball between your palms. Flatten it slightly and place on a baking sheet lined with baking parchment. Repeat with the rest of the dough, arranging the cookies on lined sheets, spaced well apart. Press one pistachio into the centre of each cookie.

Bake for 17 minutes, making sure the cookies don't take on any colour but just cook through. Remove from the oven and leave to cool down completely. Store the cookies in an airtight container for up to 5 days.

Sweet cheese

Underneath the Ethiopian church inside the ancient walls of the old city, in a rundown gloomy room, behind an unmarked iron door at the bottom of a stairway, is Zalatimo, a pastry shop like no other. People come here from all parts of town to indulge in one rare delicacy — a crisp-edged baked pastry known as mutabbaq, prepared by the Zalatimo family shops in Jerusalem and Amman. The opening hours are unpredictable and inside the ancient arched ceiling, Roman pillars and medieval flooring contrast sharply with exposed fluorescent tubes and simple Formica furniture.

Zalatimo begins by preparing the filo dough, flipping it in the air then rolling and stretching it by hand on a marbled worktop. The paper-thin dough is brushed with smen — smoked and aged clarified butter — then folded into a misshaped rectangle. The pastry is either sprinkled with walnuts and cinnamon or crumbled unsalted ewes' cheese then baked. Still warm from the oven, the crispy edged mutabbaq is drizzled with sugar syrup and the faintest hint of rose water. Around the old city, everybody knows this version simply as a Zalatimo.

PEOPLE COME HERE FROM ALL PARTS OF TOWN TO INDULGE IN ONE RARE DELICACY — A CRISP-EDGED BAKED PASTRY KNOWN AS MUTABBAQ

Mutabbaq, also known as kellaj, is one of the Palestinians' favourite sweets. It isn't quite as famous as knafeh though, which is also made with ewes' cheese. Knafeh uses semolina or vermicelli-like dough (kadaifi), food colouring, pistachios and a copious amount of sugar syrup. We prefer mutabbaq.

The use of sweetened young white cheese in desserts is widespread in the city. Ashkenazim use it for krantz cakes (SEE PAGE 284), for a range of baked cheesecakes and for blintzes — stuffed crêpes. Palestinians, however, are the only ones using sweet fresh ewes' cheese in sweets. Traditionally, the cheese is made in spring, when the pastures are lush and the milk is plentiful. Some of the milk is cooked and the cheese is preserved in jars or tins in salted water. It is later hydrated and used for a variety of savoury recipes.

Mutabbaq

130g unsalted butter,
   melted
14 sheets of filo pastry,
   31cm x 39cm
500g ricotta
250g soft goats' cheese,
   such as Rosary
crushed unsalted
   pistachios, to garnish
   (optional)

SYRUP

90ml water
280g caster sugar
3 tbsp lemon juice

Mutabbaq (SEE MORE ON PAGE 261) *is a good dessert when you have guests. It is unusual yet utterly delicious, it looks impressive and it can be made in advance, kept in the fridge and then baked to serve. Add a couple of drops of orange blossom water to the syrup if you like. An alternative, yet common, filling you can use consists of crushed walnuts (200g), caster sugar (50g), cinnamon (1 tsp) and melted unsalted butter (3 tbsp) — all mixed together.*

Heat the oven to 230°C/210°C Fan/Gas Mark 8. Brush a low-edged baking tray, roughly 28cm x 37cm, with some of the melted butter. Spread a filo sheet on top, tucking it into the corners and allowing the edges to hang over. Brush all over with butter, top with another sheet and brush with butter again. Repeat the process until you have seven sheets evenly stacked, each brushed with butter.

Place the ricotta and goats' cheese in a bowl and mash them using a fork, mixing them up well. Spread over the top filo sheet, leaving 2cm clear around the edge. Brush the surface of the cheese with butter and top with the remaining seven sheets of filo, brushing each in turn with butter.

Use scissors to trim about 2cm off the edge but without reaching the cheese so it stays well sealed within the pastry. Use your fingers to gently tuck the filo edges underneath the mutabbaq so you get a neat edge. Brush with more butter all over. Use a sharp knife to cut the surface into squares, about 7cm x 7cm, allowing the knife almost to reach the bottom but not quite. Place in the oven and bake for 25–27 minutes, or until golden and crisp.

Prepare the syrup while the mutabbaq is in the oven. Put the water and sugar in a small saucepan and mix it well with a wooden spoon. Heat up and once it boils, add the lemon juice and simmer gently for 2 minutes. Remove from the heat.

Slowly pour the syrup all over the mutabbaq the minute you take it out of the oven, making sure it soaks in evenly. Leave to cool for 10 minutes. Sprinkle the crushed pistachios on, if using, and cut into portions. Serve warm.

Semolina, coconut & marmalade cake

Semolina cakes soaked in syrup are so numerous all over the Middle East and vary in so many ways it is hard to find a single definition or an accurate enough name to fit. Some cakes have coconut in them; some have yoghurt; some bakers prefer flavouring them with citrus syrups, others with flower blossoms; some use sugar and others honey. In any case, the moist yet light texture and the aromatic flavours are what it's all about.

180ml sunflower oil
240ml orange juice
160g orange marmalade
   (fine-cut or without peel)
4 medium free-range eggs
grated zest of 1 orange
70g caster sugar
70g desiccated coconut
90g plain flour
180g semolina
2 tbsp ground almonds
2 tsp baking powder
thick Greek yoghurt,
   to serve

SOAKING SYRUP

200g caster sugar
140ml water
1 tbsp orange blossom
   water, plus a little for the
   yoghurt

These cakes will keep well for at least five days if wrapped carefully in parchment paper or foil; as a matter of fact, they improve with time. You can serve them with the yoghurt as a simple dessert, or without it if you are just having them with a cup of tea. Instead of two 500g loaves, you can make one 1kg loaf. This will take at least 20–30 minutes longer to bake.

Preheat the oven to 180°C/160°C Fan/Gas Mark 4. Whisk together the oil, orange juice, marmalade, eggs and orange zest until the marmalade dissolves. In a separate bowl, mix together all the dry ingredients and add to the wet. Mix until all is well combined. The mixture should be runny.

Grease and line two 500g loaf tins with greaseproof paper. Divide the filling evenly between them. Bake for 45–60 minutes, or until a skewer inserted in a cake comes out clean and they turn an orangey brown on top.

Near the end of the baking time, place the syrup ingredients in a small saucepan and bring to the boil, then remove from the heat. As soon as the cakes come out of the oven, start brushing them with the hot syrup using a pastry brush; you'll need to do this in a few goes, allowing the syrup to soak in for a minute or two, before you carry on brushing with more syrup. Make sure you use up all the syrup and it is all absorbed in the cakes.

Once the cakes have cooled down a little, remove them from the tins then leave to cool completely. Serve with the Greek yoghurt, flavoured with a drop of orange blossom water.

Poached pears in white wine & cardamom

Cardamom is one of our favourite spices. Like allspice and cinnamon, it has its own sweetness — not in a sugary sense, but more in an aromatic way — but it gets an extra dimension when it appears in sweet contexts. This is why it makes total sense that walking the streets of east Jerusalem you are most likely to smell cardamom near coffee sellers. Arab coffee, fiercely bitter and strong, is traditionally served with very generous amounts of sugar and often flavoured with cardamom. When grinding the coffee, the expert grinder holds in his palm just the right proportion of coffee to cardamom pods and feeds it into the machine. A scent of cardamom always surrounds young waiters walking with brass trays around the old city delivering freshly made coffee in little jugs.

500ml dry white wine
1½ tbsp lemon juice
150g caster sugar
15 cardamom pods, lightly
   crushed
½ tsp saffron threads
pinch of salt
4 firm pears, peeled
crème fraîche, to serve

We regularly teach this dessert in our classes at Leiths School in London. Students are always impressed by how simple it is to prepare and how impressive the final result is. We think it is all to do with our magic ingredient, cardamom. Cardamom pods are best crushed lightly with the side of the knife so they release their flavour. They vary in potency. Often, even pods bought freshly from supermarkets are not very aromatic, hence the large number specified in this recipe. However, if you get yours fresh from a Middle Eastern or Indian grocer you will find you may not need as many.

Pour the wine and lemon juice into a medium saucepan and add the sugar, cardamom, saffron and salt. Bring to a light simmer and place the pears inside. Make sure they are immersed in the liquid; add water if needed. Cover the surface with a disc of greaseproof paper and simmer until the pears are cooked through but not mushy, about 15–25 minutes; turn them around occasionally. Check that the pears are ready by inserting a knife into the flesh — it should go in smoothly.

Remove the pears from the liquid and transfer into four serving bowls. Increase the heat and reduce the liquid by about two thirds, or until thick and syrupy. Pour over the pears and leave to cool down. Serve cold, or at room temperature, with crème fraîche on the side or spooned on top.

Set yoghurt pudding with poached peaches

We are not big on spirits in Jerusalem. Come to think of it, we are not big drinkers at all. Arak, however, is the local spirit of choice for those who do drink. It is always associated with the famous mezze spread, where a sip of arak makes an effective palate cleanser in between bites. The diner is often served a tray with a bottle of arak, a pitcher of water and some ice, which they mix together, instantly turning the clear spirit into a beautiful milky liquid. Arak is great for cooking, mainly with fish and desserts, imparting its aniseedy flavour gently yet clearly.

---

4 gelatine leaves
  (7g in total)
200ml double cream
200ml whole milk
190g caster sugar
½ a vanilla pod, seeds
  scraped
grated zest of ½ an orange
200g Greek yoghurt
250ml water
125ml arak, ouzo or
  Pernod, plus 1 tsp to
  drizzle at the end
4 flat white peaches, or
  regular yellow peaches if
  unavailable
  (400g in total)
4 tbsp lemon juice
20g slivered Iranian
  (or crushed normal)
  pistachios

Peaches have a delicate flavour so they work well with this light and creamy pudding. You can also use pears here, apricots and even strawberries. Each fruit, though, would need a different cooking time. All the components of this dish are prepared in advance and assembled at the last minute.

Place the gelatine leaves in a bowl with plenty of cold water and leave to soften for a few minutes.

Pour the cream and milk into a small saucepan and add 90g of the sugar, the vanilla pod and half its seeds and the orange zest. Place on a medium heat, bring to a simmer and remove immediately from the heat. Remove the vanilla pod and rinse it well.

Put the yoghurt in a medium mixing bowl and whisk constantly as you add in the hot milk and cream in a slow stream. Squeeze the water out of the gelatine leaves, add them to the bowl and stir until they dissolve completely.

Pour the mixture into four 150ml individual moulds (dariol or ramekins) and leave to set in the fridge for at least 5 hours. You can also leave them in the fridge overnight, covered in cling film.

To prepare the poached peaches, put the water, arak, rinsed vanilla pod, remaining seeds and remaining sugar in a medium saucepan. Bring to the boil and add the peaches (they need to be submerged by the liquid so if they are large and plump cut them in two and remove the stones). Simmer gently for 8–12 minutes depending on the ripeness of the peaches; they need to be completely soft. Remove from the heat and leave to cool down in the pan.

Once cool, stir in the lemon juice and refrigerate for up to 2 days if you are not serving at this point. Before you use them halve the peaches, remove the stone and cut each half into 2 or 3 wedges.

When ready to serve, dip the yoghurt moulds in a bowl of hot water for a minute or two to assist in tipping out the puddings. Turn them over onto individual serving plates. You may need to shake the moulds gently but don't worry, the puddings will come out eventually. Once out, arrange the peaches and some of the syrup around the puddings, spooning more syrup over them, along with a drizzle of arak. Sprinkle with the pistachios and serve.

Cardamom rice pudding with pistachios & rose water

Rachela Shrefler, now in her seventies, came to Jerusalem from Iran as a child and later met her husband, Ezra Shrefler, a Turkish–Kurdish Jew. They are both cooks and own Azura (SEE MORE ON PAGE 166), a restaurant in Machne Yehuda market. Rachela, though, is the one cooking at home. Among the many pots she has on the stove on a Friday for the Saturday 'raid' — when dozens of hungry family members will descend on their house — is a pot with rice pudding. The rice sits on the hot platter until Saturday morning, when the family members sit together and eat it. It is simple and delicious, containing only rice, milk and sugar, with a dusting of ground cinnamon.

Rice pudding was the most common everyday dessert throughout the old Sephardi world, with variations according to community, and was eaten hot or cold, at various times of the day. Possible additions would be honey, saffron, mastic, cinnamon and other sweet spices.

Rice pudding is also common in Arab homes. Sami's mother used to prepare it for the family on occasion, causing the kids to go into serious clashes over the caramelized bits that formed at the bottom of the pot. They would have it with sugar syrup flavoured with flower blossom.

For this recipe we must thank John Meechan, a Glaswegian (!), who developed it for the menu of our London restaurant, NOPI. It is highly aromatic and rich, not muted down for the European palette.

400ml full-fat milk
120ml double cream
1 vanilla pod, seeds scraped
8 cardamom pods, lightly crushed
120g pudding rice
30g unsalted butter, diced
2 tbsp condensed milk
1 tbsp acacia honey or another mild-flavoured honey
salt
3 tbsp roasted and slivered or lightly crushed unsalted pistachios, to garnish
1 tbsp dried, edible rose petals, to garnish

SYRUP

1 tbsp acacia honey or another mild-flavoured honey
½ tbsp rose water

Put the milk, cream, vanilla (pod and seeds) and cardamom in a medium saucepan and place on a high heat. As soon as the mix is about to reach boiling point, remove from the heat, allow to cool down and leave in the fridge to infuse overnight, or at least a couple of hours.

To prepare the syrup, stir the honey, rose water and 1 teaspoon of water well until the honey dissolves and set aside.

Add the rice to the pan with the infused milk and cream, bring to the boil and simmer on a medium heat, stirring all the time, for 20 minutes. The rice should cook through but still retain a bite and the pudding should be thick. You will need to add a little bit of water, up to 50ml, towards the end of the cooking if the pudding becomes too thick before the rice is done.

Remove the pan from the heat and carefully pick out the cardamom pods and vanilla pod. Stir in the butter, condensed milk, honey and a pinch of salt. You can chill the mix now (and re-heat in a microwave oven later) or serve immediately in little flat bowls, sprinkled with pistachios and rose petals and drizzled with the syrup.

Muhallabieh

Muhallabieh, malabi, ksab, sutlaj, sahleb — these are all names for set puddings or thick sweet drinks that are dear to Jerusalemites, almost as much as the sacred stones of the old city. Well, not quite but it is fair to say that Arabs and Jews share a real fascination with these milky desserts.

In Jerusalem, before the days of coke and lattes, tamarind drink and soos (made from a liquorice twig) were the typical refreshing summer beverages (wandering vendors would carry them in ornamental vats from glass, clay or metal, attached to their backs with leather straps); their winter counterpart was sahleb.

When we were kids sahleb was sold by vendors outside Damascus gate in the Old City. In winter, we used to go there in groups, hang around and eat the warm and soothing thick beverage, topped with ground ginger, cinnamon, walnuts and desiccated coconut. The name sahleb means 'orchid' in Hebrew and Arabic as the pudding was thickened with ground orchid root. But this is now rare and expensive so today cornflour or rice flour, with no fragrance but very cheap, is used instead.

Muhallabieh or malabi (SEE PICTURE OPPOSITE AND ON PAGES 272–273) *are the dessert forms of sahleb. On the face of it, we must admit, a milk pudding doesn't sound promising at all. Imagination doesn't work here, you just need to try it. Once more, we bring in Claudine and Alison, our devoted recipe testers, who thought the description sounded horrible but actually loved it. What makes it so special is the lightness and simplicity of the base pudding (which is like a lean version of panna cotta), combined with the flavour and character coming from the condiments that are spooned on top. In Israel, both fancy restaurants and simple street stalls sell malabi and it is the topping that varies.*

We chose not to use the ubiquitous rose water for this version of the famous pudding, but a more subtle bay leaf syrup; you can easily add a couple of drops of rose water at the end if you wish. A few pomegranate seeds will also make for a beautiful addition on top. You will have bay syrup left over; it will keep for a few weeks in a sterilized sealed jar (SEE PAGE 303) *stored in a cool place. Consider spooning it over a fruit salad.*

To use this recipe to make sahleb, simply follow the instructions but reduce the cornflour to 40g. When hot and thick, pour into small glasses and top with ground ginger, ground cinnamon, chopped walnuts, desiccated coconut and a tiny drizzle of orange blossom water. Serve at once.

PUDDING

50g cornflour
500ml full-fat milk
200ml water
80g caster sugar
25g desiccated coconut, to garnish
25g nibbed or chopped unsalted pistachios, to garnish

SYRUP

60g caster sugar
60ml water
1 bay leaf, fresh or dry
¼ vanilla pod, seeds scraped

Start with the pudding. Whisk the cornflour with 100ml of the milk to make a smooth paste. Pour the remaining milk, along with the water and sugar, into a medium saucepan and heat gently so that the sugar dissolves. When the milk mixture begins to release steam whisk in the cornflour paste. Continue whisking until the mixture boils and thickens so that it resembles thick custard. Remove from the heat and pour into six individual bowls or wine glasses. Cover the top of each pudding with cling film to prevent a skin forming (the cling film should touch the surface) and place in the fridge for at least 3 hours, or until set.

For the syrup, place the sugar, water, bay leaf and vanilla pod and seeds in a small saucepan and heat gently just until the sugar dissolves. Remove from the heat and leave to cool.

To serve, top each milk pudding with coconut, pistachios and about a tablespoon of the syrup.

Walnut & fruit crumble cream

FIG COMPOTE

500g ripe figs, quartered
2 tbsp lemon juice
1 tbsp caster sugar

GUAVA AND PLUM COMPOTE

4 guava, de-seeded and cut into 3cm pieces (300g in total)
6 plums, pitted and cut into quarters (300g in total)
2 tbsp caster sugar
1 tbsp lemon juice
1 tbsp water

CRUMBLE

40g wholemeal flour
40g plain flour
50g unsalted butter, chilled and cut into 2cm cubes
50g soft brown sugar
pinch of salt
100g walnuts, roughly broken

CREAM

150ml double cream
100g Greek yoghurt
100g mascarpone cheese
1 tbsp caster sugar
½ tsp vanilla essence
½ tsp ground cardamom
½ star anise, ground

It's an old and much-loved trick — layering cream with seasonal fresh or cooked fruit — and it works every single time; but it is much more clever to spike the cream and fruit with additional layers of flavour that rhyme with each other and 'play games' with the taste buds. Here we chose fruits that grow in or around Jerusalem and some typical spices. You can opt for one of our combinations or go for something that is local and seasonal to you and enhance it with your favourite sweet spices (allspice, cinnamon, mace, clove), herbs (thyme, rosemary, marjoram, basil), various citrus peel and scented syrups. Just remember to adjust the cooking time and the amount of sugar and lemon juice to your particular fruit.

Plum and guava, we have only recently discovered, are a spectacular match. If you increase the quantity of sugar in the compote to 300g and cook the fruit longer, you will end up with the most fragrant jam.

Preheat the oven to 190°C/170°C Fan/Gas Mark 5. Start with the fruit, whichever option you choose. Mix all the ingredients together in a medium saucepan. Cook on a low–medium heat for 15–20 minutes until the fruits are completely soft, stirring occasionally. Remove from the heat and set aside to cool down.

To make the crumble, place both types of flour in a large mixing bowl with the butter, sugar and salt. Use your fingers to rub the mixture into a breadcrumb texture and then stir in the walnuts. Spread out on a baking tray lined with baking parchment and place in the oven for 15–20 minutes, until dry and cooked through. Remove and leave to cool.

For the cream, place all of the ingredients in a large mixing bowl and whisk to soft peaks, taking care not to overwhip (it is quite thick to start with so shouldn't take more than 30 seconds).

To assemble, just spoon a nice dollop of cream into a bowl, top with compôte and sprinkle with crumble. For a more fancy look, spoon one third of the crumble into the bottom of four medium glasses or glass bowls. Cover this with two thirds of the fruit then two thirds of the cream. Another third of the crumble goes on top of this, followed by the remaining fruit and then cream. Serve at once, or chill for a few hours before serving. Scatter the remaining crumble on top just before serving.

Spice cookies

During the late 19th century, as part of their Protestant beliefs, the Templers arrived in Jerusalem from Europe and established the German colony, a picturesque little neighbourhood south west of the old city that to this day feels unusually Central European. This is the 'civilized' part of town, where you go for a coffee and a slice of Sachertorte if you wish to escape the harsh Levantine reality.

Germanic influences on the city's food are evident in Christian contexts — the famous Austrian hospice at the heart of the old city serves superb strudels and proper schnitzels — but Czech, Austrian, Hungarian and German Jews arriving in the city from the 1930s have also managed to stamp their mark, opening cafes and bakeries serving many Austro-Hungarian classics (SEE ALSO PAGE 284). Duvshanyot, round iced cookies, made with honey and spices, typically for Rosh Hashana (Jewish New Year), are possibly a result of this heritage; they are very similar to Pfeffernüsse.

These are very loosely inspired by duvshanyot, or pfeffernüsse. They are actually more closely related to an Italian spice cookie and are hugely popular on the sweet counter at Ottolenghi over Easter and Christmas. The recipe was adapted from the excellent The International Cookie Cookbook *by Nancy Baggett.*

125g currants
2 tbsp brandy
240g plain flour
½ tbsp best-quality cocoa powder
½ tsp baking powder
¼ tsp bicarbonate of soda
½ tsp each ground cinnamon, allspice, ginger and nutmeg
¼ tsp salt
150g good-quality dark chocolate, coarsely grated
125g unsalted butter, at room temperature
125g caster sugar
1 tsp vanilla essence
½ tsp grated lemon zest
½ tsp grated orange zest
½ medium free-range egg
1 tbsp diced candied citrus peel

GLAZE

3 tbsp lemon juice
160g icing sugar

Soak the currants in the brandy for 10 minutes. Mix together the flour, cocoa powder, baking powder, bicarbonate of soda, spices, salt and dark chocolate. Mix well with a whisk.

Put the butter, sugar, vanilla and lemon and orange zest in a mixer bowl and beat to combine but not aerate much, about a minute. Add the egg slowly, while the machine is running, and mix for another minute. Add the dry ingredients, followed by the currants and brandy. Mix until everything comes together.

Remove the bowl from the machine and use your hands to gently knead until you get a uniform dough. Divide the cookie mix into 50g chunks and shape them into perfectly round balls. Place on two baking sheets lined with baking paper, about 2cm apart, and rest in the fridge for at least an hour.

Preheat the oven to 190°C/170°C Fan/Gas Mark 5. Bake the cookies for 15–20 minutes, or until the top firms up but the centre is still slightly soft. Remove from the oven. Once the cookies are out of the oven, allow to cool for 5 minutes only, and then transfer to a wire rack. While still warm, whisk together the glaze ingredients until a thin and smooth icing is formed. Pour 1 tablespoon of the glaze over each biscuit, leaving it to drip and coat the biscuit with a very thin, almost transparent film. Finish each with three pieces of candied peel placed at the centre. Leave to set and serve, or store in an airtight container for a day or two.

Yeasted cakes

Yeasted doughs, enriched with eggs, sugar and oil, butter or margarine, are at the heart of Ashkenazi cuisine. On Fridays, particularly in Me'ah She'arim and other orthodox neighbourhoods, you will find people queuing in bakeries for their challah (see picture on page 281) — wonderful, sweet braided Shabbat bread loved by all — just as they have done for generations in eastern and central Europe. Challah was adopted by Jews in southern Germany in the Middle Ages and spread all over the Ashkenazi world, where it was given various shapes, all having different religious significances.

Another enriched yeasted dough product is the most popular cake in the west side of Jerusalem, and probably in the whole of the country. It is the krantz cake or babbka. This archetypal cake is also known as 'yeast cake' (ugat shmarim) and as unattractive as the name may sound, the cake is scrumptiously soft and sweet, like a cross between a rum baba and a Danish pastry. People go crazy for them. There are industrial varieties sold in airtight packs in supermarkets and there are artisanal varieties baked fresh in specialized bakeries. They can be filled with a sweet soft cheese (like ricotta), poppy seeds, chocolate or nuts, to name but a few.

Like many other foods, this very Ashkenazi cake has completely crossed the lines from the world it started off in and has conquered the hearts and stomachs of the general Israeli public. Kadosh, a bakery set up in 1967 in the centre of the city, is one of the most popular joints in the city. It is run by Itzik and Keren Kadosh, he a Sephardi and she from a Moroccan family. Yotam has seen them in action. It is unbelievable! Keren and Itzik bake hundreds of krantzes every Friday, the cheese one being the most popular, and droves of Jerusalemites of every possible background come to buy them for Shabbat.

Chocolate krantz cakes

530g plain flour, plus extra for dusting

100g caster sugar

2 tsp fast-action dried yeast

grated zest of 1 small lemon

3 large free-range eggs

120ml water

⅓ tsp salt

150g unsalted butter, at room temperature, cut into 2cm cubes

sunflower oil, for greasing

CHOCOLATE FILLING

50g icing sugar

30g best-quality cocoa powder

130g good-quality dark chocolate, melted

120g unsalted butter, melted

100g pecans, roughly chopped

2 tbsp caster sugar

SYRUP (ENOUGH TO COVER BOTH CAKES)

260g caster sugar

160ml water

Making a krantz isn't easy or quick (SEE PICTURES ON PAGES 283 AND 286–7). *You need to let the dough rise overnight and then fill it and shape, which is quite an elaborate process. But, and it is a big 'but', we were guaranteed by two of our recipe testers, Claudine and Alison, that it is well worth it! (Their exclamation mark.)*

Although this recipe makes two fairly large cakes, there isn't really any risk of anything going to waste. They are just the sort of thing everyone hurls themselves at as soon as they come out of the oven. They will also keep for up to two days at room temperature, wrapped in foil, and up to a couple of weeks when frozen.

For a fabulous alternative to the chocolate filling, brush each dough half with 80g of melted unsalted butter and then sprinkle with 120g of light muscovado sugar, 1½ tbsp ground cinnamon and 50g of roughly chopped walnuts; then roll as described in the chocolate version below.

For the dough, place the flour, sugar, yeast and zest in a mixer bowl and use the dough hook attachment to stir everything together on the low speed for 1 minute. Add the eggs and water and work for a few seconds at this speed, then increase it to medium and mix for 3 minutes until the dough comes together. Add the salt and start adding the butter, a few cubes at a time, until it all melts into the dough. Continue mixing for about 10 minutes on the medium speed until the dough is completely smooth, elastic and shiny. You will need to scrape down the sides of the bowl a few times during the process and throw a small amount of flour on to the sides of the mixing bowl so that all of the dough leaves the sides.

Place the dough in a large bowl brushed with sunflower oil, cover with cling film and leave in the fridge for at least half a day, preferably overnight.

Grease two 1kg loaf tins (23cm x 10cm) with some sunflower oil and line the bottom with a piece of greaseproof paper. Divide your dough into two, keeping one half covered in the fridge.

Make the filling by mixing together the icing sugar, cocoa powder, melted chocolate and butter. You will get a spreadable paste. Roll the dough out on a lightly floured surface into a 38cm x 28cm rectangle. Trim the sides to get rid of any unevenness and place the dough so that the one short end is closest to you. Use a palette knife to spread half the chocolate mixture over the rectangle, leaving a 2cm border all around. Sprinkle half the pecans on top of the chocolate then sprinkle over half the caster sugar.

Brush a little bit of water over the long end furthest away from you. Use both hands to roll up the rectangle like a roulade, starting from the long side that is closest to you and ending at the other long end. Press to seal the wet end onto the roulade and then use both your hands to even out the roll into a perfect, thick cigar, sitting on its seam.

Trim about 2 centimetres of both ends of the cake with a serrated knife. Now use the knife to gently cut the roll into 2, lengthways (!), starting at the top and finishing at the seam; essentially, you are dividing the log into two even long halves with the layers of dough and filling perfectly showing all along. With the cut sides facing up, gently press together one end of each half, and then lift the right half over the left half. Repeat this process, with the left half lifting over the right, to create a very simple, two-pronged plait. Gently squeeze together the other ends so that you are left with the two halves, intertwined, showing the filling on top. Carefully lift the cake into a loaf tin. Cover the tin with a wet tea towel and leave to rise in a warm place for 1–1½ hours. The cake will rise by 10–20 per cent. Repeat the whole process to make the second cake.

Preheat the oven to 190°C/170°C Fan/Gas Mark 5, making sure you allow plenty of time for it to heat fully before the cakes have finished rising. Remove the tea towels and place the cakes on the middle shelf of the oven for about 30 minutes, or until a skewer inserted comes out clean of dough.

While the cakes are in the oven make the syrup by mixing the water and sugar in a saucepan. Place over a medium heat and as soon as the syrup boils and the sugar dissolves, remove and leave to cool down. As soon as the cakes come out of the oven, brush all of the syrup over them. It is important to use up all the syrup. Leave until the cakes are just warm, before removing them from the tins, and allowing them to cool down completely.

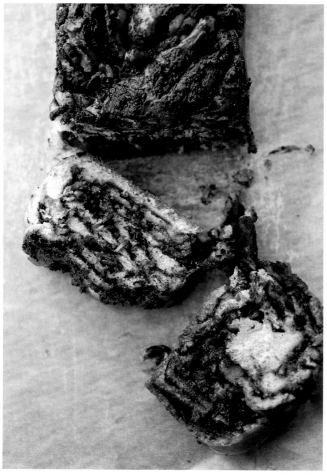

Ma'amul

During the month of Ramadan, while many shops and restaurants are closed, special pastries and confectioneries make a seasonal appearance on the streets and in the bakeries of east Jerusalem. One particular favourite is mushabak, a type of batter that is poured into hot oil and fried, then drenched in syrup and sold in bulk for the breaking of the fast feast after sunset. They are displayed piled up over a light that shines though the colourful see-through pastries.

An end-of-Ramadan specialty is ma'amul, probably the most popular of Arab cookies. Ma'amul are short biscuits made with semolina and/or flour, stuffed with nuts or dates, and daintily decorated with a special wooden mould or jagged tweezers. The date variety is round and flat, the nut one high and domed.

Sami clearly remembers a woman, whom the kids used to call 'auntie', who went around all the houses in the neighborhood towards the end of Ramadan helping housewives make the cookies. The women of the extended family used to work together in a large, chatty group gathered around 'auntie'. They had to make a lot of cookies, enough for the many guests that come and go during this time, and some for the poor or those who couldn't afford to make them. Anyone coming to the house would encounter piles of cookies everywhere, white with fresh icing sugar, like little snowballs.

350g semolina
40g plain flour
40g caster sugar
pinch of salt
180g unsalted butter, cut into 3cm cubes
2 tbsp orange blossom water
1 tbsp rose water
icing sugar, to finish

WALNUT FILLING

225g walnuts
45g medjool dates, roughly chopped
45g caster sugar
1 tsp ground cinnamon
1½ tsp rose water
1 tbsp orange blossom water

Our ma'amul cookies lack the distinctive dainty finish of the traditional version but have the typical short and dry casing with moist and nutty centre and floral aroma. We mix together nuts and dates. You can substitute the walnuts with pistachios as is common in Nablus and the Galilee. The cookies keep well (up to five days if stored in an airtight container) so consider doubling the quantities. This recipe is adapted from one by Anissa Helou, a friend and a huge expert on Middle Eastern, particularly Lebanese, cuisine.

Put the semolina, flour, sugar and salt in a large mixing bowl and stir together. Add the butter and work with your fingers until the texture is like breadcrumbs. Add the orange blossom and rose waters and ½ a tablespoon of water and use your hands to bring the mixture together into a ball. Remove to a clean surface and knead the dough until completely smooth, about 5 minutes. Cover with a damp cloth and leave to rest for 30 minutes.

To make the filling, place the walnuts, dates, sugar and cinnamon in a food processor bowl and work until the nuts are chopped quite finely but not completely ground. Add the rose and orange blossom waters and pulse quickly until you get a uniform coarse paste.

Preheat the oven to 210°C/190°C Fan/Gas Mark 6½. To mould the cookies, get a bowl of water to keep your hands damp while you work; this will help form the dough and prevent it from cracking. Remove walnut-sized pieces of pastry, weighing approximately 25g, and roll into a ball. Flatten each bowl in the cup of your hand, turning it around as you do so, using your thumb to press it flat. Lift the edges to shape a little pot. The sides need to be 3mm thick and 2.5cm high.

Fill the pastry with a heaped tablespoon, about 20g, of the filling. Pinch the dough over the filling so that the pot is sealed and then roll it into a ball again. Flatten the ball between the palms of your hands — the sides should now be 3cm high — and then place on a baking sheet lined with baking parchment. Repeat until all the dough and filling is used. Take the back of a fork and press down gently on top of each cookie to make line patterns with the tines.

Bake for 12–14 minutes. The cookies need to be cooked but must not take on any colour. Remove from the oven and transfer to a wire rack to cool down. Before serving, sprinkle liberally with icing sugar. These will keep for up to five days in an airtight container.

Helbeh (fenugreek cake)

This cake is one of Sami's childhood favourites. It is essentially a semolina cake soaked in syrup, similar to many other Levantine cakes (SEE SEMOLINA, COCONUT AND MARMALADE CAKE, PAGE 264), but the fenugreek gives it a very unusual edge. We haven't come across it anywhere else.

Sami's grandmother used to say that breastfeeding mothers must eat helbeh because fenugreek will enourage milk production. Despite their firm protests, bitter fenugreek tea was always given to kids for curing minor illnesses. It was believed to have a great medicinal effect but, unfortunately, had a flavour to match.

500g fine semolina
75g plain flour
70g pine nuts, blitzed into large crumbs
80ml olive oil
80ml sunflower oil
40g unsalted butter, melted, plus extra to grease the tin
1½ tsp fenugreek seeds
1½ tsp fast-action dried yeast
½ tsp baking powder
½ tsp salt
25g whole almonds, blanched and peeled

SYRUP

300g caster sugar
100ml water
2 tbsp lemon juice
1½ tbsp rose water
1½ tbsp orange blossom water

Helbeh cake comes with a disclaimer. Not everyone likes it. In a quick survey we did among the chefs in our restaurant, NOPI, only five out of seven approved. But those five absolutely loved it! Fenugreek, the ultimate curry ingredient, has a strong savoury association in many people's minds and some can't shake it off. However, a bit like cardamom, it works in a sweet context very well and adds magical 'exoticism' that really appeals to others. If you like cardamom, rose water and intense sweetness, you are likely to enjoy helbeh. It is fantastic with a small cup of strong black coffee.

Always make helbeh at least a day before you want to serve it and don't be tempted to tuck into it sooner; the flavours really need the time to come together properly.

Mix the semolina, flour and pine nuts in a large bowl. Add the oils and melted butter and mix well. Set aside.

Put the fenugreek seeds and 600ml of water in a medium saucepan and bring to a boil, then simmer on a low heat for about 25 minutes, until the seeds are plump and tender. Drain the seeds, reserving the cooking water, and add them to the semolina mix. Add the yeast, baking powder and salt, then gradually stir in 180ml of the hot fenugreek water; if you don't have enough liquid make it up with water. Knead the dough on a work surface until it is completely smooth.

Grease a 24cm round cake tin with butter and line it with baking paper so that the paper comes three quarters up the sides of the tin. Pour in the semolina mixture and press it down with your hand so it's levelled and smooth.

Use a small, sharp knife to score the surface of the cake with parallel lines 5cm apart, followed by another set of lines at a 45-degree angle, creating a diamond pattern. Place one almond in the centre of each diamond. Cover the cake tin with a clean tea towel and set it aside somewhere warm for about an hour. Towards the end of the resting time, preheat the oven to 220ºC/200ºC Fan/Gas Mark 7, making sure you allow plenty of time for your oven to heat fully.

Put the cake on one of the lower shelves in the hot oven and bake for 20 minutes. Reduce the heat to 200ºC/180ºC Fan/Gas Mark 6 and bake for a further 20 minutes or until it is golden brown and a skewer inserted in it comes out clean.

Prepare the syrup while the cake is in the oven. Place the sugar and water in a small saucepan and mix well with a wooden spoon. Heat up and once it boils, add the lemon juice and simmer gently for 4 minutes. Take the syrup off the heat, allow it to cool down just a little and then add the orange blossom and rose waters.

Once the cake is cooked, remove it from the oven and immediately drizzle the syrup all over it, making sure you use the whole quantity of syrup. Leave aside until the cake is completely cool before covering it well in foil or parchment paper. Serve the next day.

Tahini cookies

When it comes to food, Israelis can be very fickle. One day, without any notice, everybody discovers a brand-new favourite delight, and treats it as the absolute best thing since sliced bread. This normally doesn't last long, before something new and equally exciting makes a surprise appearance. This was the case when tahini or 'halva' cookies were at the height of their popularity a few years ago. There was no escaping them. You could find them in all the cafés, in every bakery and in the cookie jar of any avid home baker, echoing the taste and texture of local halva, the crumbly dense Arab confection made with sesame paste and honey or sugar.

Tahini is very much the local version of peanut butter (SEE ALSO PAGE 298) and this is by no means the only time it crosses sides, from savoury to sweet. Raw tahini paste, when mixed with honey, makes the most delicious breakfast spread. A staple Palestinian breakfast snack is chunks of bread dipped in tahini mixed with grape molasses. Iraqi Jews serve dates drenched in tahini to end the meal on a sweet note.

The cookie buzz has now died down, but the passion for halva lives on. These days it is served as ice cream at Machneyuda, the most creative of the city's new restaurants (SEE PAGE 205). It has also found its way into Café Kadosh's chocolate-halva krantz cake (SEE ALSO PAGE 284).

130g caster sugar
150g unsalted butter,
    at room temperature
110g light tahini paste
½ tsp vanilla essence
25ml double cream
270g plain flour
1 tsp ground cinnamon

These cookies are like a hybrid between a short biscuit and halva, with the typical melting texture of the former and the nutty, unctuous flavour of the latter. For us, who used to spread halva over white bread and gulp it down for breakfast, they are a real throwback to childhood.

Preheat the oven to 200°C/180°C Fan/Gas Mark 6. Place the sugar and butter in a mixer bowl and, using the beater attachment, work for 1 minute on medium speed until just combined but not aerated much. With the machine still running, add the tahini, vanilla and cream, then add the flour and work for about a minute, until the dough comes together. Transfer to a work surface and knead until smooth.

Pinch off 20g of the dough and roll in the palms of your hands to form a ball. Use the back of a fork to push down lightly on top of the ball so that it flattens just slightly and takes on the marks from the prongs. Place on a baking sheet lined with baking parchment (you may need 2 sheets, depending on size) and continue with the rest of the dough, laying the cookies 3cm apart on the sheet. Sprinkle a little cinnamon on each cookie and then bake in the oven for 15–17 minutes, until golden brown. Transfer to a wire rack to cool before serving or storing in a sealed container, where they will keep for up to 10 days.

Almond memories

Almonds originated in the Middle East and for centuries were a rare and expensive commodity reserved for special occasions. In Sephardi culture mazapán, or marzipan, is the pinnacle of all culinary achievements. Daniela Lerrer, owner of Sephardi bar, Barood, refers to the sweet almond paste as 'the holiest of holy'. Marzipan was, and still is to this day, prepared only for very special occasions such as births and weddings in her family. She recalls that after giving birth, her mother, in addition to passing her down the frying pan she had been using for decades, also prepared marzipan.

The Bulgarian Jews' marzipan is considered the finest. Celebrated Jerusalem-born author Meir Shalev gives a highly detailed account of marzipan-making in his book *Esau*, based on his wife's Bulgarian aunt's recipe. That same aunt showed up on his wedding day, elegant and beautiful, carrying a large tray of traditional marzipan she had made especially for the occasion. Upon noticing the groom's side of the family — a bunch of salt-of-the-earth but scruffy farmers — she held the tray close to her, tightly, and whispered to the bride, 'This, is for Bulgarians only.'

> EVERYBODY WATCHED CLOSELY AS ONE OF THE KIDS WARILY POPPED AN ALMOND INTO THEIR MOUTH AND THEN ALL BURST INTO NASTY, VICIOUS LAUGHTER AT THE SIGHT OF ONE VERY CONTORTED FACE

There were two very similar almond trees in the communal playing grounds just outside Yotam's house. School ended early in those days — around 12 or 1 p.m. — so Yotam and his friends used to spend long afternoons trying to keep themselves entertained with anything even remotely exciting, from playing with all sorts of creepy crawlies and stray cats to taunting younger kids. When they ran out of options, the almond trees supplied the all-too-necessary distraction for the gang. It was their version of Russian roulette.

As one of the trees produced only bitter almonds and the other beautifully sweet ones, and the dried nuts could only be picked off the ground, it was completely impossible to know what went into one's mouth, until it was too late. Everybody watched closely as one of the kids warily popped an almond into their mouth and then all burst into nasty, vicious laughter at the sight of one very contorted face.

Green almonds, a young nut encased in a velvety green shell that later falls off, make a fleeting appearance in markets during the spring. They are sold over ice sprinkled with salt and eaten raw; they are extremely sour. When making stuffed vegetables Sami's mother used to line the bottom of the pan with them where they would impart a sharp aroma.

Clementine & almond syrup cake

200g unsalted butter
380g caster sugar
grated zest and juice of
4 clementines
grated zest and juice of
1 lemon
280g ground almonds
5 medium free-range eggs,
beaten
100g plain flour, sifted
pinch of salt
long strips of orange zest
to garnish

CHOCOLATE ICING
(OPTIONAL)

90g unsalted butter, diced
150g good-quality dark
chocolate, broken up
¾ tbsp honey
½ tbsp cognac

This fragrant cake has a wonderful light texture and will keep, covered, for at least a week. Oranges will make an adequate substitute to clementines. A citrus zester, inexpensive and widely available, is the ideal tool for getting long, even strips of orange skin to garnish the cake.

Preheat the oven to 180°C/160°C Fan/Gas Mark 4. Lightly grease a 24cm spring-form tin and line the sides and base with baking parchment.

Place the butter, 300g of the sugar and both zests in a mixer bowl and use a beater attachment to combine everything well on a slow speed. Do not work the mix too much or incorporate much air. Add half the amount of ground almonds and continue mixing to fold through.

Add the eggs gradually, as the machine is running, scraping the bottom and sides of the bowl a couple of times as you go. Add the remaining ground almonds, flour and salt and work them until the mix is completely smooth.

Spread the cake batter inside the cake tin and level it out with a palette knife.

Place the cake in the oven and bake for 50–60 minutes. Check that it's ready by inserting a skewer inside. It should come out a little bit moist.

When the cake is almost cooked through place the remaining sugar and the citrus juices in a small saucepan and bring to the boil (the juices should add up to approximately 120ml – remove some if needed). When it comes to the boil remove the syrup from the heat.

As soon as the cake comes out of the oven brush it with the boiling syrup, making sure all the syrup is soaked through. Leave the cake to cool down completely in the tin before you remove it. You can then serve it as it is, garnished with orange strips, or store it for up to three days in an airtight container.

If you wish to ice the cake, we recommend doing this on the day you want to serve it so the icing is fresh and shiny. Put the butter, chocolate and honey in a heatproof bowl and place over a saucepan of simmering water, making sure the bowl does not touch the water. Stir until everything is melted, remove from the heat immediately and fold in the cognac. Pour the icing over the cool cake, allowing it to dribble naturally around the sides without covering the cake completely. Let the icing set and then garnish with strips of orange zest at the centre of the cake.

CONDIMENTS

Tahini sauce

150g light tahini paste
120ml water
2 tbsp lemon juice
1 medium garlic clove,
  crushed
¼ tsp salt

It is very hard to translate the local fascination with tahini to an outsider. When we filmed a documentary for the BBC in Jerusalem, we tried to get James and Lauren, the crew from England, to catch the tahini bug. We never managed, even when we sneaked it into their food behind their backs. They both spotted it and thought it just spoilt everything, whether a juicy kebab or a fresh salad. They understood the idea behind mixing it into hummus, but not having it as the star ingredient in a sauce. This was unfortunate since it was the one ingredient that always appeared on the table in both east and west Jerusalem, among Jews and Palestinians alike, at home and in fancy restaurants, fast-food outlets and local eateries. Making an appearance in a variety of guises, it was served to us in its pure state, diluted, plain or seasoned; mixed with garlic, lemon juice and olive oil; combined with peppers or parsley; served as a salad dressing and as a condiment, a sweetened confection and even in a dessert (SEE TAHINI COOKIES, PAGE 292).

Still, tahini sauces are some of the most popular among Ottolenghi customers; we serve them with roasted and fresh vegetables, as well as alongside fish and meat.

Tahini varieties range in quality, taste, colour and texture, depending on many factors, though it seems the most crucial variant is the sesame seed itself. Ethiopian seeds are considered the best, though some varieties are more suitable for oil production and others for paste. The seeds can be toasted or germinated and ground in a millstone either whole, for a darker heavier paste, or hulled, for a whiter shade and lighter flavour.

As Jerusalemites are a highly opinionated bunch, there is very little consensus on which is the best tahini between the local available brands, produced mainly in Jerusalem, Nablus and Nazereth. In the UK we opt for Lebanese, Palestinian or Israeli brands, rather than Greek or Cypriot, some of which can be purchased online.

Before starting, stir the tahini paste in its tub, scraping the bottom with a spoon, because the fat and solids tend to separate.

Put the paste into a medium mixing bowl and add the water, lemon juice, garlic and salt. Stir until you get a thick sauce, the consistency of clear honey or just a bit runnier. Add a couple of extra drops of water if you need. Store in a jar in the fridge for up to a week. Stir to loosen before using, adding a little liquid if needed.

Yoghurt with cucumber

2 mini cucumbers
   (200g in total)
500g Greek yoghurt
1 garlic clove, crushed
pinch of cayenne pepper
1 tbsp dried mint
2 tbsp chopped fresh
   mint
2 tbsp lemon juice
½ tsp salt
¼ tsp ground white
   pepper

The combination of yoghurt and cucumber uses the cooling effect of both ingredients to refresh hearty or meaty dishes. We are happy to spoon it over anything. The Palestinian version, khyar b'laban, is often served with rice dishes (SEE MEJADRA, PAGE 120) and with lamb or chicken (SEE LAMB SHAWARMA, PAGE 210, AND CHICKEN SOFRITO, PAGE 190). For Ashkenazi Jews, soured cream replaces yoghurt in dairy meals, or just the seasoned cucumbers (with oil, sugar, spring onion, dill and vinegar) are served next to meat or fish.

Peel the cucumbers and cut them into very thin slices. Mix all the rest of the ingredients in a medium bowl, add the cucumbers and check the seasoning. Leave in the fridge for 30 minutes. Serve cold.

Baharat

1 tsp black peppercorns
1 tsp coriander seeds
1 small cinnamon stick,
   roughly chopped
½ tsp whole cloves
½ tsp ground allspice
2 tsp cumin seeds
1 tsp cardamom pods
½ a whole nutmeg, grated

There's an infinite number of spice blends across the region; all vary according to spice availability, local tastes and the different uses. Baharat, literally translated from Arabic as 'spices', is used for flavouring meats, fish, stews and various pulse and grain dishes. Make your own and keep it in a sealed jar for up to eight weeks.

We recommend getting a spice grinder for this, and for plenty of other occasions; it is one of the kitchen gadgets we use the most, and it needn't be expensive. If you are using a pestle and mortar you may want to get ground cardamom as the pods will be hard to grind by hand.

Place all the spices in a spice grinder or pestle and mortar and grind until a fine powder is formed. Store in an airtight container, where it will keep for 8 weeks.

Dukkah

70g hazelnuts, with skins
2 tbsp sunflower seeds
1 tsp fennel seeds
1 tbsp cumin seeds
1 tbsp dried green
   peppercorns (or white, as
   an alternative)
3 tbsp coriander seeds
1½ tbsp sesame seeds
½ tsp nigella seeds
½ tsp Maldon sea salt
1 tsp sweet paprika

This is an Egyptian aromatic seed and nut mix that can be sprinkled over leafy salads, roasted vegetables, legume pastes such as hummus, and over simply cooked rice or lentils. It adds an exotic charm. You can prepare dukkah in advance and store it in an airtight container for a month or so. When making, make sure not to burn the seeds, removing them from the heat as soon as they begin to pop, and also not to process them much with the pestle and mortar so that they keep their texture.

Preheat the oven to 160°C/140°C Fan/Gas Mark 3.

Spread the hazelnuts on a baking tray and place in the oven for 20 minutes. Add the sunflower seeds after 10 minutes, keeping them apart from the nuts. Remove from the oven and leave to cool while you toast the seeds.

Put a cast-iron pan or heavy-based frying pan on a medium heat and leave for 5 minutes to heat up. Spread the fennel seeds inside and dry-roast them for 30 seconds. Add the cumin seeds and cook for another 30 seconds, or until they start to pop, then transfer them both to a little bowl. Keeping the pan on the heat, add the green peppercorns and cook until they start to pop, about 30 seconds. Transfer to a separate bowl. Cook the coriander seeds for up to a minute, until they start to pop. Keep separate.

Reduce the heat to low and cook the sesame and nigella seeds together, stirring occasionally, until the sesame turns light brown, then remove from the pan.

Rub the hazelnuts between the palms of your hands to remove and discard some of the skin. Use a pestle and mortar to coarsely chop them, then transfer to a medium bowl. Lightly crush the cumin and fennel seeds and add to the hazelnuts. Do the same with the coriander seeds, followed by the green peppercorns and then the sunflower seeds. Add the sesame and nigella seeds, the salt and paprika and mix well. Store the dukkah in an airtight container for about a month.

Harissa

1 red pepper
½ tsp coriander seeds
½ tsp cumin seeds
½ tsp caraway seeds
1½ tbsp olive oil
1 small red onion, roughly
    chopped (90g in total)
3 garlic cloves, roughly
    chopped
3 hot red chillies, deseeded
    and roughly chopped
½ tbsp tomato purée
2 tbsp lemon juice
½ tsp salt

Harissa, the basic flavouring agent in Tunisian cuisine, is extremely versatile. Use it as a condiment for grilled meat or fish, add it to roasted vegetables, or stir into stews and soups. We particularly like it with couscous or rice. Adjust the amount of heat by increasing or reducing the number of chillies. Just remember, it is meant to be hot!

Place the pepper under a very hot grill until blackened on the outside and completely soft, about 25 minutes, turning occasionally. Transfer to a bowl, cover it with cling film and allow to cool. Peel the pepper and discard its skin and seeds.

Place a dry frying pan on a low heat and lightly toast the coriander, cumin and caraway seeds for 2 minutes. Remove them to a pestle and use a mortar to grind to a powder.

Heat the olive oil in a frying pan and fry the onion, garlic and chillies on a medium heat. Cook to a dark smoky colour, 10–12 minutes, until almost caramelized.

Now use a liquidizer or a food processor to blitz together all of the paste ingredients until smooth, adding a little more oil if needed.

Store in a sterilized jar (SEE PAGE 303) in the fridge for 2 weeks or even longer.

Zhoug

35g coriander (leaves and
    stems), roughly chopped
10g flat-leaf parsley (leaves
    and stems), roughly
    chopped
2 hot green chillies,
    roughly chopped
½ tsp ground cumin
¼ tsp ground cardamom
¼ tsp ground cloves
⅛ tsp caster sugar
¼ tsp salt
1 garlic clove, crushed
2 tbsp olive oil
2 tbsp water

Jews arriving from Yemen in the first part of the 20th century are responsible for zhoug, the Israeli national chilli paste. It is an 'official' component of the famous pita with falafel, and shawarma.

Zhoug is a wonderful condiment that is believed to have health benefits for the immune system and the stomach. You can spoon it over anything that requires an additional kick. However, it is best served alongside some freshly grated tomatoes. Dunk a slice of white bread in each and you are in heaven. You can also spoon both over a rich piece of meat or a stew, as a Middle Eastern kind of gremolata.

The texture of zhoug is important. It needs to be coarse as if it were made traditionally — with grinding stones. It should also be very hot so use more chillies if yours aren't.

Place all of the ingredients in a small food processor bowl. Blitz in a few pulses to get a coarse paste; make sure not to overmix. Store in a sterilized sealed jar (SEE PAGE 303) in the fridge for up to 3 weeks.

Pilpelchuma

1 large ancho or pasilla
  chilli, or another dried
  chilli with a little heat
  (12g in total)
25g ground cayenne
  pepper
25g ground sweet paprika
¾ tbsp ground cumin
½ tbsp caraway seeds,
  ground
20 garlic cloves, peeled
  (75g in total)
¾ tsp salt
75ml sunflower oil, plus a
  little extra

This is an intense chilli and garlic paste that is used by Jews from Tripoli as a basic seasoning for many of their dishes, a bit like the Tunisian harissa. It is concentrated and deep in flavour so use it carefully. It can be smeared over root vegetables before roasting, or mixed with oil and herbs to marinate meats for the barbecue. It is also wonderful whisked into the eggs when making scrambled eggs.

Place the chilli in a small bowl, cover with hot water and allow it to soak for 30 minutes. Drain, deseed and cut the chilli into large chunks.

Spread the ground spices out in a frying pan. Place on a low–medium heat and dry-roast them for about 2 minutes. Put the spices in a small food processor bowl, along with the chilli, garlic and salt. Process a little, then, with the motor still running, pour in the oil until you get a sticky paste.

Spoon the mixture into a sterilised jar (SEE PAGE 303) and cover with a film of oil to prevent it drying out. Seal and store in the fridge, where it will last for up to a month.

SERVES 4

Labneh

450g goats' yoghurt
450g natural yoghurt
½ tsp coarse sea salt

Labneh is yoghurt that has had most of its liquid strained and is almost as thick as cream cheese; it has a sharp, intense flavour. You can make labneh with any yoghurt but we like mixing goats' and cows' for a good balance of flavours. You can keep the labneh for at least a week in a sealed tub in the fridge, ready to be spread over bread as a quick snack with some sliced cucumber. As part of a mezze selection, spread it out on a small plate, drizzle with olive oil and sprinkle with freshly chopped oregano or some za'atar.

Line a deep bowl with a cheesecloth or muslin. In a separate bowl, stir the two yoghurts together with the salt and pour into the cloth. Bring the edges together, form a tight bundle and tie firmly with a string. Hang the bundle over the bowl and place in the fridge. Leave the yoghurt to drain for 24–36 hours, emptying the bowl once or twice if needed. After this time much of the liquid should have been lost and the yoghurt will have turned thick and quite dry; the centre may still be creamy.

Preserved lemons

6 unwaxed lemons
6 tbsp coarse sea salt
2 rosemary sprigs
1 large red chilli
juice of 6 lemons
olive oil

We've published this recipe before, in Ottolenghi: The Cookbook, *but as pickled lemons are so central to our cooking and so much better home-made, here it is again. Just remember, the preserving process will take at least four weeks, and you really do need to give the lemons this time. The same method can be used with limes.*

Before starting, get a jar just large enough to accommodate all the lemons tightly. To sterilize it, fill it up with boiling water, leave for a minute and then empty it. Allow it to dry out naturally without wiping it so it remains sterilized.

Wash the lemons and cut a deep cross all the way from the top to 2cm from the base. Stuff each lemon with a tablespoon of salt and place in the jar. Push the lemons in tightly so they are all squeezed together well. Seal the jar and leave for at least a week.

After this initial period, remove the lid and press the lemons as hard as you can to squeeze as much of the juice out of them as possible. Add the rosemary, chilli and lemon juice and cover with a thin layer of olive oil. Seal the jar and leave in a cool place for at least 4 weeks. The longer you leave them, the better the flavour.

Quick pickled lemons

½ red chilli, chopped
3 tbsp lemon juice
3 small–medium
   unwaxed lemons, halved
   lengthways and sliced
   widthways as thinly as
   possible
35g caster sugar
½ tbsp coarse sea salt
1 garlic clove, crushed
1 tsp sweet paprika
¼ tsp ground cumin
½ tsp ground turmeric

*For these you won't need to wait four weeks as you do for preserved lemons (*SEE ABOVE*), just 24 hours. Their aroma won't be quite as perfumed but still magnificently pungent. So much so that they warrant a word of warning: a bit like chilli sauce, once you have started accompanying your food with these slices — meat, fish, lentils, couscous — you will find them seriously hard to give up.*

Use a pestle and mortar to smash together the chilli with 1 teaspoon of the lemon juice; you want to get a rough-looking paste. Transfer this to a large bowl along with all the other ingredients. Use your hands to mix everything together well so that all the flavours get massaged into the lemons. Leave in a bowl, covered, overnight. Transfer to a sterilized sealed jar (SEE ABOVE) the next day — it will keep in the fridge for 2 weeks.

Pickled cucumbers with dill

There are some foods that can be found on pretty much any dining table in Jerusalem. Pickles, particularly pickled cucumbers, are a safe bet. Their sharp, often overwhelming intensity is completely compatible with the local character

Pickles are frequently served at the beginning of meals to encourage the appetite, or alongside substantial, often fatty dishes in order to balance their richness. Palestinian and Jewish restaurants always serve pickles with hummus. The Ashkenazi cucumber pickles, which gained a mythological status, are a must next to Chopped liver (SEE PAGE 186). Sephardim serve them as appetizers before the meal and then with the meal itself, adding a touch of zest to long-cooked stews and tagines.

Both Arabs and Sephardim pickle turnips or cauliflowers in beetroot water (SEE PICKLED TURNIP AND BEETROOT, PAGE 307), which dyes them a familiar pink tinge that adds brightness to the table when placed next to dull-coloured dishes such as chickpeas, lentils and aubergine.

In general, most cuisines in Jerusalem don't add sugar to their pickling liquor and many use brine only, no vinegar, particularly for cucumbers. However, it is hard to draw many generalizations when it comes to pickles, because it is all about using up seasonal ingredients and those obviously vary. On top of that, each cuisine tends to add their own little touches — lemon skin, a spice, chilli, herbs — that are unique and distinctive.

These are easy to make and take three to six days. You need to make sure you use small cucumbers; get them from Middle Eastern grocers.

---

1 litre water
4½ tbsp coarse sea salt
1 tsp black mustard seeds
1 tsp coriander seeds
10 allspice berries
1 tsp fennel seeds
10 black peppercorns
5 whole cloves
1 tsp celery seeds
1 small dried chilli
1 large bunch of dill
  (50g in total)
7 garlic cloves, unpeeled,
  lightly crushed
6 bay leaves
10–13 mini or Lebanese
  cucumbers (about 900g
  in total)

Bring the water and salt to a boil in a medium saucepan. Once the salt has dissolved, remove from the heat.

Place all the spices, the chilli, half the dill, the garlic and bay leaves in the bottom of a 1.5-litre sterilized jar (SEE PAGE 303). Place the cucumbers vertically inside the jar, pressing them in to make sure they are tightly packed; try to get in as many as possible.

Fill the jar with the hot brine, making sure the cucumbers are completely covered. Put the rest of the dill on top and cover the jar loosely with the lid — this allows gas to escape from the jar. Store in a cool, dark place for 3 days.

After 3 days, taste one of the pickles. It should be mildly pickled. Leave to ferment for up to another 3 days if you want it sharper. In any case, once you are happy with the flavour, seal the jar and refrigerate for up to 2 weeks.

Pickled mixed vegetables with curry

¼ small white cabbage,
   cut into 3cm x 3cm cubes
   (220g in total)
3 medium carrots, peeled
   and cut at an angle into
   1cm slices (330g in total)
2 mini cucumbers, cut at
   an angle into 1cm slices
   (190g in total)
2 celery stalks, cut into
   3cm segments
¼ small cauliflower,
   divided into small florets
   (120g)
1 tbsp curry powder
1 tsp ground allspice
6 garlic cloves, sliced
2 red chillies
100ml cider vinegar
fine sea salt

Pick and choose the vegetables you want to use, based on what you like and what's available. You can add swede, radish, turnip, kohlrabi and even hard, unripe plums.

Mix the vegetables in a bowl and place about half at the bottom of a 1.5-litre sterilized jar (SEE PAGE 303). Add the curry, allspice, garlic and chillies. Top with the remaining vegetables.

Make brine by stirring together 1½ teaspoons of salt into every 200ml of warm water (you will need about 800ml of brine). Once the salt dissolves, fill up the pickle jar with enough of the solution to reach about 2cm below the edge of the jar. Add the vinegar (the vegetables should now be completely covered) and seal the jar.

Place the jar in a well lit, if possible, sunny, spot. The pickles should be ready in 5 days — they should be crunchy and full of sharp and salty flavours. Once ready, keep in the fridge for up to 2 weeks.

Pickled turnip and beetroot

10 small or 5 large fresh
   turnips (1kg in total)
3 small beetroot
   (240g in total)
1 green or red chilli, cut
   into 1cm slices
3 tender celery stalks, cut
   into 2cm slices
300ml distilled white
   vinegar
720ml warm water
fine sea salt

This is a cinch to make but must be prepared over two days. It is sharp and not too complex in flavour, perfect for serving with unctuous meats (SEE LAMB SHAWARMA, PAGE 210), *a tagine or a plate of Hummus* (SEE PAGE 114). *The bright red colour brightens up the dining table.*

Peel the turnips and beetroot, halve them if they are not small, and cut them into 0.5-cm thick slices. Place in a large mixing bowl and sprinkle with 1 teaspoon of salt. Stir well and set aside to marinate overnight at room temperature.

The following day, transfer the vegetables and their juices into a large sterilized 1.5–2-litre jar (SEE PAGE 303). Add the chilli and celery, followed by 3 tablespoons salt, the vinegar and the water. Add more water and vinegar to fill up the jar, if needed, in a proportion of 2 (water) to 1 (vinegar). Seal the jar, shake it gently for the salt to dissolve and place in a well lit spot. After 3–4 days the pickles should be ready. Keep them somewhere cool and dark for up to a month.

Index